COMMITTEE TO REVIEW THE FUNCTIONING OF FINANCIAL INSTITUTIONS

Chairman: The Rt Hon Sir Harold Wilson, KG, OBE, FRS, MP

Evidence on the Financing of Industry and Trade

WITHDRAWN FROM THE UNIVERSITY OF YORK LIBRARY

AF839748

Volume 2: Confederation of British Industry
Trades Union Congress
Association of Independent Businesses

LONDON

HER MAJESTY'S STATIONERY OFFICE

© *Crown copyright 1977*
First Published 1977

C162 3102 00 65

ISBN 0 11 630696 3

CONTENTS

UNIVERSITY
OF YORK
LIBRARY

WRITTEN EVIDENCE BY THE CBI

Industry and the City

INTRODUCTION AND SUMMARY

1. The Committee to Review the Functioning of Financial Institutions was set up in January 1977 with the following terms of reference:

- To inquire into the role and functioning, at home and abroad, of financial institutions in the UK and their value to the economy.
- To review in particular the provision of funds for industry and trade.
- To consider what changes are required in the existing arrangements for the supervision of these institutions, including the possible extension of the public sector, and to make recommendation.

The Committee will report directly to the Prime Minister. It is expected to make a first stage report on the provision of funds for industry.

2. In relation to this first stage of the inquiry the CBI were asked to give evidence on the following points:

- The relationships between the users of finance in industry and trade and those who supply it, either directly or as intermediaries.
- The different types of finance including retained profits to which firms have recourse, and the different uses to which they put it.
- Their reasons for deciding to invest—for instance how they choose between alternative projects—and whether the criteria for investment and the methods of financing it have changed in recent years, e.g. in response to changing economic conditions such as high interest rates and inflation.
- How well the demands of industry and trade for finance on reasonable terms have been met by the banking and investing institutions—for instance how often, and for what reasons, have applications for loans been refused.
- Whether there are defects or gaps in the arrangements for raising finance, and if so how they might be remedied so as to improve the flow of savings into industry and trade and stimulate investment.

3. We have consulted a wide range of CBI member companies and, in particular, the views of our Smaller Firms Council have been sought. In addition we conducted a postal questionnaire amongst a sample of companies, the results of which are presented as an appendix to our evidence.

4. **The clear conclusion of an overwhelming majority of our members is that it has not been a shortage of external finance that has restricted industrial investment but rather a lack of confidence that industry will be able to earn a sufficient return.**

5. The level of industrial investment in relation to output in this country, the evidence shows, has compared well with that of other countries, but its productivity has been much lower. To improve economic performance and safeguard employment the UK needs both to raise the productivity of existing resources and the incentive for further industrial investment. To take full advantage of the opportunities over the next few years this country must curb inflation, shift

from public to private spending, restore profitability and incentives, and improve competitiveness. (Part I).

6. Industrialists invest where there is a prospect of profit. To behave otherwise would waste resources, endanger the survival of their companies and prejudice not only their own jobs and careers but also those of their employees. (Part II).

7. Profitability remains extremely low. If industrial investment in the UK is to be raised companies must be able markedly to improve their earnings. (Part II).

8. Potential investments must be evaluated within a well-conceived corporate strategy for the future development or survival of a business as a whole. Many techniques are used for appraising individual investment proposals. The confidence with which industrialists view future prospects is crucial in determining the level of investment. (Part II).

9. Governments can help to create confidence by encouraging profit making, providing continuity and consistency in taxes, and other measures which affect industry, and permitting proper incentives for managers. In the UK governments have failed to follow such policies. Some trade unions policies and attitudes have also impeded progress. (Part II).

10. When inflation and interest rates are high, a major preoccupation of management is to find the cash necessary to maintain working capital and remain in business. (Part II).

11. Small changes in the cost of capital are unlikely in themselves markedly to affect industrial investment. However, the high and uncertain rate of inflation and associated high interest rates have made companies rightly cautious about borrowing to finance investment. (Part II).

12. The extreme financial difficulties and uncertainties experienced by companies since 1974 have forced industry to cut back its fixed investment and stock-building. The problems resulting from inflation on the scale experienced in the UK, together with continuing uncertainty about the future rate, must rank as the most serious of the forces which limit investment at the present and damage confidence in the future. (Part III).

13. Equity capital is the risk capital of a company bearing the brunt of variations in profits and providing a basis for borrowing. In recent years the income and capital gearing of UK companies have been under severe pressure. Despite this, there is no evidence that companies have found difficulty in raising sufficient external funds to meet profitable investment opportunities. It has not been a shortage of external finance that has restricted industrial investment but rather a lack of confidence that industry will be able to earn a sufficient return. (Part III).

14. The working of the capital market could be improved by ending dividend control. (Part III).

15. Companies generally have been able to raise external finance to the extent that they have tried to do so through the existing financial arrangements. There is no need for any extension of public sector involvement in the provision of finance for investment. (Part III).

16. Industry generally is not merely satisfied with, but often complimentary about, its relations with those who supply it with funds. Industry would welcome a closer link with all its shareholders. Further consideration should be given as to how this might be achieved. (Part IV).

17. Smaller companies have some special problems. The efforts by the banks and others to increase the provision of financial advice to such companies is welcomed and it is hoped that such facilities can be strengthened and extended. There should be a fundamental change in the tax system to encourage saving and investment in productive industry, and to reduce the mounting burden of taxation on capital and its impact on the productive assets of smaller companies. (Part V).

18. For many companies investment overseas is a vital and integral part of their activities, necessary to develop and protect markets which would otherwise be lost. The alternative to overseas investment is often not to invest at all. As the current account of the balance of payments moves into surplus, the present exchange control on overseas investment should be relaxed. (Part V).

19. Industry generally supports the assistance provided by ECGD but would welcome the improvement and extension of some of the recent schemes. (Part V).

20. Appendix I summarises the results of our postal survey. Appendix II provides a management view of the major factors influencing the investment decision. Appendix III lists the members of the CBI Working Party which, with help from the CBI Financial Policy Committee, CBI Smaller Firms Council and other CBI Standing Committees, prepared this Evidence. The CBI Council approved the main lines of the Evidence in July 1977.

PART I: THE BACKGROUND

21. In comparison with other industrial nations the UK's economic performance since the war has been poor: output per head has risen more slowly than in all other main European countries and the UK share of world trade in manufactures has fallen by more than half.

22. Some critics have argued that a primary reason for this disappointing economic performance has been a lack of industrial investment, and that this is partly due to the failings of the "City". Neither of these views is supported by the evidence. For example, during the 1960s fixed investment by manufacturing industry after allowing for replacement increased at an average rate of about 4 per cent a year in real terms which was higher than the growth in manufacturing net output of nearly 3 per cent a year. Chart I.1 shows that in relation to net output, gross investment by UK manufacturing industry during the 1960s was broadly in line with West Germany and the USA.

23. More, profitable investment would certainly have helped the UK economy, but these and other comparisons show that the main problem has been our failure to use existing resources effectively. Chart I.2 shows that the increase in output the UK has achieved from a given amount of investment has been about half that of West Germany, and two thirds that of France, Japan, USA and Sweden. The impression given by these statistics is supported by other international comparisons of productivity: even where the plant and equipment is similar, UK output per employee tends to lag. The UK needs to raise both the productivity of its existing resources and the incentive for further industrial investment.

CHART I.1 Manufacturing investment*

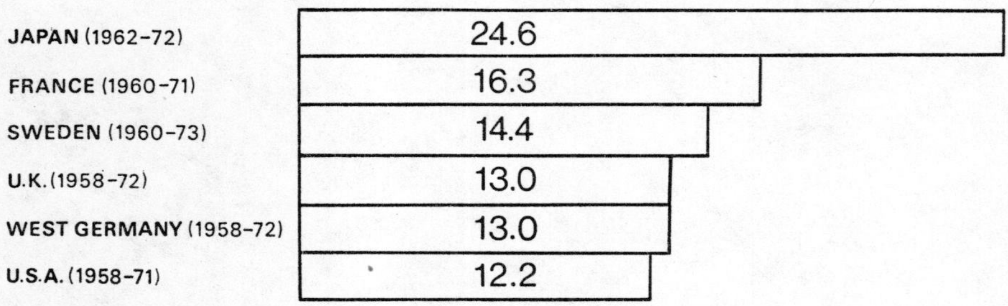

Source: Derived from Economic Trends, OECD National Accounts and Deutsche Institut für Wirtschaftsforschung.

*Manufacturing gross fixed investment as a percentage of value added. The time periods for each country have been chosen to eliminate, as far as possible, distortions due to cyclical influences, by calculating the figures for each country between troughs of the business cycle.

CHART I.2 The effectiveness of investment*

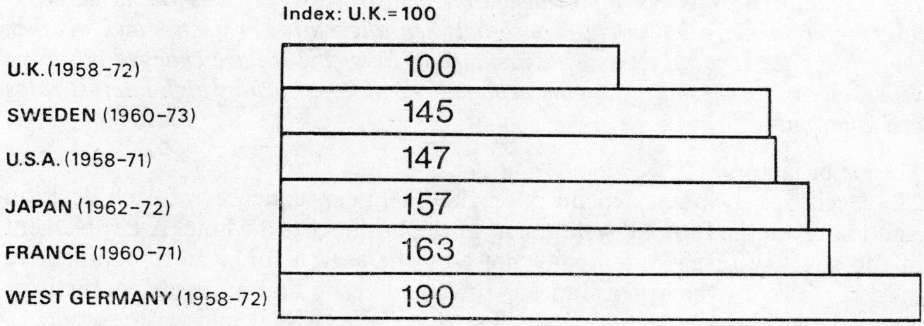

Source: Derived from Economic Trends, OECD National Accounts and Deutsche Institut für Wirtschaftsforschung.

*The increase in net output associated with a unit of investment. This incremental output-capital ratio (IOCR) is the increase in value added divided by investment at constant prices in manufacturing industry over the period. The higher the IOCR, the greater the rise in output associated with each unit of investment. The time periods for each country have been chosen to eliminate, as far as possible, distortions due to cyclical influences, by calculating the figures for each country between troughs of the business cycle.

24. In *The Road to Recovery* and *Programme for Action 77* we set out in detail the policies which we consider necessary if the UK is to take full advantage of the opportunities open to it over the next few years.

25. Action is needed:

- **To curb the rise in costs and prices to a rate at least no higher than that in competitor countries:** this will require moderation in pay increases in the year from July 1977, strict control of the money supply, and, in the longer term a fundamental reform of the pay determination system[1];
- **To bring about a major shift from public to private spending:** the Government must firmly adhere to its 1977–78 spending plans and further reduce those for later years, and steadily reduce the burden of taxes. Government, management and unions must all give priority to rebuilding company profitability so as to increase investment, exports and import-saving.
- **To restore incentives:** UK rates of income tax should be brought down into line with the average of other European countries, and plans for a Wealth Tax dropped.
- **To improve the UK's competitiveness:** management must continue to improve product development and the effectiveness of marketing, unions must cut out manning practices that add to costs, and management and unions together must strive to improve efficiency and quality and to meet the production and delivery schedules and after-sales service customers want.

26. **It is action on these points that is required, not changes in the organisation and control of the financial system.**

27. We now turn to the specific questions on which the Wilson Committee asked for comments.

[1] See *The Future of Pay Determination* Confederation of British Industry June 1977.

PART II: REASONS FOR INVESTMENT

The Committee asked us for evidence on industrialists' reasons for deciding to invest—for instance how they choose between alternative projects—and whether the criteria for investment and the methods of financing it have changed in recent years, e.g. in response to changing economic conditions such as high interest rates and inflation.

The major factors

28. Decisions to invest depend upon the likely consequences of each decision as it relates to the future development of the business as a whole. A key element in the strategy of each company must be the search for a more competitive market position which gives an edge over domestic and overseas competitors and provides the prospect of profit. To behave otherwise would waste resources, endanger the survival of businesses and prejudice not only the jobs and careers of industrialists but also those of the people they employ.

29. Prospective profits—and hence investment—depend on such things as technologies, the tastes of consumers, the strength of demand and wage costs. Many of the empirical relationships that have been developed indicate that changes in investment are responsive to changes in output (sales) and capacity utilisation. This is mainly because expected returns on projects are sensitive to changes in demand.

30. Chart II.1 shows the past connection between profitability and investment. Recent articles in the *Bank of England Quarterly Bulletin*[2] establish a link also between the "valuation ratio", which is defined as the real rate of return relative to the real cost of capital, and industrial investment. The Bank also shows that the real post-tax profitability of industrial and commercial companies has declined even faster than pre-tax profitability. But for the introduction of stock appreciation relief the real post-tax return would have been close to zero in the last few years.

31. Expectations about the future are influenced by recent experience. Thus the deplorably low real profitability achieved by companies in the last three years or so will have had an influence on expected profitability and hence on the prospects for investment[3]. Chart II.1 shows how the real profitability of industrial and commercial companies—before allowing for the payment of taxes and interest—has fallen in recent years, from an average of about 10 per cent during the 1960s, to about 3½ per cent in 1975 and 1976. This return has been inadequate to compensate for the risks involved. It is therefore not surprising that, in aggregate, industrial companies are currently valued at approximately half the replacement value of their assets.

32. The reasons for this marked decline in profitability include changes in the bargaining power of employees, increased foreign competition, and the economic recession. Recently the rapid increase in the rate of inflation coupled with the use of conventional historic cost accounting and pricing must have played a major part. Price and profit controls—based largely on inappropriate historic cost principles—have also damaged profitability. Depressed levels of profitability, whether caused by recession, inflation or specific government measures such as price control, are a deterrent to investment.

---

[2] March 1976, June 1976 and June 1977.

[3] The available data relates only to the profitability of the whole capital stock of industrial and commercial companies; information about the profitability of additions to the capital is not available.

CHART II.1: Investment and pre-tax profitability of industrial and commercial companies: 1960-76

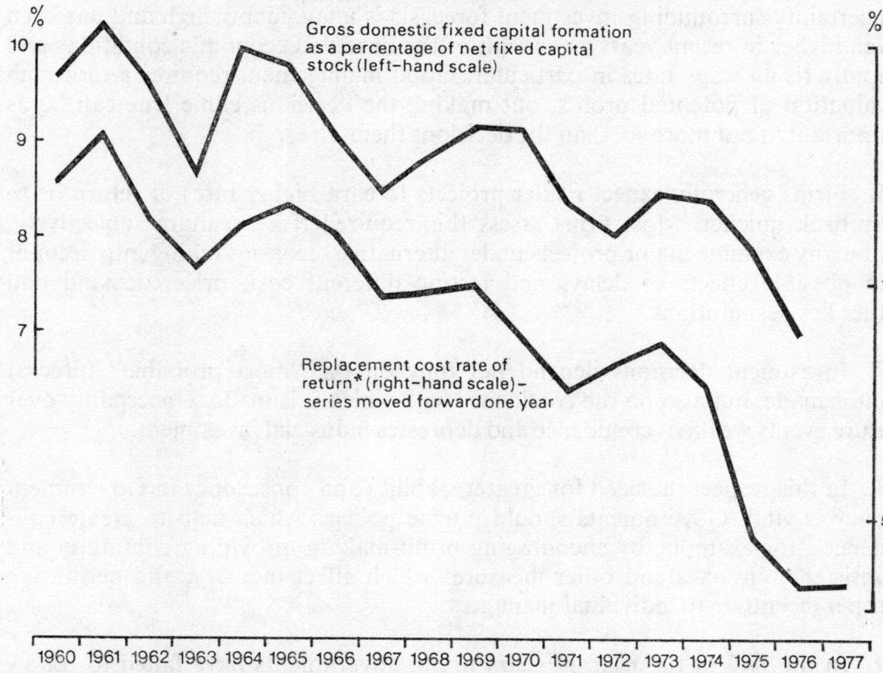

Source: Derived from National Income and Expenditure Blue Books and CSO Statistics.

*Gross trading profits plus rent received less stock appreciation and capital consumption at replacement cost as a percentage of net fixed capital stock at replacement cost plus book value of stocks.

33. Some trade union policies and attitudes can also adversely affect industry's confidence and impede progress towards improving our productivity. Industry's competitiveness cannot be improved without the co-operation of the workforce. Employees and unions must not undermine the effectiveness of machinery by limiting its use and increasing costs. There must be a greater willingness to accept re-deployment of skilled workers and, where full skills are no longer needed, the replacement of skilled by unskilled workers. A more co-operative attitude from more trade union leaders at national level would encourage flexible responses from employees generally.

Investment appraisal

34. Although some companies are highly dependent on one product or a group of closely related products, many firms aim to have a 'portfolio' of products at differing stages in their life-span, so that a failure in any one will not jeopardise the whole business. Particular emphasis is often placed on protecting the core of a company's activities and major projects are usually submitted to separate marketing, business, financial and technical appraisals. In times of particular difficulty, with rapidly changing inflation rates and shortages of retained earnings, investment is concentrated on projects necessary for survival; investments to improve productivity are likely to receive higher priority than those which would increase capacity.

35. Although individual investments may be subjected to formal appraisal techniques, projects which form part of a well conceived corporate strategy are

more likely to be taken up. This is partly because of the greater confidence which top management has in the assumptions on which the appraisals are based. The uncertainty surrounding investment forecasts is unavoidably high and has been even higher in recent years as a result of the unsettled economic conditions and rapidly rising wage rates in particular. Good management requires a thorough evaluation of potential profits, but making the decisions come true can be as important, if not more so, than the decisions themselves.

36. Firms generally expect riskier projects to earn higher rates of return or to pay back quicker. Most firms assess this required risk premium subjectively, but many examine major projects under alternative scenarios taking into account the possible effects of delays and testing different cost, price, demand and other key assumptions.

37. Investment decisions depend not only on the "most probable" forecast that is made, but also on the confidence with which it is made. Uncertainty over future events weakens confidence and depresses industrial investment.

38. In this respect the need for greater stability and consistency in Government policy is vital. Governments should pursue policies which help to create confidence—for example, by encouraging profit-making, providing continuity and consistency in taxes and other measures which affect industry, and permitting proper incentives to individual managers.

39. In the UK in the past 20 years or so, governments have failed to follow such policies. For example:

- Since 1950 there have been 33 changes in the form, rates or coverage of purchase tax or value added tax, and 19 changes in HP controls.
- Pay and price controls were introduced in 1966, ended in 1970, re-introduced in 1972, ended for pay in 1974, effectively re-introduced in 1975 and radically altered in mid-1977.
- The steel industry was nationalised in 1949, denationalised in 1953 and renationalised in 1967.
- The Industrial Reorganisation Corporation was set up in 1966, abolished in 1971 and replaced with extended powers by the NEB in 1975.
- Dividend controls were introduced on a voluntary basis for 1947–51 and again during 1961–62 and 1965–66, on a statutory basis for 1966–67, going back to a voluntary basis for 1968–69 and re-introduced on a statutory basis for 1972.
- Regional incentives changed frequently during the 1950s and 1960s both in the form and coverage of the incentives and in the boundaries of the regions eligible to receive aid; and there were more major changes made without notice earlier this year.

40. Industry is currently concerned about the likely consequences of the changes in price control which came into effect in August of this year. The 1976 Price Code although inflexible did have clearly established procedures and guidelines. The consequences of replacing it by a discretionary system of control, without effective safeguards for companies, will not be known for some time. This very uncertainty could be damaging to business confidence, investment and jobs.

41. As for appraisal techniques, considerable use is now made by UK firms of discounted cash flow (DCF) methods; there appears to have been a significant increase in their use since the early 1960s[4]. However, DCF techniques are normally used as only one among several approaches. Another commonly used test is the length of the playback period with alternative projects also being examined with regard to their cash flow properties. Increased uncertainty and pressures on prices and margins in recent years have led some companies to attach more importance to pay-back and cash flow and less to DCF techniques.

42. Although the rate of return has fallen so dramatically in recent years, most companies have not reduced their target returns (after taking account of inflation) on new investment. Large firms generally take account of changes in relative prices as well as of general inflation in their investment appraisals, but rapidly changing prices have created difficulties. The target rate of return is increasingly conceived in real terms.

43. Usually there is no difference in principle between the appraisal techniques applied to new and replacement investment proposals except to take account of the different risks involved. Relatively minor routine projects are not subjected to detailed testing.

44. Many firms divide their investments into productive and non-productive categories and projects which are expected to yield a low or zero return to the company (such as those required by environmental legislation) are assessed subjectively. Their costs need to be covered by the returns earned from productive investment.

45. Many firms attempt to evaluate investments after allowing for grants and tax allowances but may ignore or discount heavily those measures which are subject to frequent changes. Full account is usually taken of the first year investment allowances and regional grants. Managers usually assume that the firm will be profitable enough to take full advantage of the tax allowances associated with a project as they fall due. However, as profitability has fallen so markedly in recent years many companies will not have been able to make full use of such allowances, and this may influence their future investment appraisals.

Cost of capital

46. Some people have suggested that as nominal interest rates have been below the rate of inflation, the "real" interest rate has been negative, and that companies should therefore be willing to borrow more heavily. This is a misconception. Company income has not risen in line with inflation; indeed, rapid inflation has in many cases made it more, not less, difficult to meet high interest charges. When interest rates are high and the rate of inflation uncertain, companies are rightly reluctant to commit themselves to medium or long-term fixed-interest borrowing, as the interest charges on such debt could be extremely burdensome. In addition, companies are particularly conscious of the "front end loading" effect when interest rates are high and there is a heavy interest cost in the early years. Since it is common for investments to make losses in early

---

[4] See, for example; B Carsberg and A Hope *Business Investment Decisions Under Inflation* The Institute of Chartered Accountants in England and Wales 1976: C A Westwick and P S D Shohet *Investment Appraisal and Inflation* The Institute of Chartered Accountants in England and Wales (Occasional Paper No 7) 1976.

years, the effect of financing new investment with loans at high fixed interest rates can be to damage a company's creditworthiness significantly.

47. In the short term small changes in interest rates are unlikely to have a large effect on corporate fixed investment behaviour, although particular sectors may be more responsive. However, if rates remain high for a sustained period industrial investment programmes will be affected.

48. In the past industry's investment in stocks has not appeared to be particularly sensitive to changes in the rate of interest but the dramatic increase in the cost of stocks[5] has placed a major cash-flow burden on companies. Management are now more responsive to changes in the cost of holding stocks.

49. Companies cannot easily estimate the rate of return required by shareholders, especially when expectations of inflation and future profitability are uncertain. Companies generally aim to maintain a consistent distribution policy of steadily increasing dividends over a longish period, and to relate the cost of retained earnings to the yield that could be obtained by investing the funds elsewhere. The calculations are in practice very complicated as tax, transaction costs, and different degrees of risk have all to be taken into account.

50. **Industrial confidence in the stability of the economic outlook and the prospect of making an adequate profit are however more important than small changes in the rate of interest.**

Factors limiting investment

51. Since January 1972—through the troubled period discussed in detail in Part III of our evidence—we have asked a representative sample of manufacturing companies about the factors limiting their investment in buildings, and plant and machinery. We have reported the main conclusions as part of our Industrial Trends Survey releases[6]; we now give the results in detail.

52. New investment is, as we explained above, less likely to be profitable or justified in any way if existing capacity is adequate to meet expected demand. The survey results show that this has been the major factor limiting investment throughout the period (see Table II.1).

53. Shortage of internal finance—mainly from profit—has been a serious constraint even for firms which had adequate capacity but saw additional investment opportunities. This problem was greatest in 1974 and 1975, as the figures in Table II.1 line b.i. show. It also prevented investment by firms in which capacity was not considered adequate (see Table II.1 line c.ii).

54. The relative unimportance of shortage of external finance is also clear from these results. At no time did more than 8 per cent of firms name this as a constraint—and outside the 1974–75 period the proportion has normally been about 2 or 3 per cent.

---

[5] The book value of stocks and work in progress held by industrial and commercial companies rose from £13,720 million at end 1970 to £32,575 million at end 1976.
[6] Available on subscription from CBI Print and Publications Department.

55. These survey results support our view that if conditions for investment become more favourable—with improving profitability and demand—then investment will be increased without any radical change in the present system of private sector financial institutions. The most recent CBI forecasts show manufacturing investment rising this year and next—reflecting at least partly an apparent improvement in business prospects over the last year or so; the latest Department of Industry forecasts[7] show a similar picture. The size and duration of the recovery will depend on whether that greater confidence proves to be justified.

[7] Published in June 1977.

TABLE II.1 Factors likely to limit Capital Expenditure Authorisations on

	Jan 1972	*Apr 1972*	*Jul 1972*	*Oct 1972*	*Jan 1973*	*Apr 1973*	*Jul 1973*	*Oct 1973*	*Jan 1974*	*Apr 1974*
a. I have adequate capacity to meet expected demand	83	80	79	76	71	64	57	56	63	60
b. Although I have adequate capacity I have also capital investment opportunities which would be profitable at the present cost of finance, but I shall not be undertaking some of them for the following reason or reasons:										
i. Shortage of internal finance	14	11	10	9	9	8	4	6	8	11
ii. Inability to raise external finance	3	2	1	1	1	1	1	1	2	2
iii. Shortage of managerial and technical staff	2	2	2	3	3	3	4	4	2	4
iv. Shortage of labour	2	3	3	4	7	8	13	15	8	12
v. Other (please specify)	3	4	4	3	3	2	4	4	10	3
c. My capacity is not adequate to meet expected demand but I do not intend increasing my capacity. This is for the following reason or reasons:	2	3	3	3	5	7	9	12	11	11
i. Not profitable because of the cost of finance	†	1	†	1	1	2	1	2	3	3
ii. Shortage of internal finance	1	1	1	1	1	1	2	2	2	4
iii. Inability to raise external finance	†	†	†	†	†	†	1	†	†	1
iv. Shortage of managerial and technical staff	†	†	†	†	1	†	1	2	1	1
v. Shortage of labour	†	1	†	†	2	3	5	7	4	4
vi. Other (please specify)	1	1	1	1	2	3	4	5	5	4
d. None of the above is applicable	15	17	17	20	24	29	34	32	27	29

Source: CBI Industrial Trends Surveys.
†Positive response of less than 0·5 per cent.
Note: All figures up to first column for April 1975 are unweighted percentages of the total sample. From second column for April 1975, figures are weighted percentages.

buildings and plant and machinery over the next twelve months (%)

Jul 1974	*Oct 1974*	*Jan 1975*	*Apr 1975*	*Apr 1975*	*Jul 1975*	*Oct 1975*	*Jan 1976*	*Apr 1976*	*Jul 1976*	*Oct 1976*	*Jan 1977*	*Apr 1977*	*Jul 1977*
67	71	80	82	81	84	84	82	82	74	75	73	74	76
14	22	22	21	24	21	18	15	15	9	11	11	10	7
3	6	6	4	4	3	2	2	4	1	2	3	3	1
3	2	2	1	2	2	1	1	2	2	2	2	3	2
12	9	4	3	2	1	1	1	1	1	2	2	2	3
4	4	4	4	3	5	4	3	4	5	4	3	2	2
10	11	7	5	4	3	1	2	1	4	3	3	3	4
3	4	2	1	1	†	†	†	1	1	2	1	1	1
3	6	4	3	2	1	†	1	1	1	1	1	1	1
1	2	1	1	1	†	†	†	†	†	†	†	†	†
1	1	1	†	†	†	†	†	†	†	†	†	†	1
5	3	2	1	1	†	†	†	†	†	1	†	†	1
3	3	1	1	1	1	†	1	†	1	†	1	1	1
23	13	13	13	15	13	14	16	17	21	22	24	23	20

PART III: TYPES OF FINANCE

The Committee asked us to discuss the different types of finance including retained profits to which firms have recourse, and the different uses to which they put it.

Recent financial pressures

56. In the last few years, industry has been through grave financial difficulties, caused mainly by high inflation and falling profitability. This has had important effects on the types of finance sought, and the way it has been used.

57. We start by discussing the "financial account" of industrial and commercial companies and the "financial balance"[8] struck between the total of their undistributed income or saving[9] (plus net capital transfers) and their spending on investment in the UK on fixed assets and stocks.

58. This shows that in the 1960s spending on fixed investment was broadly in line with saving, with changes in the financial balance mainly reflecting changes in stockbuilding. In 1970, however, industry recorded a substantial financial deficit of £759 million. As a result of the slowdown in economic activity and consequent cutback in investment spending, this was followed by a recovery through 1971 and a substantial surplus of £1,022 million in 1972. The improvement in order books and industrial confidence in 1973 led to a marked increase in industry's investment intentions[10]. However, the sharp rise in commodity and oil prices and the rapid increase in the rate of inflation dramatically increased the cash required to maintain industry's stocks, and there was a marked fall in profitability at a time of rising fixed investment expenditure. Thus in 1974 the industrial and commercial company sector was once again faced with a substancial financial deficit—of an unprecedented £3,187 million. The increase in the value of stocks and work in progress by industrial and commercial companies was £6,092 million, of which £4,908 million[11] was attributable to stock appreciation. That November the Chancellor of the Exchequer recognised the difficulties being faced by companies and announced a (temporary) scheme to relieve the major part of the increases in stocks from tax.[12]

59. As a result of the necessary retrenchment during 1974 and 1975 industry's financial position improved somewhat, with the deficit falling to £329 million in 1975. Industry as a whole was able to contain the situation but only because

---

[8] The financial surplus (deficit) equals undistributed income *plus* net capital transfers *less* gross domestic fixed capital formation and *less* the increase in the value of stocks and work in progress.

[9] Company saving is defined as total income (including income from abroad) before providing for depreciation and stock appreciation, *less* taxes, dividends and interest payments.

[10] The August/September Department of Industry survey of investment intentions forecast a 15 per cent increase in the volume of manufacturing fixed investment 1974 on 1973 (revised down to 12–14 per cent in their November/December survey), whilst the NIESR, as late as November 1973 forecast a rise of 23·5 per cent. The subsequent fuel crisis and financial problems for industry caused a cut-back in these plans, so that the actual increase was only 8 per cent.

[11] This accounted for 42 per cent of gross trading profits and 58 per cent of undistributed income (91 per cent of undistributed income after allowing for depreciation at replacement costs) for industrial and commercial companies.

[12] However, it should be remembered that measures announced in the March 1974 Budget had intensified the pressures on cash flow and liquidity by imposing the surcharge on Advance Corporation Tax, raising employers' National Insurance contributions and (as a consequence of increasing the basic rate of Income Tax) increasing the rate of Advance Corporation Tax.

there was a much lower level of activity: working capital, fixed investment, and employment were all sharply reduced. The increase of profits net of stock appreciation in 1976 fell short of expectations with virtually no improvement in the real rate of return and although industry continued to de-stock and undertook less fixed investment, the financial balance worsened slightly to a deficit of £588 million (see Chart III.1).

CHART III.1 Financial balance* of industrial and commercial companies 1960-76

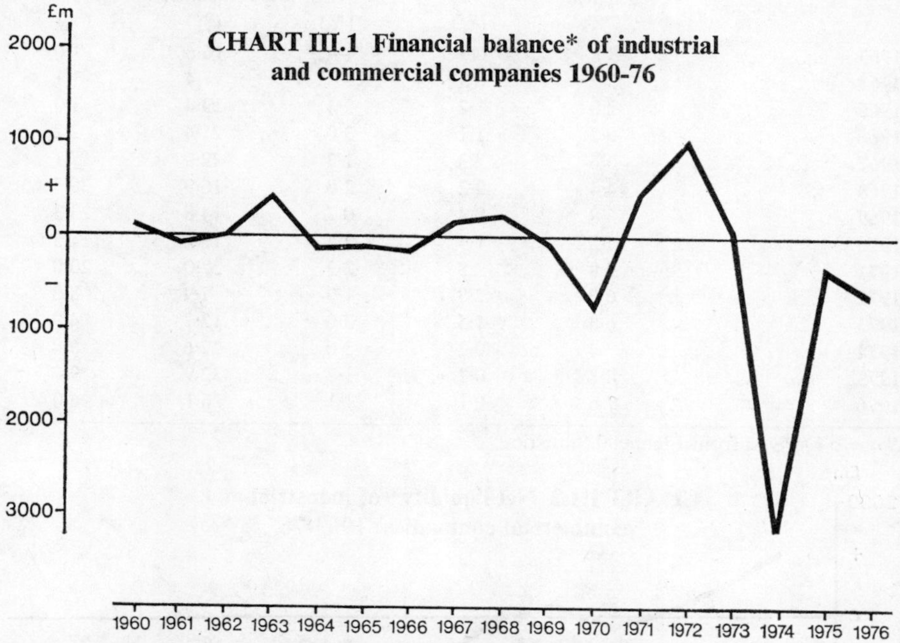

Source: Bank of England, Economic Trends and Financial Statistics.
*The financial balance is undistributed income plus net capital transfers less gross domestic investment in fixed assets and stocks.

TABLE III.1 Sources of external finance: industrial and commercial companies

	Bank borrowing (%)	Other loans and mortgages (%)	UK capital issues (Listed companies) Ordinary Shares (%)	UK capital issues (Listed companies) Debentures and preference Shares (%)
1963	42·4	9·8	9·7	16·8
1964	48·1	13·6	10·1	16·2
1965	33·4	17·9	4·2	23·2
1966	15·8	8·8	10·5	38·1
1967	24·2	2·5	4·7	25·4
1968	25·5	6·9	13·6	8·2
1969	25·9	7·7	7·1	13·1
1970	36·9	10·5	1·4	5·2
1971	24·6	8·0	5·4	7·2
1972	58·7	3·1	6·4	5·7
1973	59·5	10·5	1·4	0·7
1974	61·2	0·8	0·6	–0·8
1975	14·4	10·5	21·2	1·2
1976	38·4	8·8	11·6	0·4

Source: Derived from Financial Statistics.

TABLE III.1 Sources of external finance: industrial and commercial companies

	Overseas				
	Import credit and advance payments on exports (%)	Capital issues overseas (%)	Direct investment in securities (%)	Intra-Company investment by overseas companies (%)	Capital transfers (%)
1963	3·8	0·5	—	16·6	1·0
1964	3·2	0·3	—	7·4	1·1
1965	2·0	1·2	3·4	13·4	1·3
1966	–0·7	1·1	3·0	21·4	2·2
1967	–0·6	2·3	1·3	22·9	17·1
1968	4·4	2·2	2·0	16·9	20·3
1969	6·8	0·4	0·7	14·8	23·3
1970	5·2	1·3	2·4	19·7	17·3
1971	7·8	2·8	2·3	22·0	20·0
1972	6·0	2·3	1·9	7·9	8·0
1973	6·8	1·5	2·0	12·7	4·9
1974	7·4	0·2	3·0	22·6	5·0
1975	8·1	0·2	1·7	32·9	9·7
1976	7·6	–0·1	1·1	26·1	6·0

Source: Derived from Financial Statistics.

CHART III.2 Net liquidity* of industrial and commercial companies: 1963-76

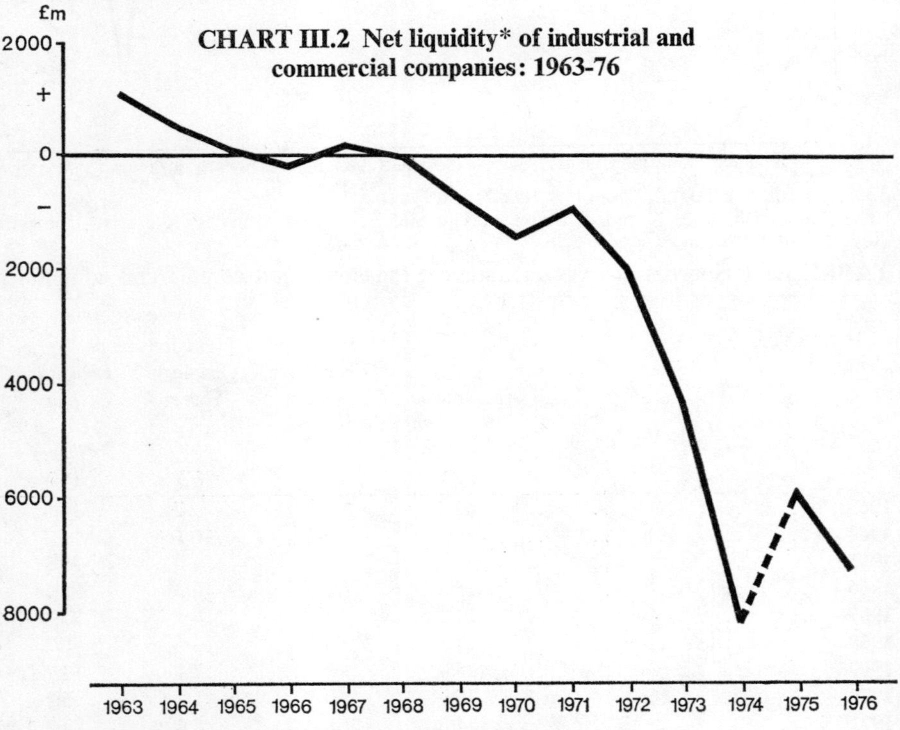

Source: Derived from Economic Trends and Financial Statistics.

*Net liquidity equals gross liquidity less bank advances. Gross liquidity equals *end of period* holdings of identified financial assets which includes deposits with the banking sector (main item) plus tax deposit accounts, Treasury Bills, tax reserve certificates, local authority temporary debt and deposits with building societies and finance houses. The composition of the series has been revised several times during the period. The principal revision occurred in mid-1975, with the exclusion of some companies now classified as financial companies, which "improved" net liquidity by about £1,800 million.

60. This does not mean that industry may operate satisfactorily and continue to expand its investments only if its financial account is balanced or in surplus. If profits are rising and are expected to continue to rise, deficits can be covered by loans or equity raised from external sources. But if profits are depressed when the financial account moves into substantial deficit there is little incentive to seek external finance and equity or long term debt is unlikely to be readily available on attractive terms.

61. The deterioration of industry's net liquidity[13] position imposed a further constraint on investment. During 1973 and 1974 the major part of companies' external finance was borrowing from the banking sector. But in 1975 conditions in the financial markets encouraged them to raise more longer-term finance from non-bank sources (see Table III.1) most notably by way of rights issues as share prices improved, to restore corporate balance sheets. The second half of the year also saw a clear recovery in net liquidity from the crisis position reached in 1974, but the position deteriorated again through 1976 (see Chart III.2).

TABLE III.2 Internal funds as percentage of total funds—industrial and commercial companies*

	Before deducting stock appreciation and depreciation at current replacement costs	*After deducting stock appreciation and depreciation at current replacement costs from internal and total funds*
1964	68	55
1965	71	56
1966	75	57
1967	77	62
1968	73	57
1969	72	53
1970	68	40
1971	75	55
1972	59	38
1973	59	36
1974	65	15
1975	80	26

Source: Trade and Industry—4 February 1977.

***Internal funds** are defined as trading income and other revenue income plus capital receipts less tax, dividend, and interest payments. **Total funds** are made up of internal funds plus bank borrowing, issues of ordinary shares in the UK for cash, issues of preference shares and debentures for cash and other loans and mortgages.

62. Table III.2 shows the relative importance of retained earnings as a source of funds during this period. Between 1964 and 1975 retained earnings averaged 70 per cent of total funds, and at no time fell below 59 per cent. Concentration on the proportion of internal funds can, however, be misleading: for example, in 1975 the **proportion** of internal funds increased markedly but their actual **value** increased only slightly. The increase in the proportion of internal funds occurred principally as a result of a reduction in the total value of funds received from all

[13] Net liquidity is defined as holdings of identified financial assets (including deposits with the banking sector) *plus* tax deposit accounts, Treasury bills, tax reserve certificates, local authority temporary debt and deposits with building societies and finance houses, *less* bank advances.

sources. Tables III.3 and III.4, taken from *Trade and Industry*[14], give the values and percentages involved for the sources and uses of finance by the industrial and commercial companies' sector for the period 1964 to 1975.

63. Business thrives on profitability and confidence. Companies will invest more readily when the general economic and industrial outlook appears settled and confidence is high, but will naturally be less inclined to do so when the prospects are highly uncertain. With the experience of a period during which profit margins have been under severe strain and profitability has fallen well below target, and with many companies trading at a loss in real terms, it would be surprising if companies were not cautious of committing themselves to ambitious investment programmes. **If there is to be a sustained improvement in industrial investment in the UK then companies must be able markedly to improve their earnings.** The impact of the 1974 profitability and liquidity crisis and recent experience has served to remind businessmen of the importance of maintaining prudent gearing ratios to safeguard corporate viability.

Gearing

64. Capital gearing is the relationship between a company's indebtedness and the value of its equity capital. "Secondary gearing" is the relationship between short and long-term debt. Interest cover (or "income gearing") is the relationship between earnings and interest charges: with high interest rates and low profitability this becomes a more significant test.

65. When calculating a company's capital gearing there is no universal method for treating "intermediate" capital such as preference shares or deferred tax, and the treatment may depend on who is making the judgement about the company.

66. The situation has been complicated by the build up of large deferred tax balances in company accounts. Although stock relief has overcome most of the difficulties which historical-cost taxation would have caused for industry, there remain uncertainties over its future form. This makes it difficult for lenders to judge a company's ultimate credit worthiness, and as a result some companies have found it more difficult to raise external finance. It is therefore important for the uncertainty about the tax treatment of stock relief to be removed as soon as possible, and for steps to be taken to meet the problems caused by the present deferred tax liabilities. For example, the notional liabilities arising from the first years of stock relief could now be cancelled[15].

67. Industrialists are generally pragmatic about what constitutes optimal capital gearing. The optimal ratio varies between companies and also with the current and expected financial position of a company. There is, however, within each company, an accepted range above which it is considered imprudent to go. Appendix I, question 3c, shows that 56 per cent of the respondents to this question in our questionnaire considered their current debt/equity ratio to be

---

[14] *Trade and Industry:* 4 February 1977.

[15] For the future we would favour a system under which relief is given on a once and for all basis each year (this could be achieved by the use of a cost of sales adjustment calculated on current cost accounting principles). Under the present system, a reduction in the value of stocks results in the clawback of prior relief. This is likely to fall due at a time when the company is least able to afford it, for example when it is cutting back on capital during a period of retrenchment. Clawback should not be a feature of any future form of stock relief.

TABLE III.3 Sources and uses of funds of industrial and commercial companies 1964–75 (£ million)

	1964	1965	1966	1967	1968	1969	1970	1971	1972	1973	1974	1975
Sources of funds												
Gross income[1] [4]	5,975	6,303	6,142	6,462	7,570	8,181	8,779	9,975	11,468	15,496	19,274	18,122
Tax payments[2]	−1,595	−1,682	−1,641	−1,935	−2,154	−2,423	−2.927	−3,179	−3,345	−3,533	−5,620	−4,320
Dividend payments	−821	−939	−886	−860	−842	−913	−810	−930	−933	−1,396	−1,517	−1,483
Interest payments	−564	−689	−847	−866	−995	−1,148	−1,238	−1,253	−1,448	−2,326	−3,299	−3,242
Total internal funds	2,995	2,993	2,768	2,801	3,579	3,697	3,804	4,613	5,742	8,241	8,838	9,077
Bank borrowing	752	497	187	333	569	664	1,126	732	2,988	4,504	4,411	700
Share issues[3]	630	743	727	500	733	745	636	765	988	1,216	274	1,576
Total external funds	1,382	1,240	914	833	1,302	1,409	1,762	1,497	3,976	5,720	4,685	2,276
Total source of funds	4,377	4,233	3,682	3,634	4,881	5,106	5,566	6,110	9,718	13,961	13,523	11,353
Uses of funds												
Gross domestic fixed capital formation	2,289	2,447	2,424	2,359	2,617	2,992	3,354	3,470	3,796	4,718	5,848	7,028
Stocks[4]	892	710	565	356	822	951	1,331	759	943	3,526	6,089	2,382
Acquisition of domestic financial assets[5]	516	443	207	835	807	164	694	1,794	3,344	4,164	856	2,900
Net investment abroad[6]	146	181	109	−3	50	386	−474	−628	−70	−71	−703	−1,352
Other identified and unidentified assets	534	452	377	87	585	613	661	715	1,705	1,624	1,433	395
Total uses of funds	4,377	4,233	3,682	3,634	4,881	5,106	5,566	6,110	9,718	13,961	13,523	11,353

[1] Gross income net of unremitted profits overseas, of profits due abroad and of current and capital transfers. [2] Including tax on dividends.
[3] Proceeds of issues of ordinary shares for cash in the UK and issues of preference shares and debentures for cash and other loans and mortgages.
[4] Including stock appreciation. [5] Cash acquisitions of subsidiaries and trade investments plus bank deposits and other financial assets.
[6] Intra-company investment by UK companies overseas net of unremitted profits held abroad and by overseas companies net of unremitted profits held in UK plus import deposits and export credit less import credit.

TABLE III.4 Sources and uses of funds of industrial and commercial companies, 1964–75 (%)

	1964	*1965*	*1966*	*1967*	*1968*	*1969*	*1970*	*1971*	*1972*	*1973*	*1974*	*1975*
Sources of funds												
Gross Income[1] [4]	136·5	148·9	166·8	177·8	155·1	160·2	157·7	163·3	118·0	111·0	142·5	159·6
Tax payments[2]	–36·4	–39·7	–44·6	–53·2	–44·1	–47·5	–52·6	–52·0	–34·4	–25·3	–41·6	–38·1
Dividend payments	–18·8	–22·2	–24·1	–23·7	–17·3	–17·9	–14·6	–15·2	–9·6	–10·0	–11·2	–13·1
Interest payments	–12·9	–16·3	–23·0	–23·8	–20·4	–22·5	–22·2	–20·5	–14·9	–16·7	–24·4	28·6
Total internal fund	68·4	70·7	75·1	77·1	73·3	72·4	68·3	75·5	59·1	59·0	65·4	80·0
Bank borrowing	17·2	11·7	5·1	9·2	11·7	13·0	20·2	12·0	30·7	32·3	32·6	6·2
Share issues[3]	14·4	17·6	19·8	13·8	15·0	14·6	11·4	12·5	10·2	8·7	2·0	13·9
Total external funds	31·6	29·3	24·9	22·9	26·7	27·6	31·7	24·5	40·9	41·0	34·6	20·0
Total sources of funds*	100·0	100·0	100·0	100·0	100·0	100·0	100·0	100·0	100·0	100·0	100·0	100·0
Uses of funds												
Gross domestic fixed capital formation	52·3	57·8	65·8	64·9	53·6	58·6	60·3	56·8	39·1	33·8	43·2	61·9
Stocks[4]	20·4	16·8	15·3	9·8	16·8	18·6	23·9	12·4	9·7	25·3	45·0	21·0
Acquisition of domestic financial assets[5]	11·8	10·5	5·6	23·0	16·5	3·2	12·5	29·4	34·4	29·8	6·3	25·5
Net investment abroad[6]	3·3	4·3	3·0	—	1·0	7·6	–8·5	–10·3	–0·7	–0·5	–5·2	–11·9
Other identified and unidentified assets	12·2	10·7	10·2	2·4	12·0	12·0	11·9	11·7	17·5	11·6	10·6	3·5
Total uses of funds*	100·0	100·0	100·0	100·0	100·0	100·0	100·0	100·0	100·0	100·0	100·0	100·0

Source: Derived from *Trade and Industry* 4 February 1977.

[1-6] see footnotes to Table III.3. *Numbers have been 'rounded', thus totals may not sum to exactly 100 per cent.

about right; 25 per cent too high and 19 per cent too low. Question 3b shows that the average debt/equity ratio of the respondents was 47 per cent.

68. Constraints on capital gearing arise from lenders who impose particular limits and also from the fact that companies may be required under their Articles of Association to ensure that their dependence on borrowed funds does not exceed some stipulated level. In the past the income and capital gearing ratios of the average UK company have been well below these limits as managers have adopted more prudent positions. It is the risk of insolvency which makes gearing a critical aspect of a company's balance sheet. Attitudes to this risk—by both potential lenders and borrowers—are central to the determination of the most appropriate level of gearing in given circumstances. The financial strains of 1974, when companies borrowed £4,411 million from the banks, indicated the importance of companies maintaining prudent ratios. Table III.5 shows that capital gearing ratios have risen steadily over the last 20 years or so.

TABLE III.5 Manufacturing industry capital gearing*

(%)	
1954	18
1955	18
1956	18
1957	20
1958	21
1959	20
1960	20
1961	21
1962	22
1963	25
1964	26
1965	28
1966	30
1967	36
1968	40
1969	45
1970	49
1971	55
1972	54
1973	54
1974	57
1975	59
1976 (estimate)	48

Source: Diamond Commission. Report No 2. Table 32, and Mr E J Goodwin, of the accountancy staff of the Monopolies and Mergers Commission, in a personal capacity.

*Long-term loans plus bank borrowing as a percentage of ordinary and preference shares plus revenue, capital and tax reserves plus minority shareholders' interest (short-term loans are excluded because figures are not available for the whole period).

The ratios are based on book values rather than current prices.

69. Secondary gearing, the ratio of short-term to long-term debt, was relatively stable in the range of 51–63 per cent up to 1972. But the pressures of 1974 made it necessary to finance fixed assets, in part, by short-term financing and caused a marked deterioration in this ratio from which companies have slowly retreated (see Table III.6).

TABLE III.6 Secondary gearing (%) listed companies in manufacturing and distribution

	A	*B*	*C*
1960	51		
1961	57		
1962	51		
1963	53		
1964	55		
1964	57		
1965	63		
1966	59		
1967	51		
1968	52		
1969	56		
1970	63		
1971	55	73	64
1972	54	74	62
1973	68	88	68
1974	94	118	80
1975*	83	109	67

Source: Derived from Business Monitor M3 Company Finance.

* Based on accounts received up to 30 September 1975 only.

A: Bank overdrafts and loans as a per cent of long-term loans.

B: Bank overdrafts and loans plus other short-term loans as a per cent of long-term loans.

C: Bank overdrafts and loans plus other short-term loans as a per cent of long-term loans plus deferred tax.

70. In the 1960s institutional lenders generally required individual companies to have long-term debt interest covered about four times by available income: the average cover was well over twice this requirement during the period. The marked increase in bank borrowing in 1974 and the rise in interest rates, combined with low industrial profits, has resulted in interest payments taking a much larger proportion of corporate income than during the 1960s. Table III.7 illustrates that there was a steady decline in the degree of interest cover during the 1960s but that the dramatic events of 1974–75 resulted in a marked worsening, from which industry has yet to recover.

71. Although international comparisons show that the capital gearing of UK companies is low compared with that of some other industrialised nations,[16] this does not mean that UK companies should increase their debt/equity ratios. International comparisons of gearing need to be treated with great care and should not be viewed in isolation from the experiences of each individual country.[17] The major reason for the higher gearing of companies in many other countries is that their market for equity capital is not as wide as that in the UK. In the UK companies have a better choice of financing methods. The success of the USA, whose industrial and financial structure is similar to that in this country, should be noted.

[16] See, for example, the Royal Commission on the Distribution of Income and Wealth *Report No 2* (Cmnd 6172) Appendix R; or Samuels J M, Groves R E V and Goddard C S *Company Finance in Europe*. The Institute of Chartered Accountants in England and Wales 1975.

[17] See, for example, "On Misunderstanding Capital Markets" I J Fraser *The Banker* June 1976; or "The British Capital Market and Banking System—Some Criticisms Examined" H B Rose *Barclays Bank Review* August 1976.

TABLE III.7 Interest cover: industrial and commercial companies

	Total income[1] divided by interest payments[2]	Gross trading profits divided by interest payments[2]	Gross trading profits after deducting stock appreciation divided by interest payments[2]
1960	10·5	8·8	8·6
1961	9·0	7·5	7·3
1962	8·6	7·0	6·8
1963	9·4	7·8	7·6
1964	9·1	7·6	7·2
1965	8·0	6·6	6·3
1966	6·5	5·4	5·1
1967	6·4	5·3	5·2
1968	6·4	5·3	4·9
1969	5·9	4·8	4·3
1970	5·9	4·7	4·1
1971	6·5	5·4	4·7
1972	6·7	5·5	4·8
1973	5·7	4·4	3·3
1974	4·6	3·5	2·1
1975	4·5	3·5	2·3
1976	4·9	3·9	2·5
Seasonally adjusted			
1974 Q1	4·9	3·7	1·4
Q2	4·6	3·5	1·9
Q3	4·5	3·5	2·5
Q4	4·5	3·5	2·4
1975 Q1	4·5	3·5	2·0
Q2	4·3	3·4	2·2
Q3	4·4	3·4	2·3
Q4	4·9	3·8	2·7
1976 Q1	5·2	4·1	2·8
Q2	5·0	3·9	2·5
Q3	4·8	3·8	2·3
Q4	4·7	3·7	2·3

Source: Derived from *Financial Statistics.*

[1] Gross trading profits *plus* rent and non-trading income *plus* income from abroad (net of taxes paid abroad).

[2] Including dividends on preference shares. Prior to 6 April 1973 the dividends on preference shares are gross of tax; after this date they are actual payments.

72. **Moreover, even in the very difficult period through which we have been passing, with gearing ratios strained, there is almost no evidence that companies in the UK have found difficulty in raising sufficient external funds to meet the profitable investment opportunities open to them. It has not been a shortage of external finance that has restricted UK industrial investment but rather a lack of confidence that industry will be able to earn a sufficient return and investors a sufficient after tax yield.**

New equity and loans

73. The Diamond Commission clearly identified the role which equity plays in the capital structure of a company, drawing particular attention to the

significance of shareholders funds. They constitute the risk capital of a company and bear the brunt of variation in profits, so helping to reconcile fixed liabilities with variable income. The Commission concluded that: "Given the uncertainty of a company's future income, and the fact that fixed interest borrowing entails a contractual liability to make regular payments to creditors, there is a need for enterprises to obtain some part at least of their finance in a form which admits of variable remuneration. Equity capital meets this need in the private sector and can thus be seen as providing a basis for borrowing".[18]

74. Although the role of equity is primarily related to the degree of risk of a company, equity is suitable for particular types of long-term investment. Where investments have a long or uncertain lag between the initial expenditure and returns, there is a case for finance which does not have to be remunerated initially. Long-term investment which is subject to fluctuation in its income also requires some element of risk capital.

75. UK companies' two traditional means of finance for fixed investment, retentions and new capital issues, are not optional alternatives. In practice, companies often work out their investment programmes and calculate how far they would be covered by retained earnings. If retained earnings are insufficient then long-term borrowing will be considered. If a company is at the limit of what it considers to be its "safe" long-term borrowing then it may need to raise more equity. It must also ensure that its dividend policy is consistent with its expected earnings and financing needs. In deciding its long-term dividend policy a company can opt to build up retentions for investment use, but this limits flexibility in external fund-raising.

76. In certain cases a company may raise finance for a specific investment but in general a precise identification of any part of the total finance raised with a particular activity is not possible, since the finances of a company are treated as a pool from which expenditure on all of its activities is financed. However, certain types of finance (e.g. grants and loans from governmental sources) can normally only be utilised for specific investments. A company's financing programme should be viewed as a whole and in relation to the position it has reached in its development, its current financial position and its investment plans.

77. Some investments have features which can influence the shares of equity and debt (and the term structure of the debt) which are sought for financing the project. But, even where finance may be associated with a particular investment the ability to remunerate it depends on the overall performance of the company rather than just on the returns from the particular investment. The choice of finance will therefore be limited to those alternatives which keep the individual company's overall capital structure within acceptable bounds.

78. Bank overdrafts, although often containing a "core" element which is effectively medium term, may have to be reduced in relation to companies' needs if banks are squeezed. A company pursuing a sound financial policy will have this in mind in building up short-term debts. The question of inflation apart, the choice for financing long-term investment is thus between equity and

---

[18] Royal Commission on the Distribution of Income and Wealth. *Report No 2: Income from Companies and its Distribution*. July 1975 (Cmnd 6172) Paragraph 189.

long-term debt (at either a fixed or variable interest charge). The nature of the operations in which a company is involved will affect the extent to which its profits fluctuate and will thus influence the extent to which it can prudently finance its activities out of debt. Debt financing is hazardous in a period of uncertain future income.

79. There is a general convention, as a first approximation, that companies use short-term bank loans for financing current assets and use long-term borrowing or equity for fixed assets. The development of a number of new loan facilities by the banks and others, such as medium-term loans and leasing, has become increasingly important to companies and provides them with an added degree of flexibility in their financing arrangements. Industry generally considers that financing variable working capital needs by short-term financing gives more flexibility, especially during periods of great uncertainty and inflation.

80. There is a place for long-term (20–25 years) fixed interest loans, at acceptable rates, and indeed, there was an active new issue market in loan stocks until the recent crisis. A return to long-term fixed interest financing is unlikely until both the inflation rate and general business uncertainty decline. A lower inflation rate and a reduction in the demand for such funds by the Government should bring the fall in interest rates that would be needed to revive this market.

81. We draw attention to the fact that holders of gilt-edged securities are not liable to Capital Gains Tax on such securities, so long as the securities have been held for more than one year, whilst capital gains accruing to holders of industrial debentures are liable to tax. This places industrial financing at a disadvantage[19].

82. In recent years there has been an increase in the use of variable interest rate[20] medium-term loans by industry, although there are problems in their use relating to interest cover and existing loan stock covenants. Industrialists generally consider that issuing indexed loan stocks or long-term variable rate bonds is not in the interests of companies, at least at the present time[21]. The extensive use of such open-ended financial commitments, especially at a time of great uncertainty about inflation and corporate profitability, should be avoided because of the cashflow risks involved. **It is stressed that the need is not for measures that mitigate the effects of inflation but rather for the rate of inflation to be reduced.**

83. As noted earlier, companies not only require debt finance but also need to raise additional equity finance. Equities are risk investments and thus have to offer the possibility of high returns to compensate for the uncertainty of return. As the Diamond Commission noted: "we accept the view that capital values are based on expected future returns from shares, which are in part at least, related to future dividends. The prospect of increased future dividends, therefore, will increase the share price and thus facilitate equity issues."[22] The imposition of a ceiling on returns by way of dividend controls, if sustained,

---

[19] We recognise, however, that pension funds are not affected by it.

[20] Usually linked to London inter-bank rates.

[21] See Appendix I questions A 4d(i) and A 4d(ii).

[22] Royal Commission on the Distribution of Income and Wealth *Report No 2* July 1975. (Cmnd 6172). Paragraph 328.

UNIVERSITY
OF YORK
LIBRARY

ultimately reduces the capital values and attractiveness of equities in general and of relatively risky equities in particular.

84. Detailed exemptions to the dividend limits have been permitted by the Treasury to alleviate some of the worst effects; but this is a very poor second best. Because the exemptions are only allowed in certain short-term qualifying situations companies are prevented from pursuing long-term dividend policies which are consistent with their desired pattern of finance for investment. We would stress the damage which dividend controls do, particularly over a long period. The efficiency of the capital market is reduced and business decisions are unnecessarily distorted.

85. From time to time activity in the new issues market falls to very low levels. Such periods are usually those of low share prices and in which the business outlook has seemed particularly unfavourable. In 1974, for example, share issues were generally considered to be inappropriate because of the low level to which share prices had fallen as a response to the adverse economic and industrial expectations at that time. As the outlook improved and confidence returned it became desirable, and proved possible, for companies to undertake long-term equity funding to restore corporate gearing to more normal levels.

86. The attitude of a company board to the company's share price is typically that it should be broadly in line with that of other companies similar in size, growth and character. If the share price is too low, it may make raising funds expensive, involve the risk of take-over and hinder the company from making necessary acquisitions; if too high, there is a danger that a fall in price could result in market disappointment, to the possible prejudice of future activities.

87. The influence of share prices on investment decisions is complex. As far as a general fall in share prices is concerned, it is often difficult to distinguish its direct effects from its indirect effects as an expresion of investors' views concerning the outlook for activity and profits. Short-term fluctuations in share prices may affect the timing of share issues but are not considered to be a material factor in the investment decisions of our members. Investment plans are usually based on a longer-term view of strategy, sales and profits.

88. The timing of approaches to the market will depend upon judgments about when the company might secure the best terms for itself. This may lead companies to make long-term financing arrangements in advance of major spending programmes or to rely upon short-term financing whilst awaiting a better moment for long-term borrowing or equity financing. Whatever the period ahead for which cash plans are made there will be regular revision and up-dating, with consequent changes in external financing plans, including the balance between various forms of external finance.

State finance

89. There is, of course, also a certain amount of State finance. The Government as a source of funds has been helpful in some industries especially where there has been consistency of policy and where there have been known and well-understood criteria applicable to all. We should note that some of our members report that Government agencies are much slower in giving decisions in response to financing requests than are private sector institutions, thus reducing their

potential effectiveness. As our evidence to the Wilson Committee clearly demonstrates, **there is no need for an extension of public sector involvement in the provision of finance for investment.** The services provided by the private-sector providers of finance have been adequate and, given freedom of action, can be expected to continue to meet the demands of industry.

90. The Government may provide assistance for research and development, in support of its regional policies, to ease structural change, and in some cases to assist temporarily larger firms facing serious financial difficulties which may lead to high unemployment and serious disruption to other companies and industries while assessment is made of whether they can succeed in the future.[23] However, selective support has often had the effect of bolstering companies which have failed, to the deteriment of competitors whose own efforts to survive have thereby been prejudiced. Selective Government interference in industrial decisions has repeatedly been shown to result in considerable waste, supporting inefficient production of unwanted goods, the net effect of which must be to slow the creation of wealth and the improvement of living standards.

91. It has been suggested that the present system of investment allowances should be withdrawn and replaced by an investment reserve scheme. This would be a major mistake. We should emphasise that one of the prime requirements of investment incentives is that industrialists should be confident that the incentives will not be subject to frequent changes in either rate or form. The first-year allowance has been a valuable incentive to industry and if the hoped for recovery in industrial investment is to be encouraged then the Government should seek an early opportunity to reassure industrialists that this incentive is to continue.

---

[23] CBI views on the limited conditions under which State finance should be available are set out in *The Road To Recovery*.

PART IV: RELATIONSHIPS BETWEEN THE SUPPLIERS AND USERS OF EXTERNAL FINANCE

The Committee asked for views on the relationships between the users of finance in industry and those who supply it, either directly or as intermediaries. We are also asked how well the demands of industry and trade for finance on reasonable terms have been met by the banking and investing institutions.

A vote of confidence

92. Considering the enormous burden of interest charges, and the nature of the relationship, there are bound to be some complaints by industrial borrowers about those supplying finance. To get these into perspective, we asked a sample of industrial companies to tell us what they thought of the services provided to them by the banks and other financial institutions.

93. The result is a considerable vote of confidence. Table IV.1 sets out the results in full: it speaks for itself.

Future developments

94. The private and public sector pension funds, insurance companies, investment trusts, unit trusts and charitable trusts between them own approximately a half of the equity of British quoted public companies. They exist to serve the interests of a very large number of people, often of small or modest means, and have a duty to ensure that their funds are properly used.

95. We believe that it is in the interests of all concerned that there should be a regular, continuing, two-way relationship between a company and its shareholders in which shareholders of all kinds adopt a questioning and stimulating role, and directors endeavour to consult their shareholders both formally and informally on difficult questions of policy or practice. All shareholders should

TABLE IV.1: The CBI questionnaire: question 5

In general, how do you assess the services provided to you by the following as sources of finance:

	Size group (No. of employees)	*Good*	*Fair*	*Bad*	*Not applicable*	*TOTAL (No. of respondents)*
(i) **Clearing banks**	0 – 199	20	7	0	3	30
	200 – 499	21	7	1	1	30
	500 – 4,999	39	4	0	3	46
	5,000+	60	10	1	3	74
	All respondents	141*	28	2	10	181*
(ii) **Other British banks**	0 – 199	7	3	0	20	30
	200 – 499	9	3	1	17	30
	500 – 4,999	16	8	0	22	46
	5,000+	41	13	1	19	74
	All respondents	73	27	2	79*	181*

*This includes one respondent who did not indicate size of company.

	Size group (No. of employees)	Good	Fair	Bad	Not applicable	TOTAL (No. of respondents)
(iii) Overseas banks	0–199	4	1	2	23	30
	200–499	3	2	1	24	30
	500–4,999	22	2	0	22	46
	5,000+	55	15	0	4	74
	All respondents	84	20	3	74*	181*
(iv) Consortium banks	0–199	0	0	1	29	30
	200–499	2	0	0	28	30
	500–4,999	3	4	1	38	46
	5,000+	21	15	0	38	74
	All respondents	26	19	2	134*	181*
(v) National Giro	0–199	0	0	0	30	30
	200–499	0	0	0	30	30
	500–4,999	0	0	0	46	46
	5,000+	0	1	1	72	74
	All respondents	0	1	1	179*	181*
(vi) Issuing houses	0–199	0	1	0	29	30
	200–499	0	1	0	29	30
	500–4,999	6	1	0	39	46
	5,000+	25	14	2	33	74
	All respondents	32*	17	2	130	181*
(vii) Accepting houses	0–199	1	0	1	28	30
	200–499	0	2	0	28	30
	500–4,999	9	6	0	31	46
	5,000+	35	15	0	24	74
	All respondents	45	23	1	112*	181*
(viii) Insurance companies	0–199	3	2	0	25	30
	200–499	6	3	0	21	30
	500–4,999	4	7	0	35	46
	5,000+	9	12	3	50	74
	All respondents	22	24	3	132*	181*
(ix) Pension funds	0–199	2	1	0	27	30
	200–499	6	1	0	23	30
	500–4,999	1	5	0	40	46
	5,000+	6	6	2	60	74
	All respondents	16*	13	2	150	181*

*This includes one respondent who did not indicate size of company.

	Size group (No. of employees)	*Good*	*Fair*	*Bad*	*Not applicable*	*TOTAL (No. of respondents)*
(x) **Factoring companies**	0 – 199	2	0	2	26	30
	200 – 499	11	2	2	15	30
	500 – 4,999	0	0	4	42	46
	5,000+	0	2	1	71	74
	All respondents	13	4	9	155*	181*
(xi) **Leasing companies**	0 – 199	7	4	1	18	30
	200 – 499	11	4	0	15	30
	500 – 4,999	15	6	2	23	46
	5,000+	22	19	2	31	74
	All respondents	55	33	5	88*	181*
(xii) **Hire purchase companies**	0 – 199	9	4	1	16	30
	200 – 499	10	4	0	16	30
	500 – 4,999	9	5	1	31	46
	5,000+	5	4	2	63	74
	All respondents	34*	17	4	126	181*

*This includes one respondent who did not indicate size of company.

be involved in the task. Institutional shareholders, because of their strong position and greater expertise in investment matters, can be expected to take a leading role in this process.

96. Various proposals have been put forward as to how a closer relationship could best be achieved. This subject is now being given further consideration and we shall submit additional evidence to the Committee at a later date.

PART V: DEFECTS AND GAPS

The Committee asked us whether there are defects or gaps in the arrangements for raising finance, and if so how they might be remedied so as to improve the flow of savings into industry and trade and stimulate investment.

Smaller companies

97. The importance to the economy of smaller companies, and new companies, is very great. Firms with under 200 employees contribute directly about 18 per cent of the net output of British manufactures; this rises to 26 per cent if "small" is taken to mean under 500 employees. They provide a wide variety of essential goods and services; they are the source of many valuable innovations; they employ a great many people (29 per cent of manufacturing industry employment is in firms with less than 500 employees); their industrial relations are often extremely good; and their adaptability and resourcefulness are essential to industrial and commercial life. All this means that particularly in the present economic difficulties it is very important to make conditions as favourable as they can reasonably be for these companies.

98. It is often harder for a small company, or a company being started, to obtain money than for an established, successful, large company. The risks are greater and the administrative costs to a lender are a higher proportion of the money provided. More depends on the ability of the few key people running the small business, and this is hard for the outsider to judge. The very fact that a company is small means that the business is likely to be less diversified and more vulnerable to ill fortune.

99. These are facts of life. They mean that people lending money to a small company, putting up equity—or, indeed, providing trade credit—look for a higher return on their money; an extra 3 per cent on borrowed money is not untypical. They also mean that small companies will find more problems in raising money, even at a higher cost, than large ones.

100. Improvements could certainly be made in the present arrangements for raising finance by smaller companies.

101. The first priority should be to create a better general business climate, so that confidence and profitability can be greater. This requires action to reduce the rate of inflation, to provide more stable policies, and to encourage profitability. The complexity and burden of legislative and other controls on business need to be reduced. Public expenditure and taxes must be lower. Profit margin controls and dividend controls should be abolished—they discourage the search for better profitability, raise the cost of capital and distort business decisions.

102. More specifically, but still outside the narrow field of external finance, Government policies should pay more regard to the importance of allowing and encouraging smaller companies to prosper. Planning controls and IDC controls should be simplified, and made more practicable. Although we are fully in favour of fair competition, which may result in closures of unsuccessful companies, prices of large companies should not be held down artificially by the Price Commission in disregard of the likely consequences for smaller competitors. The burden of form-filling for administrative as well as statistical purposes

should be reduced. The VAT threshold should be further raised, to relieve small businesses of unnecessary bureaucratic chores.

103. We need to create a new climate to allow smaller businesses to flourish. Tax changes are essential for this.

104. The tax system should give greater encouragement to smaller companies and to entrepreneurs. The rewards for success in business need to be drastically improved. First and foremost, income tax rates must be reduced on higher incomes. The UK cannot afford to have marginal tax rates higher than in competing countries. 60 per cent should be the maximum rate of tax on income from employment to bring it into line with the weighted average of the highest marginal rates in EEC countries. This new top rate would compare with an effective maximum marginal rate on earned income of 54 per cent in France and 56 per cent in West Germany. Tax on income from investments must be correspondingly reduced. Capital taxes also need to be reduced. Capital Gains Tax should no longer be levied on increases in asset values merely reflecting inflation; nor should Capital Gains Tax and Capital Transfer Tax both be levied on the same gift, as happens at present.

105. Capital Transfer Tax should be reformed: to allow transfer to other members of a family (consanguinity relief); to provide further relief for business assets; levied at lower rates; and levied according to the amount received by each individual, rather than by the total amount transferred by the donor. Proposals for a wealth tax should be firmly rejected. "Shortfall" provisions designed to penalise close companies wishing to retain profits in the business should be abolished as the marginal rates of Income Tax are reduced. One particular technical matter, the deferred tax liabilities resulting from the form taken by the interim system of stock relief and other factors, has been referred to elsewhere in this evidence (para 66). It presents particular problems for smaller companies, in discouraging investment decisions and in deterring lenders.

106. The tax system must make better allowance for the needs of small business. Owners are regarded as wealthy individuals and so are taxed at exorbitant rates on earnings, on dividends, on capital gains and on capital transfers; yet it is in practice almost impossible to get enough money out of the small business to pay such taxes without a crippling effect on the funds needed inside the firm—for expansion or even maintenance of present production and employment levels.

107. This is because with very high tax rates a huge multiple of the sum required has to be withdrawn from the firm. For example, someone paying income tax at the top rate and wishing to transfer his business to somebody else would have to pay 98 per cent of any dividends he took from the business to pay Capital Transfer Tax (CTT) in Income Tax. This means that to pay a CTT bill of, say, £100,000 he would need to take out of the business no less than £5,000,000 in dividends. If he tried to save the £100,000 out of his salary over a period it would still cost the firm no less than £588,000.

108. Such rates of tax effectively prevent the owners of small businesses from making sensible arrangements to transfer ownership. There can be a hard choice between doing nothing (at potential disadvantage to the business) or seeking

more or less artificial arrangement or damaging the business by withdrawing relatively huge sums of money for the Inland Revenue.

109. The fairer tax treatment and a better general climate for industry and commerce, and the specific emphasis on smaller companies which we are seeking, would do far more to improve the financial position of smaller companies than any possible modifications to the financial institutions or their practices.

110. Smaller companies replying to our survey (Appendix I), like larger companies, are in general very complimentary about their relations with the financial institutions. Although smaller companies taking part in the CBI Industrial Trends Survey over the last few years have reported an inability to raise external finance as a factor limiting their investment opportunities, this has not been a problem particular to small firms. The average response since October 1974 (see Table V.1) has been 4 per cent for small firms (under 200 employees) compared with 5 per cent for large firms (over 5,000 employees). Replies to another question in the "Trends" survey show how many firms find "shortage of credit or finance" (whether internal, external or both) to be a factor limiting output in the short term. The results are available since 1965; the average for small firms is 12 per cent, for large firms 4 per cent.

111. Some improvements in the arrangements for raising external finance by smaller companies could, however, be made.

112. Firstly, there are now so many different specialist financial institutions, and so many varied forms of finance, that it is a real problem for the smaller company to know whether it is asking the right people for the right form of finance for the particular circumstances. Advice is of couse available from accountants and brokers as well as from banks and other financial institutions and CBI and others have published guides. Nevertheless, a new, comprehensive guide, offering practical advice on terms and forms of finance, would be valuable; it might also cover the best ways to present applications for different forms of finance. The evidence submitted by the financial institutions to the Committee provides a source of up-to-date material on which such a guide could be based. The guide should cover the NEB, and the subsidy schemes offered by Government departments, as well as the private sector financial institutions. It should also include advice from the Stock Exchange on the possibility of a public issue of shares.

113. Secondly, more information should be published by Government departments about the criteria which they apply when deciding whether or not to accept applications for any support schemes. Where these criteria include a minimum size of application they should be changed. Such schemes should discriminate as little as possible, and certainly not against smaller companies.

114. Thirdly, we welcome the fact that the banks have been putting increasing effort into training their staff, particularly to advise companies. For the smaller company, the quality of service given by local bank managers is extremely important; mutual understanding needs to be fostered.

115. Turning to the forms of finance, there is a question about the availability of equity capital. The grave decline in industrial profitability has reduced

TABLE V.1 Percentage of firms listing their inability to raise external finance as a factor likely to limit their capital expenditure authorisation on buildings and plant and machinery over the next twelve months

	Size group 0 – 199 *Employees*	*Size group* 200 – 499 *Employees*	*Size group* 500 – 4,999 *Employees*	*Size group* 5,000+ *Employees*
1974				
October Survey 54	6	12	6	12
1975				
January Survey 55	6	8	8	11
April Survey 56	4	5	4	7
July Survey 57	4	3	2	4
October Survey 58	2	4	2	3
1976				
January Survey 59	3	2	2	3
April Survey 60	2	2	1	7
July Survey 61	4	3	1	0
October Survey 62	3	2	2	2
1977				
January Survey 63	4	3	1	4
April Survey 64	3	2	2	4
July Survey 65	3	3	1	1

Source: CBI Industrial Trends Surveys.

Note: From Survey 56 inclusive the replies are weighted by net output and employment size. Prior to Survey 56 the figures are unweighted.

the internal generation of shareholders' funds. High rates of tax on capital and upper incomes and dividend controls have reduced the availability of private capital which might otherwise have helped to meet the need for equity, perhaps particularly for new and expanding businesses. Small private investors may be willing to take greater risks and lower returns in the short term when helping to start a new business, if the after-tax possibilities are greater in the long term.

116. The remedy lies mainly in reducing taxes and in rebuilding profitability, but we welcome the development by the financial institutions of new ways of helping to meet the need for equity capital.

117. A contribution might also be made by the introduction of an effective over-the-counter market in securities such as exists in the USA, or by other ways of improving the marketability of shares in smaller companies. This is a question to which we shall return in further evidence to the Committee.

118. The banks have been increasing their medium-term lending to industry, and this is welcome, although whilst inflation and interest rates are high there will be limits on the ability of companies to take on medium-term fixed interest liabilities. Some assistance might nonetheless be given by the Government providing some refinancing facility (as has been done for export credit and shipbuilding loans); we hope that this possibility will be explored by the Committee.

119. We have mentioned the fact that smaller companies generally have to pay higher interest rates than larger companies. It would be helpful to have more information on whether this difference is more or less than can be explained by the greater risks and administrative costs of lending to smaller companies.

120. One of the suggestions considered by the Bolton Committee[24] in its investigation into this field was the establishment of an organisation similar to the Small Business Administration which operates in the USA. This proposal has recently received further attention. The main purpose of setting up such a scheme in the UK might be to guarantee medium and long-term loans by the banks to smaller companies and to serve as a means of providing financial advice and information. Such a guarantee would help to make loans more readily available to small firms, without by-passing the banks or setting up yet more bureaucracy. There may be a case for a more explicit subsidy element to help very small, or starting, firms with small loans (measured in tens of thousands of pounds) if only as a temporary expedient until the problems of tax and inflation have been dealt with. We shall consider this further in our later evidence.

121. A recent comparative study[25] of the development of new technology-based firms in the United Kingdom and the Federal Republic of Germany concludes that "The City of London is much more responsive to the needs of the individual entrepreneur and the small firm than the German financial community". The study says the main reasons why the level of activity in this area has declined are; the poor performance of the economy which has reduced the number and attractiveness of investment opportunities; the low success rate of venture capital investments and the absence of "big winners"; the collapse of the stock-market in 1974 and the impossibility of "going public"; the failure, or lack of success, of a number of venture capital organisations; the shock waves of the secondary banking crisis in 1973 and 1974; and adverse changes in taxation, including the introduction of Capital Transfer Tax. The study suggests, however, that although the private sector organisations are willing to take on a high level of commercial risk—and are receptive and positive towards new and developing ventures with high growth potential—they are generally unwilling to accept technological risk in addition (partly because of the high failure rate, and the absence of notable successes, from such investments). The Committee may wish to consider whether the facilities provided in this area[26] are sufficient.

122. Recent CBI studies of the financing of smaller companies have not been confined solely to the United Kingdom. We have also led a UNICE[27] study of the financial problems of, and sources of finance for, small and medium-sized enterprises throughout the EEC, the Report on which will be available in October and will be submitted to the Committee as part of our supplementary evidence.

---

[24] *The Report of the Committee of Inquiry on Small Firms* (The Bolton Committee). November 1971 (Cmnd 4811).

[25] *New Technology-Based Firms in the United Kingdom and the Federal Republic of Germany* by Arthur D Little Ltd., Anglo-German Foundation for the Study of Industrial Society.

[26] Technical Development Capital Ltd., (TDC) is the largest venture capital company in Europe.

[27] *Finance for Small and Medium-sized Enterprises* Union des Industries de la Communaute Europeenne. Available October 1977.

123. This study has revealed that although the problems faced by small enterprises vary in degree from one European country to another, the principal problems are similar throughout the EEC. Most importantly, small enterprises now find it more difficult to build up their own resources, either by earning an adequate rate of profit and being able to retain a sufficient proportion of their earnings after tax, or by obtaining more risk capital from their existing owners and their relatives, friends and business associates, as their real incomes and capital have been eroded by inflation and taxation. There are common problems also with the exchange of information between small enterprises and the sources of finance: too often those in search of external finance are unaware of the range of sources of finance available to them, or of the best procedures for applying for credit or capital. Third, small enterprises are repeatedly concerned that the costs to them of external finance are regularly higher than those charged to large concerns by a greater margin than may be justified by reference to differences in administrative cost or commercial risk. Fourth, they regularly experience difficulty in obtaining venture capital on terms which are acceptable in respect both of cost and of the period for which funds are offered.

124. Smaller firms throughout the EEC share the view that improvement of their financial situation is dependent upon improved profitability and lower taxation. Stronger internal finances will help them to obtain more external finance on acceptable terms. They want less rather than more State intervention in arrangements for providing credit and capital; though they would never deny that Governments may be able to help by offering, for example, loan guarantees to lending institutions, provided that such assistance is made generally available, and is unconditional.

125. Some features of the fiscal and financial systems of other countries covered in our study might usefully be considered for adoption or imitation in the United Kingdom. For example, the reform of the Italian fiscal system begun in 1974 made several concessions to small businesses with regard to accounting procedures and the frequency of tax returns, and offered additional tax allowances for the owners of some small unincorporated businesses in respect of the income which they receive from their businesses. In France it is now proposed that the incomes of new small industrial companies should be subject to lower rates of tax in their first three years of operation (though it is doubtful whether relatively speaking, this would provide any greater assistance than the existing small companies rate of Corporation Tax in this country).

126. Also in Italy, where there is clearly the greatest concern among small businesses over the availability of short-term bank credit, there are now some 6,000 small firms participating in "credit guarantee consortia" organised by small firms themselves, the banks, local Chambers of Commerce and professional associations. Similar arrangements are being introduced in France to assist the supply of medium-term credit for new industrial enterprises and are already in use, for the benefit of small enterprises in some sectors, in Denmark. The Danish arrangements involve some assistance from public funds, but in general smaller firms are opposed to Government involvement in such credit guarantee schemes.

127. The supply of medium-term bank credit appears to be improving through-

out the EEC, though it remains to be seen whether this is a permanent change in the banks' policies or only a temporary development which will be reversed when activity levels and the demand for short-term credit begin to pick up. In the Netherlands the provision of medium-term bank loans for smaller firms for certain specified purposes has long been assisted by the Government by means of guarantees to the lending banks. Formerly these guarantees were available only to the Nederlandse Middenstandsbank NV, but since March of this year they have been extended to all major banks. This assistance has been welcomed as the Government has made no attempt to influence the banks' lending policies, and indeed has allowed to the banks full discretion in granting credit except in respect of loans in excess of a certain amount, now equivalent to £150,000, which must be approved by the Ministry for Economic Affairs.

128. Few arrangements have been made for the provision of either medium-term credit or risk capital by non-bank institutions especially for the benefit of smaller firms which compare favourably with those which already exist in this country. Most "special arrangements" for smaller firms have involved some assistance from public funds which has led, sooner or later, to Government interference with institutions' lending and investment policies, disregard for normal economic and commercial criteria, and a clear waste of public funds. An exception may be made, however, of the support which the German Federal Government provides by way of guarantees to Deutsche-Wagnisfinanzierungs Gesellschaft mbH (WFG), a venture capital company recently established by the major banks. Contrary to the view often expressed in this country, the German banks are not revealed as either significant or willing providers, on their own account, of risk capital for small or new enterprises.

129. One of the major lessons which may be learned from the experience of other EEC countries regarding the financing of smaller firms concerns the bridging of "information gaps" between those firms and the financial community. Close attention should be paid to the activities in the Netherlands of Centraal Institutt voor het Midden- en Kleinbedrijf (CIMK), established with some help from public funds not as a source of finance but to assist small businesses with information on sources of finance, advice on financing methods, investment appraisal, and the preparation of applications for credit and capital from outside sources. While there is some similarity between the work of CIMK and that of the Small Firms Information Centre Service and the pilot Counselling Service operated in this country by the Department of Industry, CIMK has the advantage in the eyes of small businesses of operating independently of any Government department.

130. Particular problems in obtaining finance can be experienced by smaller companies expanding their export business. Complaints are made about banks being unwilling to provide additional credit on the security of firm export orders or Irrevocable Letters of Credit obtained from overseas customers, even where the status of the issuer of the Letter of Credit is unexceptionable. While we would not share the view of some critics of the banks that they should make separate credit facilities available, on top of those which they have already provided, related to the working capital requirements of production to meet particular export orders, but believe that creditworthiness should be judged and credit limits set by reference to the totality of the enterprise's operations, we do feel that there is sufficient evidence to prompt concern that some bankers are

unduly cautious in increasing their lending to small businesses which can demonstrate a clear increase of their exporting business.

131. As for provision of export credit insurance, we have on many occasions pointed out how some of the facilities provided by the ECGD are beyond the reach of small exporters, and have called for the lowering of thresholds in respect of, for example, cost escalation cover.

Par value of shares

132. We would like to see fresh consideration given to the possibility of introducing shares with no par value. Although, as Appendix I shows, par values create problems in only a minority of cases, we wonder whether the advantages of the system justify its retention. We shall return to this question in our later evidence to the Committee.

International operations and their financing

133. It is sometimes alleged that investment by British companies overseas has been at the expense of exports or investment in the UK. This has not been the case, for direct investment overseas and exports are normally complements not substitutes.[28] The alternative to overseas investment is often not to invest at all. This is supported by the response to question B2 of our survey which indicates that for 95 per cent of those companies which considered additional investment abroad in recent years, their investment in the UK has been unchanged or lower as a result of the restrictions on investment abroad.

134. British companies need to make direct investments overseas to develop new markets, expand existing ones, and to protect markets which would otherwise be lost. Import regulations, administrative procedures or political factors frequently favour the establishment of local companies and commercial pressures may require joint ventures with local companies already in the market.

135. Only a very small proportion of the UK's overseas investment is in sectors where there might be a conflict with exports and over 80 per cent of new investment in the period 1965 to 1975 was financed by reinvested profits earned abroad or by overseas borrowing.[29] Under current exchange control rules the financing of direct investment overseas does not draw upon the official exchange market except in special cases which promote a quick and continuing benefit to the balance of payments. The net effects of overseas investment on the UK's reserves has been both favourable and massive, averaging some £2,250 million a year over the period 1973–1975 when account is taken of overseas investment in the UK private sector.[30] As the current account moves into surplus the present exchange control on overseas investment should be relaxed.

136. Industry supports the assistance provided by ECGD but ECGD must be more flexible when considering, and faster when processing, applications. If credit limits were revised upwards at frequent intervals in order to reflect inflation, this would help. We would welcome an extension to some of the recent schemes devised to cope with the problems arising from high rates of

---

[28] See *Effects of UK Direct Investment Overseas—Final Report* W B Reddaway et al. Cambridge University Press 1968.

[29] The average for the period 1971–75 was 109 per cent.

[30] Economic Progress Report. HM Treasury September 1976.

inflation in the UK, the magnitude of risks associated with large projects and the stringent contractual conditions being demanded by some overseas customers. ECGD has recently had largely to replace the sterling buyer credit scheme with a foreign currency scheme. They should operate this with flexibility and an understanding of the difficulties exporters will have to face as a result of the new measures, especially those arising from the foreign exchange risk in the period between tendering and the signing of the contract of sale. It was announced on 28 July that ECGD would introduce a new scheme aimed at mitigating such risks; this came into effect on 1 August. Our first reaction is that the scheme appears to leave uncovered a number of important areas.

137. As we mentioned earlier, there is considerable resentment amongst smaller firms that some ECGD facilities are not available to support export contracts of a size open to them. The eligibility criteria for cost-escalation, pre-shipment finance, performance bonds and project participants' insolvency cover should be improved.[31]

138. UK exporters, contractors and consultants face a number of problems in 'jumbo' projects overseas involving complete package deals and quite different sectors of industry. We welcome the work undertaken to see what can be done to enable British industry to bid for such contracts more easily and to promote active UK participation in multinational consortia, and early action is essential. As a means of mitigating some of these problems and to enable European industry to compete on a basis of equality with US and Japanese industry we would support the early establishment of a European Export Bank.

139. The Government should use 'crédit mixte' more positively. On occasions a limited use of aid funds to soften commercial credits would help British industry to secure important overseas projects, especially those which involve penetration of new markets. Used carefully, dispositions of this kind need not lead to increased competition in credits or the assumption of obligations by the borrowing country which exceed its capacity to repay.

Profitability

140. The main 'gap' in the arrangements for raising finance is the shortage of profit. After tax and interest, many companies are still operating at a loss in real terms. While industry is so unprofitable, there are bound to be some problems in raising new external finance. The remedy lies in the policies we have outlined earlier—reducing cost inflation, removing artificial controls on profit margins and prices, restoring incentives and cutting taxes.

---

[31] The existing eligibility criteria for the cost-escalation scheme of a minimum contract of £2 million, minimum manufacturing period of two years and minimum unit value of £500,000 should be amended to £1 million a year (value of the contract times delivery period) and a minimum unit value of £20,000.

CONCLUSIONS

141. The CBI supports the need for a periodic general review of the factors which bear on the performance of industry and commerce. We particularly welcome the Committee's decision to give priority in their work to an examination of the provision of funds for industry and trade. The performance of wealth-creating activities in the private sector is fundamental to the recovery and development of the UK economy over the next few years. Any possible impediments to that recovery should be identified and action taken to overcome them.

142. The main conclusion to emerge from our wide consultations with companies is that given sound economic policies and industrial confidence in the future, industry will be able to meet the demands that will be made on it without major changes to the "financial system". In particular, it is clear that there is no justification for an extension of state involvement in the provision of finance for investment. The promising, but fragile, improvement in industrial investment that is now evident can only be expected to develop within an acceptable economic environment. This means that the rate of inflation must be markedly reduced and corporate profitability restored. In addition a reduction is needed in the burden of taxes, especially income tax, to restore incentives and spur on expansion, and there must be a drive for improved productivity.

143. There are, however, a number of specific improvements in the field to be covered by the Committee which we consider would aid industrial recovery, some of which require early action. These include:

- A reduction in the mounting burden of taxation on capital, to protect the productive assets of smaller companies and to encourage private savings and investment.
- An improvement in the financial advice and information available to smaller companies.
- A closer relationship between companies and their shareholders.
- The removal of the uncertainty about the tax treatment of stock relief and the notional deferred liabilities shown in company accounts.
- The abolition of dividend and profit margin control.
- An extension to some of the recent schemes introduced by ECGD.
- A relaxation of the exchange controls on overseas investment.

144. The message which comes through from our wide consultations is clear, though it will not be easy to achieve. The rate of inflation must be reduced and industrial profitability improved. Industry's internally generated funds, suitably complemented by private-sector external funds, will then be adequate to finance the industrial recovery.

APPENDIX I: THE CBI QUESTIONNAIRE

The results of the questionnaire sent to a sample of industrial companies during April 1977, are set out below.

Total number of questionnaires sent out	306
Total number of questionnaires returned	181
Response rate	59 per cent

The companies which responded have been classified into four size groups according to the number they employ.

Except where otherwise indicated, the figures in the tables refer to the actual number of respondents.

A. Investment and finance in the UK

QUESTION 1

In recent years have you been prevented from carrying out what you considered to be a potentially profitable investment project because it has not been possible to raise sufficient finance on acceptable terms from outside your company or group?

Size group	*"Yes"*	*"No"*	*No response or not applicable*	*TOTAL*
0–199	4	26	0	30
200–499	8	22	0	30
500–4,999	2	44	0	46
5,000+	3	69	2	74
All respondents	17	162*	2	181*

*This includes one respondent who did not indicate size of company.

Of those 17 companies which indicated that they had been prevented from carrying out what they considered to be a potentially profitable investment project because it had not been possible to raise sufficient finance on acceptable terms from outside their company or group, three had not been "prevented" but rather were deterred from investing because they felt it inadvisable to raise further finance at that time. From the other 14 companies there were 6 references to the rate of interest required as being a principal obstacle, 8 to gearing, and 5 to profitability/cash flow. Other reasons given were: a reluctance to become a public company, (which was a condition required by ICFC), lack of adequate security or proven company performance, political uncertainty and a lack of local authority funds.

The difficulties in raising finance were not restricted to one particular form of finance: they included short, medium and long-term loans, (secured and unsecured), preference shares, ordinary shares, convertible loan stock and hire purchase.

QUESTION 2

Please indicate, to the nearest 10 per cent, the percentage distribution of your sterling debt at the following dates, as between short-term borrowing and term borrowing (clearing banks and other sources).

The figures show the average percentage distribution of debt. The number of responses for each group is given in brackets.

	Short-term borrowing	*Term borrowing*	
		Clearing banks	*Other sources*
Size group 0 – 199	(%)	(%)	(%)
(21) Mid–1974	56	22	22
(20) „ 1975	57	27	17
(20) „ 1976	50	30	20
Size group 200 – 499			
(27) Mid–1974	53	22	25
(27) „ 1975	54	17	29
(27) „ 1976	53	17	30
Size group 500 – 4,999			
(39) Mid–1974	63	10	28
(40) „ 1975	56	16	28
(41) „ 1976	52	12	35
Size group 5,000+			
(70) Mid–1974	39	7	53
(69) „ 1975	34	11	55
(68) „ 1976	30	14	57
*All respondents**			
(158) Mid–1974	50	13	37
(157) „ 1975	46	16	38
(157) „ 1976	42	16	42

*This includes one respondent who did not indicate size of company.
Figures may not sum to 100 due to rounding.

24 companies either did not respond or indicated that they had no sterling debt at the above dates.

QUESTION 3A

For each of the years indicated, please give your impression as to whether, on average, your debt to equity ratio (i.e. bank borrowing and long-term debt in relation to share capital and reserves) was higher/unchanged/lower than in the previous year.

Size group 0 – 199	*1974*	*1975*	*1976*
Higher	9	9	9
Unchanged	8	4	6
Lower	7	11	9
No response or not applicable	6	6	6
Total	30	30	30

Size group 200 – 499			
Higher	14	14	8
Unchanged	5	8	6
Lower	9	6	14
No response or not applicable	2	2	2
Total	30	30	30

Size group 500 – 4,999	*1974*	*1975*	*1976*
Higher	29	20	19
Unchanged	6	7	5
Lower	9	17	20
No response or not applicable	2	2	2
Total	46	46	46

Size group 5,000+	*1974*	*1975*	*1976*
Higher	47	20	21
Unchanged	10	10	15
Lower	14	41	35
No response or not applicable	3	3	3
Total	74	74	74

All respondents	*1974*	*1975*	*1976*
Higher	100*	64*	58*
Unchanged	29	29	32
Lower	39	75	78
No response or not applicable	13	13	13
Total	181*	181*	181*

*This includes one respondent who did not indicate size of company.

QUESTION 3B

To the nearest 5 per cent what is your present ratio of debt to equity?

Size group	*Number of respondents*	*Mean debt/equity ratio (%)*
0 – 199	18	41
200 – 499	23	54
500 – 4,999	40	40
5,000+	69	50
All respondents	151*	47

*This includes one respondent who did not indicate size of company.

The 7 respondents quoting debt to equity ratios of 200 per cent and above were excluded as "untypical". Their inclusion would have yielded the following mean debt to equity ratios: 131, 92, 46, 57, and 70 per cent, respectively. In view of the small sample size and the wide range of debt to equity ratios quoted, great care should be taken in interpreting the results for the smaller size groups.

QUESTION 3C

Please indicate whether you consider your debt to equity ratio to be too high/about right/too low.

Size group	*Too high*	*About right*	*Too low*	*No response or not applicable*	*TOTAL*
0–199	8	11	7	4	30
200–499	12	12	4	2	30
500–4,999	11	23	9	3	46
5,000+	11	47	12	4	74
All respondents	42	94*	32	13	181*

*This includes one respondent who did not indicate size of company.

QUESTION 4A

Have you at any time been prevented from making an ordinary share issue?

Size group	*"Yes"*	*"No"*	*No response or not applicable*	*TOTAL*
0–199	1	21	8	30
200–499	1	26	3	30
500–4,999	7	38	1	46
5,000+	9	59	6	74
All respondents	18	145*	18	181*

*This includes one respondent who did not indicate size of company.

Of the 18 companies which indicated that they had been prevented from making an ordinary share issue 11 cited low share prices or unfavourable conditions in the stock market as the cause. 5 companies felt unable to demonstrate sufficiently favourable future prospects, and 2 cited restrictions on private companies.

The most commonly cited consequences of this inability to raise equity capital were increased borrowing from other sources (8 references) and the deferral of investment plans (6 references).

QUESTION 4B

Has the requirement to have a par value on your shares ever hindered your ability to make an equity issue?

Size group	*"Yes"*	*"No"*	*No response or not applicable*	*TOTAL*
0–199	1	14	15	30
200–499	1	22	7	30
500–4,999	4	33	9	46
5,000+	3	58	13	74
All respondents	9	127	45*	181*

*This includes one respondent who did not indicate size of company.

QUESTION 4C

If your debt to equity ratio is equal to or exceeds what you consider to be its desirable upper limit, why have you not increased your borrowing base by raising more equity?

Of the 43 respondents to this question, 2 had recently raised new equity and 7 did not wish to do so because they felt that the high debt to equity ratio was only temporary. Of the others, 7 said that their business performance did not justify a new issue; 6 did not want to lose control of a family concern and a further 5 wanted to remain a private company. 4 respondents cited the high cost of servicing additional equity and another 4 the low level of quoted share prices.

QUESTION 4D

Do you believe it would be in the interests of your company to issue:

(i) **Index Loan Stocks**

Size group	*"Yes"*	*"No"*	*"Don't know"*	*No response or not applicable*	*TOTAL*
0–199 ..	1	9	2	18	30
200–499	2	15	5	8	30
500–4,999	0	26	10	10	46
5,000+ ..	3	49	10	12	74
All respondents	6	99	27	49*	181*

(ii) **Variable Rate Bonds**

Size group	*"Yes"*	*"No"*	*"Don't know"*	*No response or not applicable*	*TOTAL*
0–199 ..	1	9	2	18	30
200–499	3	12	7	8	30
500–4,999	0	26	10	10	46
5,000+ ..	15	37	8	14	74
All respondents	19	84	27	51*	181*

*This includes one respondent who did not indicate size of company.

QUESTION 5

The full response to this question is given in Part IV of this Evidence.

B. Investment and finance overseas

QUESTION 1

Please rank in order of importance the sources of finance used for your investment overseas in recent years.

The figures in each cell of the matrix show the number of respondents ranking a particular source of finance either 1, 2, 3 or 4. A number of respondents did not give a complete ranking from 1 to 4.

Size group 0 – 199

	Ranking 1	2	3	4
Loans/capital raised overseas†	1	1	0	0
Overseas retained earnings	1	0	1	0
Loans/capital raised in the UK†	1	1	0	0
UK retained earnings	1	1	0	0

24 respondents indicated that they had not invested overseas in recent years.

Size group 200 – 499

	Ranking 1	2	3	4
Loans/capital raised overseas†	2	1	1	0
Overseas retained earnings	2	1	0	1
Loans/capital raised in the UK†	0	1	0	0
UK retained earnings	4	0	1	0

23 respondents indicated that they had not invested overseas in recent years.

Size group 500 – 4,999

	Ranking 1	2	3	4
Loans/capitalraised/overseas†	5	3	2	1
Overseas retained earnings	9	4	4	0
Loans/capital raised in the UK†	3	6	1	0
UK retained earnings	5	3	1	5

23 respondents indicated that they had not invested overseas in recent years.

Size group 5,000+

	Ranking 1	2	3	4
Loans/capital raised overseas†	34	20	6	3
Overseas retained earnings	18	22	14	6
Loans/capital raised in the UK†	16	10	17	5
UK retained earnings	2	5	13	22

6 respondents indicated that they had not invested overseas in recent years.

All respondents

	Ranking 1	2	3	4
Loans/capital raised overseas†	42	25	9	4
Overseas retained earnings	30	27	19	7
Loans/capital raised in the UK†	20	18	18	5
UK retained earnings	12	9	15	27

†Outside the company or group concerned.

QUESTION 2

Have the restrictions on investment abroad as a result of UK legislation or direction meant that your investment in the UK has been:

	Size group 0 – 199	200 – 499	500 – 4,999	5,000+	*All respondents*
Significantly higher	0	0	0	0	0
A little higher	0	1	1	2	4
Unchanged	5	8	23	59	96*
A little lower	0	0	1	4	5
Significantly lower	1	0	3	1	5
Don't know	0	0	0	0	0
No response	1	0	0	2	3
I have not considered additional investment abroad in recent years	23	21	18	6	68
Total	30	30	46	74	181*

*This includes one respondent who did not indicate size of company.

APPENDIX II: MEMORANDUM BY SIR ARTHUR KNIGHT CHAIRMAN OF THE CBI WORKING PARTY

Much of our main submission is necessarily expressed in general terms by reference to aggregate statistics. This reflects the wide-ranging documentation and consultations which we have had to undertake to give a valid assessment for UK industry as a whole. Now with our first-stage evidence completed I think it worthwhile to bring together some comments from individual managers in order to give the added perspective which comes from recognising that these general statements express the outcome of numerous individual and sometimes highly personal decisions. Given limits on time and resources the approach in this Memorandum is necessarily selective; but if it had been possible to proceed by studying a sufficiently wide collection of individual investment decisions, the overall picture which would have emerged would be the same as that derived from the more generalised approach. This alternative approach brings vividly to view that in investment decisions, as in all other decisions, the personal attitudes of the decision-maker are crucial.

People, not money, the crucial factor

Again and again, managers make the point that successful investment depends on the commitment, flair, morale, and intelligence of the individuals concerned. The individuals who are prepared both to create challenges for themselves and face those which come their way are those who are willing, for whatever reasons, to put themselves at risk. People who have lost their capacity or desire to face a challenge, or whose main objective in life is a quiet life, will not be much use in assessing new products, markets or production methods, the introduction of which is always difficult and disruptive, even if it succeeds.

There have been a number of adverse developments in this country in recent years. First, the very high rates of taxation and the severe incidence of recent pay policy have hit the living standards of middle and senior managers seriously. Second, lack of labour with the right skills in the right place can be just as crucial a limiting factor on investment as the availability of money; and when labour is available, difficulty often faces managers in the ultra-conservative and restrictive attitudes of many trade union representatives to new initiatives and new patterns of work.

There is a widespread feeling of being victims of discriminatory government policies, at the same time as having to cope with ever-increasing difficulties and pressures, especially those of dealing with the workforce and its representatives. These together represent a combination of circumstances which many feel are sapping morale and therefore are a far more serious obstacle to investment than any financing problems.

Investment inseparable from business management as a whole

Again and again, managers warn against conceiving of investment as a separable activity, separately definable, apart from the rest of the job of managing a business. Often, this inseparability was expressed in semantic questions. What is investment? Is product development investment, or better marketing, or a new system of quality control, or a swifter tendering procedure, or better advertising or after sales service? Obviously, you cannot draw a line around plant and buildings, as if decisions to buy a new tool or take on a new building were of a different kind from any others taken for the future good of the business.

Investment, in the sense of the use of a society's savings for future production, rather than immediate consumption, is an aggregate concept derived from macro-economics. It is not a particularly useful category of thought for the manager on the job. Funds, whether from inside or outside a company, may be spent on a programme designed to meet or develop a market opportunity which may take in every aspect of the business. That is why managers frequently argue that the whole climate in which business operates is relevant to investment—from the widest political and social environment down to the details of the situation facing the company—and not just the behaviour of suppliers of funds.

Profitable sales essential

Managers confirm time and time again that investment, the spending of money on the maintenance or improvement of a company's prospects, always originates in a view of what the future market situation will be like. If profitable sales, allowing for capital to be rewarded at a level comparable to that offered by rival opportunities, were in reasonable prospect, suppliers of funds would not be so stupid as to hold back. If they were not, the suppliers would not be so stupid as to waste their money.

The manager's own energy and skills, and his track record; the labour force's commitment or otherwise; the business, economic and political environment; all have to be assessed when it comes to judging future markets, and managers describe their many different criteria for doing so. No assessment system can hope to avoid the subjective nature of this process, or do other than formalise it. There will always be bad investment decisions by managers and by suppliers of capital, as well as good.

A reasonably competitive and diverse capital market exists in the UK, and British managers show no inclination, given reasonable incentives, towards less dedication than their counterparts abroad, so that any shortfall in investment in this country must be blamed on the social and political background against which both investors and managers have to work. No country will have much of an investment programme if managers and investors alike feel themselves to be under attack.

APPENDIX III: THE CBI WORKING PARTY

This appendix lists the members of the CBI Working Party which, with help from the CBI Financial Policy Committee, CBI Smaller Firms Council and other CBI Standing Committees, prepared this first-stage Evidence. The CBI Council approved the main lines of the Evidence in July 1977.

The Working Party which prepared the CBI's evidence to the Wilson Committee was:

Chairman

Sir Arthur Knight	Courtaulds Limited

Members

M C Ashworth	Burrell & Company Limited
J Bateson	British Institute of Management
I G Bonas	Bonas Machine Company Limited
W M Clarke	City Communications Organisation
D Davis	Garton, Sons & Company Limited
E Frye	The Plessey Company Limited
D W Hardy	Tate & Lyle Limited
G T Holdsworth	Guest Keen & Nettlefolds Limited
Sir Emmanuel Kaye	Lansing Bagnall Limited
A J W S Leonard	Shell (UK) Limited
Q M Morris	British Petroleum Company Limited
A W P Stenham (alternate R W Archer)	Unilever Limited
Professor H B Rose (Until 24 May 1977)	Barlcays Bank Limited

Secretary

P S Taylor	CBI Company Affairs Directorate

Research Secretary

G J Burgess	CBI Economic Directorate

Committee to Review the Functioning of Financial Institutions

Note of a meeting held at the Guildhall, London, on Tuesday, 11 October 1977

PRESENT:

The Rt Hon Sir Harold Wilson, KG, OBE, FRS, MP (*Chairman*)
The Lord Allen of Fallowfield, CBE
Professor A D Bain
Mr G V Bayley, CBE
Sir Kenneth Bond
Mr Z Brierley, MBE
Mr K R Cork
Professor R Dahrendorf
Mr A Graham
Mr R E B Lloyd
Mr L A Mills
Dr J E Mitchell
The Rt Hon Lionel Murray, OBE
Sir David Orr, MC
Sir John Prideaux

Mr B P Hudson (*Secretary*)

Witnesses:

Sir Arthur Knight
Mr I G Bonas
Mr G T Holdsworth
Mr T R S Lyon, TD
Mr John Methven

on behalf of the CBI

Note taken by CSD Reporter

Chairman: Sir Arthur and gentlemen, you are very welcome to this evidence session. Considering the width of subject raised in your evidence and the questions, obviously the time is going to be all too short. But you can assume that the committee have not only read, but re-read, the very full evidence which you have submitted. I would like to say to you, as we have had occasion to say to others—and I have said it publicly—that we have all been extremely gratified by the very high quality and detail of the evidence.

We thought that we would try to cover five main subjects, which very much follow your paper: the broad question of the relationship between the supply of funds to industry and industry's demands for funds; the relations between industry and lending institutions; the relations between industry and sources of equity capital; public sector sources of finance; and, of course, the financing problems of small firms. Later in the day we are meeting the AIB as far as small firms are concerned. We naturally want to hear the emphasis of any points in the evidence on this. I would like to begin, having mentioned those five points, by asking whether there is anything in your evidence which you particularly want to highlight at the outset.

—A: (*Sir Arthur Knight*) The main point, chairman, that we want to highlight at the outset is this: that over many years now investment in manufacturing industry in this country has been satisfactory by comparison with what has gone on else-

where. The proportion of our national wealth which has gone into industrial development compares well. The performance has been unsatisfactory, and it is here that we believe our main problems arise. The actual cash that people have needed to support their investment plans has by and large been available through the channels which exist. There are problems on the small firms side, which we can come to. But the main point that we want to emphasise is that it is the managers who are pivotal, as we see it, in this process and it is their confidence which leads them either to invest or not to invest. That confidence has been lacking to the required degree for all sorts of reasons. Those are the main points that we wish to bring out in our evidence.

Chairman: Thank you. Mr Bayley, would you like to come in?

Mr Bayley: Thank you, chairman. Sir Arthur, my question would follow on immediately from what you are saying. In your evidence, part I, the output capital ratios for the UK are shown in your chart 1.2. Could you give the committee an impression as to what you believe to be the main reasons for the low ratios in the UK? Can you help us in getting our perspective right?

—*A:* Yes. Output capital ratios have been low for quite a number of years. The reasons are many. I think we have had, over the last 15 years or so, a much more competitive market situation. Governments, rightly, have followed policies of reducing tariffs and of opening up world trade; and there was legislation about restrictive practices. Therefore, from the pricing side, industrialists have been under pressures that may not have been there in the 1950's. This has happened elsewhere. One has seen other countries' profits go down. But the biggest single factor applying to the British situation, as we see it, is the productivity of labour. The productivity at the workplace compares unfavourably with that elsewhere. From all the consultations that we have had—and we have had masses of consultations within the CBI in preparing this evidence—from all of these, this one theme comes through: the problems that managers have in getting the labour productivity which they know should be possible; and, side by side with this, the problems they often have in getting the results from the investments which they have made, which they had expected and feel they should be able to achieve.

Other factors: we have had price control, and I note that the Price Commission themselves in one of their reports—I think it was in 1975—said that something like £4000 million of potential profit had been lopped off by reason of their activities. We have had recession in recent years; and we have had inflation. But I do stress, above all, chairman, this question of the productivity of labour.

Q: Sir Arthur, in paragraph 32 you talk about changes in the bargaining power of employees. Are you really saying that compared with our competitors not only are we baking a smaller cake—this follows from part 1—but that the slice of it which is demanded, as it were, by labour is getting greater and that therefore there is a 2-fold reduction: a smaller cake, and a smaller part of that cake going to the reward of capital?

—*A:* I think the problems which we are talking of here are of very long standing, and that the adverse effect in the last 15 years or so has been a consequence of the increased competivity in the world situation, which I talked about: the fact that we have become a more open market means that in this situation our low productivity becomes a much greater handicap than it may have been before. This is seen in export performance as well as in the volume of imports. In practice—and I talk here from experience—it comes in the way in which one's negotiations have to take place. I think it is fair to say that the union officials, with whom managers have to deal, regard their role, reflecting the wishes of their members, as negotiating and fighting for each, as they say, concession in terms of manning. This of course means that managers spend a lot of their time in negotiating; whereas the interest of the members ultimately lies in accepting the changes which lead to higher productivity.

The reasons for this British attitude one can perhaps find in the past, but it does, to my mind, provide the main reason for the problems that we have.

So when you put it in those terms, as you did, of demanding an increased share of the cake, I think it is much more in terms of the way in which on the shop floor the practices which have been there for a long while have had a greater impact in the last 15 years or so.

As I have, chairman, talked in terms of personal experience, I wonder whether Trevor Holdsworth might want to add from his experience.

—A: (*Mr Holdsworth*) Certainly in the realm of mechanical engineering, or the nuts and bolts of industry, literally, one can see over 10 or 15 years this worry that the increased competition, particularly the Far East competition, has been eating into traditional manufacturing, things like bolts and nuts for example, and we have had to try to get manning on a realistic basis to compete, and it just has not been possible. In fact, we have in one area been struggling for 10 years to get realistic manning, and the business is just deteriorating until we are losing out. And you can repeat that in many other fields: car imports, steel imports—all these areas in which Britain had a very, very low import content—are now gradually being taken over. I think that is because we have not got the productivity situation right.

Chairman: We hear a lot about the car industry, including various disputes at local level. You are saying that the car industry is only one of many, are you? You do not know any distinction of it being more liable to trouble than, for example, the mechanical engineering side you are talking about?

—A: It may be more liable to trouble because of having massive numbers of people in one site. But fundamentally it is no different: it is a mechanical assembly industry. It is no different in principle from the others.

Mr Bayley: Just to clarify paragraph 33, sir, where in the evidence it says that some trade union policies can adversely affect confidence and impede progress—and you give some examples there. What you are now saying is that this does in fact happen and is damaging productivity in a way which is injurious?

—A: (*Sir Arthur Knight*) Very right.

—(*Mr Methven*)*:* Could I add one thing, sir, and it is something which always worries me: that the UK gets out of each new unit of investment approximately half the volume of output compared with all our major continental competitors. I think that applies right across the board with very few exceptions.

—(*Sir Arthur Knight*)*:* And a very telling example does come from the car industry. I do not know whether you have seen, in the so-called "Think Tank" report, that in Germany, with exactly the same equipment as in the UK, in a plant which they studied in some detail, the productivity was twice as high.

Mr Murray: We are talking somewhat of chickens and eggs here. You have emphasised, Sir Arthur, that the price competitiveness of this country has been improved in recent years—in the last 15 years. May it be that the relatively low wages paid in this country and the very small real increases produce the picture of what you are talking about? And may it be that the reasons for some of the phenomena which you have been describing, and which exist, we know, arise from rather deeper causes than the trade union policies and attitudes that you talk about in paragraph 33? May these not reflect the low productivity of capital and, if I may go back to the point you make in your general personal comment at the end, to the importance of the manager as such in this situation?

—A: I think there are three elements in what Mr Murray has raised there. Yes, it is a fact that wages have been low in this country. But I see no way in which they can become higher unless we achieve it through higher productivities. So that, to the extent that you have to have a chicken before you can have an egg, I would regard the productivity as the primary factor, and we are all seeking ways of paying higher wages providing the productivity is there. There is, of course, the fundamental point that if one had had much more consistent and higher rates of economic growth in this country there would have been, no doubt, an atmosphere in which changes would have been much

more acceptable than they have been. But I do not suppose, chairman, you would want us here to get involved in talking about our economic policies on the national scale, which clearly have been a factor.

If I can come to the third point. Yes, management has a key role. I can think of no manager anywhere who has not wanted to get the higher productivities. So that in that respect I can think of nowhere where managers, having done what they have done, want to get less than they should. I do accept—and this is no doubt what Mr Murray is getting at—that there are cases in which managers, faced with their own objectives, may not always go about achieving them in the right way—the best way.

Q: Could I come back to this question of capital investment. The impression I get—and it is no more than an impression—is that in many areas our prices are far superior. Where we sometimes fail is with such non-price factors as design, quality, delivery dates, and so on. Is it, in your view, right to suggest that we have gone rather down-market in terms of the type of product we have been offering? One so often hears that prices sometimes are not as relevant in terms of the purchase of machinery, and so on, than these other qualities which Britain has been renowned for in the past but is less renowned for at the present time. Is it that the investment which has taken place has not been in the areas where we could have best benefited, either in terms of exports, or whatever it may be? Are there any lessons to be drawn from this about the way the attitude of the providers of investment capital has affected this whole area?

—*A:* There are three points there, I think, chairman. First I would make this point: that we have a diversity of industries and there are those in which, as Mr Murray says, delivery date and design are primary factors. But there are other large ones, big exporters, in which price is the key factor. I would mention chemicals; I would mention textiles; and, because I happen to be a director of Rolls-Royce, aero-engines. So there are large areas of our export performance where price is a key factor. But if one looks at Germany and their success one picks out these kinds of industry to which Mr Murray is referring. I think one must come back to our general rate of economic growth, because it does seem that the ability to adapt, to invest in new expanding industries, is a by-product of policies which make for growth. So, to that extent, if there is validity in this argument about our having gone down-market, yes, it would be, I would have thought, what one might expect of a country which has had a very poor general economic expansion in this period.

—(*Mr Methven*): Chairman, I wonder if I could come back on to Mr Murray's first question about managers. I think all of us feel that management alone can lead to change. Sir Arthur said that managers are pivotal in investment, which is what we believe, and I think all of us feel that managers' morale is not as high in the UK as it should be at the present time. They have enormous problems with their unions: with getting new equipment in; and with adequate manning levels. Both Trevor Holdsworth and Sir Arthur can give practical examples. We need to get managers turned on properly, with an open style of management that they are going to need in the years to come, because participation, involving them in a practical way, has to come if we are going to motivate the shop floor. Managers will have to be better turned on than they are at the moment. I know this is outside the terms of this inquiry, but there is a morale problem for managers which is related to taxation and incentives, and I for one would certainly feel that a large part must come from them because they are going to lead change.

Chairman: Are there any questions?

Lord Allen: Sir Arthur, you have mentioned the question of productivity in paragraph 33 of your document very slightly, and of course all of us know that productivity comes from managerial expertise, the workpeople and, perhaps, last but not least, good quality investment. Some time ago we heard that the greatest restraint on growth was the inability of management to pick up money because the interest rate was so exorbitant. Would you now say that the greatest deterrent to growth, as seen by you, is the productivity question; or is it now investment? And if we get productivity right —because I know the emphasis is on productivity now, whereas some months ago the emphasis was on investment— what is going to be the third crisis, after we get productivity right?

—*A.* (*Sir Arthur Knight*) Lord Allen has, I think, given the answer in his question. We have talked about general economic policies, and these general economic policies are pretty fundamental. And although we, chairman, here talking as CBI, are stressing productivity, I think it would be wrong to suggest that changes of some kind in relations between managers and trade unions about productivity arrangements, that those changes, by themselves, would provide a solution to our problems. We have talked in our evidence about continuity of policy towards industry and we give in one of our paragraphs a list of the ways in which governments of both sides have swung in their attitudes—ways which affect industry pretty profoundly.

There has been no continuity, and it is important here that we bring this to the surface—there is a pragraph in our evidence which does this. But there is a wide swing of economic policies generally which did not quite go along with the flavour with which the question was put, because the flavour does in fact touch on something which is worrying—that we do appear to go from year to year from discussion of one nostrum on to another nostrum.

Q: Might I just pursue that, if I may, chairman, and say, as Sir Arthur has touched on it, that if high interest rates, as we have been told some months earlier, are a deterrent to investment, why is there no boom now?

—*A:* May I respond to that, chairman, and then invite my colleagues to add their comments. I am reminded of Mr Heath when he was Prime Minister and made certain changes in investment incentives. As a result of these he did not see the increases in industrial investment which he had hoped—this was 4, 5, 6 months after—and he got rather angry with industrialists. But it is the timescales on which firms have to plan their investments, and the fact that we have been as we have in the last year or so does not of itself change attitudes about investment policy. It is much more fundamental; and the timescales on which we all think are much longer than that. Shall I invite my colleagues to intervene at this stage?

—(*Mr Methven*)*:* Chairman, there are a number of causes for profitability or unprofitability: low productivity is one of them; high interest rates may contribute to it. But the graph on page 9, which is chart II.1, shows the close relationship which there has been between profitability and investment in the UK.

On the other point, I would merely reiterate what Sir Arthur has said. If you are putting down a really large ethylene cracker, which has very high technology although it is a very base chemical, many ethylene crackers we have in the UK have skilled technology and the timescale is an enormously long one: it may be 4 or 5 years, and one may be taking very great risks in putting that new technology in. So not only is one looking backwards at what profitability one has had—and profitability, as you know, is one-third of what it was in the 1960's in real terms— but one is also looking forward as to when that plant may come into beneficial operation and what the circumstances are going to be then. That is again a manager's judgment. If you have had low or declining profitability in the past, low profitability in a highly competitive world, these are the sort of things that are going to cause people to look more carefully. I am surprised that the investment intentions in this country have remained as high as they have. They are not as high as anyone would wish to see; but they are unjustified by the profitability of British industry at the present time.

—(*Mr Holdsworth*)*:* Could I add that from a recent study of investments that we have done I was surprised to find, even talking about relatively minor investments—£100,000 was one in the study—that it takes 2½ years from inception to realisation. Even if that level of investment is possible it seemed very small. We are not talking only about huge steel plants and so on; but even some way below that level it takes that sort of time. The UK seems slower than Germany and the other countries on some aspects, but not all that much. In this country we always seem to be pulling up the plant every so often to see whether it is growing: if the policy is not working, do a shuffle and change it.

—(*Sir Arthur Knight*): May I put a slightly different angle, chairman, on this question and refer to the company I know best. Here we have a company which has carried on an active investment policy over quite a number of years. In the last few years it has had to cope with inflation, and last year, to take that last year, as a result of large investment, and as a result of having to find the cash to deal with inflation, we had a cash deficit of £96 million, which in our context is a lot of money. This, in a company which had already borrowed to the extent of £350-odd million—again, quite a lot of money. This year we have had to take various steps to get our cash position under control, one of which has been a cut in our investment programme. The fact that interest rates for the time being are lower than they were does not lead us to feel able to invest at this moment of time, because we have much more fundamental things to deal with in our company than that at this stage. We have to get away from the problems which have been created over the last two or three years, and that is a long haul.

Sir David Orr: Mr Methven has answered to some extent the point I was going to raise. On this question of declining profit, about which there is no dispute—and the CBI in their paragraph 32 mentioned some of the reasons—could the group give us any idea of how they see the importance of these various reasons? What has led to low profitability? You have mentioned poor labour performance; but there are other factors, like management, perhaps looking at their results on historic terms rather than on replacement terms. It can be inflation; it can be government policies, price controls, and so on. Can you give us any priorities, which are the more important factors which have caused this low profitability?

—*A:* Taking industry as a whole, productivity is the top: no doubt at all. Price controls have been a major factor for a number of companies for some years; and the general state of the nation is a major factor. It is difficult to put it in terms of priorities because one could argue this, perhaps, from the industrialist's point of view, that it is productivity as he sees it. So let us leave it at those three. Those are my three, chairman.

—(*Mr Methven*): Could I add one, which I think applies to the smaller sector very often, and that is the amount of legislation that firms have had to deal with. Legislation in this country has increased by about three times over the last 10 years—the actual weight of it. The fact is that our managers spend twice as long on industrial relations as their continental counterparts. If that got a lot of increased productivity, which it clearly does not, then that would be helpful. But I am sure that both Mr Lyon and Mr Bonas, who run small firms, will tell you that the administrative burden which is imposed by legislation and so on is in fact inhibiting the development of smaller firms.

Chairman: On price control, which you have just mentioned, suppose that were to be phased out: would you expect that to lead to substantial increases in prices; or is industry generally facing such a competitive situation, partly from imports and partly from the deflation side of inflation, that prices would not rise very much?

—*A:* (*Sir Arthur Knight*) Our evidence is that in the last year and a half to two years price control overall is a less powerful factor, and the general state of trade is the more important factor.

—(*Mr Methven*): That is absolutely right, sir.

—(*Mr Holdsworth*): I am actually operating in an area which has no price control—steel—and we cannot sell the stuff.

Mr Graham: I am a little puzzled about one feature, because I want to discover what it is that is constraining industrialists. You have mentioned so far the long lead times in investment, and you also make quite a lot of play of the increased uncertainty in recent years. Yet when you come to talk about variable interest rate bonds, or indexed bonds, most industrialists come up with a negative answer and say they do not want to see that. I was not quite sure, when I looked at the appendix to your evidence, whether one could not also read it to say that a very large number of people just did not think it was relevant to them and perhaps had not thought about it. My question is: why, if there has been this increase in uncertainty, are industrialists so uninterested in something which would apparently go some way to reduce it?

—A: I personally was very interested in the indexed bonds, naturally. We had a scheme which was turned down, but most people seem to be worried about them simply because they are open-ended: they cannot measure the consequences of them in the long-term, even though in the short-term they may appear to deal with a particular problem. I think it is the uncertainty.

Q: I can see that, when one wants an ideal situation with everything sewn up: but of course the future is unknown. So I am still rather puzzled because presumably the difficulty about present interest rates is that there is an open-ended commitment, in the sense that the inflation rate could mean that they will go negative. I do not say that the increase in uncertainty which occurs in shifting to an indexed bond or a variable interest rate bond is ideal, but it seems to me that it is better than the present situation.

—A: It is not certain that these things are necessarily logical. A new mechanism in an uncertain world in the future—these two things combine to make people think that they are rather fancy, irrelevant things.

Q: Is there, therefore, a distinction between what industrialists are thinking, as reported in your appendices, and what, so to speak, the CBI's view would be, having thought about these things?

—A: (Sir Arthur Knight): There is probably, amongst us who have been working on this topic for some months, an awareness of the possibilities. If you take not index linking, but variable interest rate borrowing, then of course a lot of this medium-term lending which has expanded so much is of that variable kind and to that extent is some move towards what you would describe as index linking, perhaps; and people have gone for this to some degree. As Trevor Holdsworth has said, we see now perhaps the beginning of a policy which is getting us away from the high rates of inflation. We hope it is going to succeed; none of us can be sure at the moment that it will. And therefore the greater uncertainty that is imposed on a person who is thinking of taking on index-linked borrowing is a major constraint in his mind. When you talk of certainty, I wonder whether you might have in mind an all-embracing inflation-adjusted economy?

Mr Graham: I was not thinking of that; I was thinking simply of an adjustment of interest rates at this stage.

Chairman: Sir Arthur, it used to be a fairly common complaint, I think, about new investment that there was an unwillingness on the part of labour to work that very expensive piece of equipment right through the 24 hours, but to work it only 7½ or 8 hours. One does not hear that point quite so much now. Would you say that situation has improved?

—A: It is still very troublesome and if you wish we could quote cases where one is not getting what one ought to be getting and is having to do deals, to apply manning levels, which are unsuitable but which are the most that are acceptable at this stage.

—*(Mr Holdsworth):* Yes, you are quite right that there is not so much discussion about it. But I do not think it has gone away; I think it has been accepted. It is one of these examples where perhaps management has given up a little.

Q: I would like to follow Mr Murray's reference to down-marketing some of our products. Certainly we have found, in the machine tool sector, for example, that what the world was wanting was not what we were geared to supply. And there was also a special Treasury scheme to modernise the textile machinery industry following the NEDDY report, which was put into effect. Would you say that was general, or not?

—*A:* There is one very good example where it is not true, and that is the automotive components industry, which has really swept through; and they are high precision components. Even though the automotive industry is the other way round, the actual component suppliers have traded up much more generally. So it is not true in that field.

Q: Would you say, Sir Arthur, something about the second and third points: on the relations between industry and lending institutions, and the relations between industry and sources of equity capital.

—*A:* (*Sir Arthur Knight*) Certainly. In relations between industry and the lenders one thinks firstly of commercial banks, and I suppose I have to admit that as a result of having been involved in this for six months or so, the extent to which industry is not only satisfied with, but is complimentary about, its relations, came as something of a surprise. But it was overwhelming; and it came through in all sorts of ways. There is an exception, which we will come to in dealing with small firms. But in relation to the large, as I say, there is great satisfaction. There is a recognition that in the last 10 or 12 years the arrival in London of the American banks has provided a competitive spur to which the commercial banks here have responded. Most of us who have been involved in large-scale operations with the banks have welcomed the arrival here of these foreign banks, and commercial banks have modified themselves in some ways: perhaps that increase in medium-term lending has something to do with the arrival of the Americans.

The other big factor, of course, is the long-term lending which in the past most of us have engaged in, and where we look to the institutions, and particularly the insurance companies, as buyers of our long-term securities. This market has disappeared because of the extraordinarily high rates of interest which we have had and which none of us were prepared to accept and take commitments of 15 and 20 years ahead. The market disappeared, I am sure, not because lenders would have been unwilling to lend, but because industrialists on low profit rates could not see any prospect of profit which would justify them in paying that sort of price for money.

Q: They have not been proved wrong.

—*A:* They have not been proved wrong. Those are the relations with the lenders. Moving on to relations with the equity suppliers. Here again, in our consultations there was a warm response to the questions that we had to put and the discussions which we had with people. The Stock Exchange, as an instrument, is regarded by the industrialists as highly effective, the envy of people in European countries who do not have such a highly developed Stock Exchange; it has enabled companies to raise large sums at moments of their choosing. I would like to ask Trevor Holdsworth to supplement on that one.

—(*Mr Holdsworth*)*:* I can really only reinforce what you are saying on that. Speaking from my own experience there has never been any problem in getting the financial resources for anything we have wanted to do, either lending or equity. I would have said that two or three years ago the equity market was dead; but it flows fairly quickly when needed.

Professor Bain: I would like to take up one or two points to do with loans, before we move on to equity. We are concerned to explain why the gearing of UK industry is lower than its continental counterparts, and we are led to believe that industry generally takes care not to reach the limits that the financial institutions impose upon it. My question is, if the financial institutions were generally prepared to allow gearing ratios to rise, without imposing any additional commitment, would you expect companies gradually to take advantage of this and to increase the gearing of their capital structure?

—*A:* (*Sir Arthur Knight*) First, chairman,

if I may say so, I find the discussion about gearing interesting because, as we have said—and the evidence is overwhelming—companies have found the money they have wanted in one way or another. So to that extent, one asks oneself, why the emphasis on gearing? But, leaving that aside, it is a fact that we have all, in the last 15 years or so, increased our gearing. It is also a fact that in the last two or three years, with high interest rates, our income gearing has become unpleasantly high; the income gearing being that proportion of our total income before interest which is already tied up. And you get to the point where you begin to feel worried when you see that your interest charges are getting over one-third of your income before interest. This has nothing to do with what the lenders impose: it has to do with self-preservation, because liquidation is a painful process, not just for the managers but for the workers, with the uncertainties that it introduces. It is an effective mechanism; but it is one which one tries to avoid! In the last couple of years or so, by reason of high interest rates, it has been income gearing that has worried most of us. Therefore, any change in practice on the part of the institutions would be unlikely, I would have thought, to change our attitudes. As best I can see we now have gearing ratios which look comparable with those of the United States. One can point to much higher figures, for example in Germany, but the Germans themselves recognise how much they suffer from the lack of a good, effective Stock Exchange—and these high gearing ratios are a consequence of that.

First, then, I do not myself regard the gearing argument as all that vital to our main theme; and secondly, I would not have thought that it would change our attitude all that much. It is a matter of business prudence rather than what the institutions impose on us.

—(*Mr Holdsworth*): Gearing is a result of lending; and lending is high risk to the borrower. Therefore you have to have fairly high profitability to enter into these higher realms of gearing. We have not had that, so you want a much more stable, more certain, environment against which you can then perhaps take the risks. Then the gearing would go up. The gearing might go up in those circumstances; but not simply by the instituions saying, "Here is the money; we will lend it to you".

Q: What you are saying, effectively, is that the strength of the British equity market allows British industry to avoid risks which their continental counterparts are bound to take. It has been put to us that the fact that your continental counterparts are forced to take these risks imposes disciplines on them which can be lacking in this country. Would you accept that?

—*A:* (*Sir Arthur Knight*) No. As one involved in a company which has borrowed heavily, the risks that we have taken have been the investment risks—the investment decisions that we have taken. Being active in the textile industry, which has had a difficult past, we have been vigorous and the results of what we have done have not yet been fully proven. The choice of gearing was a matter of it being, in the situation that we had to deal with, a cheaper way, as we saw it, of financing what we were doing; not a matter of running away from risks, but having taken the risks and then minimising the cost.

Professor Dahrendorf: Table IV.1 on page 23 is in a sense a little puzzling to the social scientist, because all tables which are almost too good to be true are. There are two related points which I would like to raise in this context: one is assuming that perhaps the term "fair" is used by the respondent in the sort of way in which pilots use it when they describe the weather at the point of destination, that is, when they distinguish between "fine" and "fair", "fine" means good and "fair" means bad. The interesting points are of course insurance companies and pension funds. If I interpret "fair" to mean "not good", one wonders about the relationship to these to sources of finance. I would be very interested to hear more about the problems which you see.

The other question is, if you ask people, "How do you assess the services provided to you by the following as sources of finance?", they reply in a way that assumes that these sources of finance are supposed to provide services and nothing else. What would have happened if you had asked them, "How do you assess the understanding of your needs on the part of the institutions listed here"—that is, the needs of industry on the part of the institutions listed here—"above and beyond providing funds; above and beyond the obvious services?" Indeed, if you had asked, "What would you like to see changed in the relationship between industry and these financial institutions?", there might have been some interesting answers as well: I am just wondering about it.

—*A:* Taking the first question first: our survey produces results very much the same as those produced by surveys carried out by NEDO in 1975 when they did a report on investment and industry. So that I for one did not find these results all that surprising. On the point you make about the pension funds and the long-term lenders—and we are talking here, of course, of long-term lenders—one has to recognise that the relations between the industrialists who answer and these long-term lenders are handled through merchant banks and stockbrokers. So that the direct relationship which you have with a commercial bank is seldom present when you are raising a long-term loan. Therefore I find this result that we get here a little difficult to interpret because, as I see it, it cannot reflect direct evidence.

If I can move on, though, to your point about supposing we had put a different question, would we have got a different answer? Taking my own experience, I think yes. I think that one looks upon this City mechanism, this machine that provides us with finance, as a machine that does provide us with finance. And in terms of understanding what we are up to in our strategies and our commercial policies I would not have, in my experience, said that I have seen a lot of that. But I would like to ask Trevor Holdsworth.

—*A:* (*Mr Holdsworth*) All I can add is that I do in fact see a lot of shareholders' representatives and I find the contact useful and helpful. But on the first point you made, there is not direct person-to-person contact with the insurance companies as financiers. That is why you have this rather less than good impression here.

Q: Would you value more direct contact with the lender; would it be helpful to industry to deal more directly with the parties and to have them understand more what you are about?

—*A:* (*Sir Arthur Knight*) This, chairman, raises an issue which, if I may, we want to come to in later evidence. We are not talking so much of the provision of funds, as of the relationship of industry with its shareholders and the role of the shareholder—a subject on which we are having discussions in the CBI—and, if it is convenient, we would like to give you some evidence on that.

Mr Mills: I would like to ask two questions: one in particular to follow up the question of gearing which was made; and another more general question. We are given a table for capital gearing ratios for the last 13-14 years. Is it not the case that one of the reasons for the increase in the percentage of capital gearing is because of the lack of availability of equity finance? You say that constraints on capital gearing arise from lenders who impose particular limits. Is it not a case where perhaps the suppliers of funds are a little too cautious; not only in connection with small firms, but generally? Gearing ratios are not only higher in West Germany but they are higher, as you know, in a number of EEC countries. Is there anything sacrosanct about our current gearing?

—*A:* No, sir, there is nothing sacrosanct about our gearing ratios at all. Our evidence is that gearing ratios have gone up because of the reasons of the kind I mentioned—that some of us who have been handling these things have seen it as a cheaper way of financing our activities. We could at any moment have raised equity—I am sorry, let me correct that, not at any moment; one has to choose one's timing. But if we had chosen our timing any of us could have financed our expansion with equity. We chose to do it the way we did because it looked a cheaper way of doing it. There is nothing sacrosanct about the ratios which we have.

—(*Mr Methven*): Could I add one point, chairman. It really relates back to Professor Bain's point, that in fact continental companies take greater risks because the gearing is higher. First, manufacturing investment in the UK in relation to the increase in GDP is just as good as in continental countries. The second thing is that our profitability is so low anyway—it is one-third of what it was 10, 15 years ago—that I do not see how we could have taken more risks, because the likelihood is that profitability would have been even lower. I thought I would just try to answer that point. One goes back to the basic fact that the amount of investment that has gone on in relation to GDP does not appear to be at fault: it is what we get out; it is the use of the investment which is involved.

Q: The other point, chairman, is a general question. You have made a lot of play about profitability and the factors for that. In paragraph 63 you make the general point that business thrives on profitability and confidence. You have explained what you mean by profitability and the factors. Could you encapsulate your definition of confidence: confidence in whom and of whom?

—*A:* (*Sir Arthur Knight*) Encapsulate a definition of confidence? No, I cannot encapsulate a definition of confidence. What I say is this: that running a business is a risky activity anyway. One is at risk in one's battles with one's competitors; and one is at risk in the investment decisions one takes. What we mean here when we stress confidence is that added to these risks in our situation in the UK there have been other hazards, other uncertainties, which, as we see it from the industrial side, need not have been there. We have had additional hazards imposed on us—in government policies, and from our problems in dealing with our workforce. But these are removable. We are there to cope with the inevitable hazards of business. Therefore, although I cannot encapsulate it, that is what I mean by looking for a higher degree of confidence: imparting into the system a greater feeling that in terms of policies and attitudes there was more on our side, so that we could cope with the inevitable risks of business with a feeling that the system was a little more congenial.

Lord Allen: Would you say there is great risk all the time, that one develops a state of mind about the absence of confidence as distinct from dealing with it in the manner in which some of your European competitors are dealing with it?

—*A:* (*Mr Methven*) On any capital project there are a number of tests which are automatically applied—return on capital, DCF, risk analysis—and it is a fairly scientific business if in fact you are putting many millions down, and these have been developed in British industries as they have in continental industries over the years. At the end if it is touch and go—and those are the sort of projects one is talking about—one is weighing a number of factors: should you adjust your net sales income, which very often affects the whole of the profitability of the project; what are those extraneous circumstances which might make it less successful than you believe? Whilst you go down the road of doing these provisional analyses, in the end you weigh it up. If I can put it this way, the answer to Lord Allen's point is that a number of us see investment going on in the UK at the present time on more blind belief that the future is going to be better than the past than I have ever seen before. That shows that people are prepared to take risk, risk that I do not believe the Germans or French would take at this point in time. I am glad to see it because it makes the prospect better for this country, but I would say that there is a risk of over-confidence rather than under-confidence at this point on investment intentions.

Dr Mitchell: I should like to raise three points, please, Mr Chairman. On the first one can I make an observation for Sir Arthur to make an observation back? I am made very suspicious of the story that everything is 100 per cent marvellous if I also observe that, with the various Government support schemes under the Industry Acts and the various things that have been done during the recession, the Government departments have not failed to find clients, and there are also spectacular rescue cases from time to time so that something goes wrong, and the something that goes wrong must surely have a financial input. What is the CBI's view about this and, particularly, do you investigate these bad cases to see what really goes wrong in order to formulate a policy to put it right, perhaps?

—A: (*Sir Arthur Knight*) I am slightly surprised at anyone getting from us any feeling that things look 100 per cent marvellous. Indeed far from that—and I thought Lord Allen's question reflected this—we are very conscious of the number of problems and the number of difficulties which we have got. Perhaps Dr Mitchell was referring to the specific point about the availability of finance. There we have not said 100 per cent marvellous but we have said, and we believe, that this is not a major factor and that all of our evidence supports the assertion that people have been able to find finance, except for the small ones where we come on to problems.

Certainly if we take your next point about the way in which these state bodies are faced with all sorts of clients, yes we do say—and we want to talk to you later about this, chairman—that there is an information gap, that people do not know enough of the facilities which are available and, of course, the government publicity behind some of these arrangements which now exist does produce a lot of clients. One also has to add that some of these people who are queueing and going from one agency to another are those who have failed to find the money through the normal processes, and one has to add from personal experience that, when some of these agencies have been misled into giving these people money, those of us who have struggled hard to establish our competitive position have had our lives made more difficult because companies that should have gone to the wall have been kept alive for a bit longer and have gone to the wall later at the expense of the public, so yes of course there are clients if there is money available for those who ought not to have it. This is not to say, by the way, that I am generalising because I do not know enough to generalise. I am quoting cases that I know of where this has happened.

Mr Murray: Do you put Rolls-Royce in this category?

—A: No, I put Rolls-Royce in a very different category, if you want to open up that discussion. I think Rolls-Royce's situation was that of taking a risk on a project in a one-product company where, if the costs went high—and they often do for all of us in our projects—or anything else went wrong then the whole company was at risk, so I do regard this Rolls-Royce case as a rather special one, indeed one where one has to ask oneself whether the private sector is capable of handling investments of this magnitude and this timescale. If I look at the American aero-engine industry and see the extent to which government money is provided to keep our two competitors alive then I ask myself, is this a private sector activity at all?

Coming back to Dr Mitchell's question, do we take note of the failures, yes—and this is something, chairman, which I would hope we could go back to when we come to give evidence about the relations between the investments and industry. I do believe that there are lessons here which we at the CBI will want to take note of.

Chairman: When do we expect to see that?

—A: We were planning to get that done by the end of November,* if that is convenient.

Chairman: Thank you.

Dr Mitchell: Can we look forward to recovery not in any particular context—let us say whatever is reasonable? It is my belief that these trends are extremely deep-seated and it is very difficult, if not impossible, to shift them. The first part of the question is do you think it is possible—conceptually possible if you like—that there should be a total shortage of supply of finance? I find this a very difficult idea. Secondly, will you comment on the terms and forms in which the finance is available to various customers who need it? As a tail-piece, you produced evidence and you clearly agree that the forms of finance were very satisfactory. I get this, I think, from every representative of industry that one meets in this sort of environment—I have never had any difficulty in borrowing

***Subsequently changed to December.**

money in any form or manner—but this is not the environment in which one would meet businessmen who had had difficulties and were having difficulties, so it is not very surprising. I just finish by observing that the City seems to be an activity in which their customers, who after all are the large and sophisticated, do not seem to be represented very directly, which is rather surprising.

—*A:* (*Mr Methven*) Can I try and answer the first question, chairman, and leave those on my left who are more expert to the second and third. The first thing I would say is that any recovery that comes, whether for the world or the UK, is likely to be reasonably slow. If one looks at the increase in world trade in manufactured goods, which is a good test if one goes back over the last 20 years, most people believe that the increase is going to be at the low end rather than at the top end—that is somewhere around 7 per cent to 8 per cent rather than up to 11 per cent. It might well be said that we have had a double-bottomed recession this time and the signs of climbing out of it for the world as a whole, even though reflationary measures are being taken, are slow.

The second point I would put is that there is a NEDC committee on finance for investment with which Mr Murray is very familiar which has looked two or three years ahead and sees no shortage of finance except, I think I am right, Mr Murray, if we have quite gross rates of inflation—that is the general effect of what it said—so from what one can see on the world scene and what the NEDC committee itself has done I do not think there is any reasonable likelihood of shortage of finance over the next two or three years.

Q: And you go along with the NEDC analyses?

—*A:* Yes I do, because I believe the increase in trade in manufactured goods is going to be at the bottom end rather than the top end, taking the last 20 years, and it is going to climb up pretty slowly.

Mr Murray: May I make one very brief comment on this. Would Mr Methven agree that the doctrine that supply equals demand can be found in any chapter 1 of any economic text book, and is basically tautological? The connecting factor, in fact, is the price.

—*A:* Yes I would agree that it is found in most chapter 1s of most economic text books. After that, chairman, I would prefer to argue with Mr Murray on the side, if I may!

—(*Sir Arthur Knight*)*:* If I may take Dr Mitchell's second point, chairman, it has now been answered. She said she found it difficult conceptually to conceive of an absolute shortage. It is merely price.

Dr Mitchell: But there is not one price. It is then a question of forms and terms, is it not?

—*A:* In relation to that we keep putting off the discussion on the small firms, because we did look a little at that subject and we did come to the conclusion that the additional costs involved on the small were probably a reasonably fair reflection of the costs and risks to the lender, but that is a topic which, when you are ready, chairman, we can take in some more detail.

Mr Cork: The big conflict of views that comes to this committee is one side saying that industry's poor performance is due to lack of investment, and the other side, which you are supporting today, that the poor performance is lack of productivity. I must just put this question to you—lack of productivity can be caused by a lack of demand for goods because people will not work themselves out of a job. Therefore it could be argued that if more investment were made and more suitable goods produced at a better price then the productivity would go up and, therefore, your lack of productivity might be a lack of investment. You have answered everything extremely clearly, and I would like to have your clear evidence on that particular argument.

—*A:* Chairman, it does come back to an answer I gave to Mr Murray, which is that the evidence on our side stems entirely from our experience about economic policy and the absence of growth in this country over a long period of years. Each will have his own analysis of the reasons: our excessive preoccupation for many years with past overseas commitments; crucifying ourselves on the cross of the sterling area; taking a high proportion of our resources in welfare policies to the point where even one of our present Cabinet ministers says that we have really failed to recognise that what people want is more money in their own pockets to spend in their own way. As I say, these are matters on which each of us would have his own personal analysis, and I can do no more, chairman, than bring it back to the general answer I gave to Mr Murray—yes, you would get the bigger investment as soon as you get policies here which provide an environment in which that becomes attractive. As John Methven was saying, we are beginning now to see one or two ways in which those policies might be coming through in one or two little ways.

Chairman: Have any of my colleagues any more questions on items 1-4 before we pass on to the small firms?

Mr Graham: One very quick one—what would the CBI like to see in terms of this environment happen to the exchange rate?

—*A:* The CBI have not yet formulated a final view on this. There are one or two strands in our thinking and, in that, we see clearly the need to follow policies which over a period of the next 10 years or so will foster manufacturing industry and exports, and those policies will include opening up overseas investment because the evidence we have got supports the view that a lot of our export performance is helped and furthered by the relevant types of overseas investment, so one is talking perhaps selectively now about investment. There are other strands to this discussion which I could perhaps ask my colleagues to talk on. We have got a CBI submission which we are preparing although not for this committee, unless you would like it, chairman.

—(*Mr Methven*): Chairman, I think one significant thing about the last year is that the UK has held its share of world trade in manufactured goods, which has been quite unusual (as you know, we have steadily gone down—we have lost one per cent over the last four years) at a time in fact when the exchange rate has gone up, and I think most industrialists, certainly short-term, were hoping for what they have had, which is a steady exchange rate. It has slightly appreciated in fact. The number of respondents to the CBI survey who are now showing price as being an inhibition on exports has gone up rapidly, and that is because our rate of inflation is still at least twice that of our major competitors. Long-term we would believe that we must get the rate of inflation down to that of our major competitors because, with the balance of payments surplus, the pressure to keep the pound up where it is will be very considerable, and to have an inflation which is running at least twice that of countries like Germany we believe would be disastrous for industrial investment.

Mr Murray: If I may, Mr Chairman, I would like to put one point on the question of the form of public sector finance. Is it in the CBI's view right to think of such agencies as the NEB, the SDA and the WDA as part of the market and as having a continuing role to play, and in what particular areas do you think they have this continuing role to play? Some of them are enjoined to take into account factors other than short-term profitability. Given the need for long-term profitability they are enjoined to take into account these other factors too. Does not this provide a problem for you in terms of seeing profitability as perhaps the sole criterion for investment decisions?

—*A:* It is a very fundamental point that Mr Murray has raised. Our belief is that the greatest incentive to efficiency is the market economy, and the market tends to choose winners better than governments do. That is not to say that there is not a role for government. Other nations have seen that role—Japan, for example—but this has very often been of a temporary nature to help particular industries through, and then they have been exposed to competition again when the rationalisation has taken place. We certainly believe that there is room for government assistance on things like research and development and regional policy, and as I say to assist the industries temporarily which are meeting what we regard as unfair competition. So far as the NEB is concerned we believe there is a role for the NEB, first to help particular companies which maybe are meeting unfair competition, secondly to hold government shareholdings, but we believe that as many of these as can be should be returned to private ownership in due course.

If I might add, chairman, one of the most interesting problems for the UK is going to be how the benefits of North Sea oil in terms of government revenues are used. They could be used for selective investment by government or they could be used to bring our tax rates down to those, particularly in direct terms, of our continental competitors. We would wish to say very firmly that we believe the right solution is the second, because if this country is going to be successful in its business it needs the same business environment as its continental competitors, and that means incentives by way of tax cuts, not just for the owners and managers of business but particularly for skilled people, which is one of the problem areas in the UK where we are seeing shortages yet again because skilled people are not doing their skilled jobs. They are going elsewhere.

Lord Allen: I wonder if Mr Methven could say what evidence there is to lead us to believe that if there were a reduction in tax that in itself would result in more risk-taking and improved economic and industrial performance?

—*A:* The first thing, chairman, is that the tax cuts, whilst directed at the top end, are most expensive at the bottom end. It costs roughly £500 million to take 1 per cent off the basic rate of tax. It is lowering the tax rates, the direct tax rates, to the level of our competitors that we believe most important. It will be more expensive at the bottom end but it is just as much needed as at the top end. One can only make comparisons. That is the most one can do, chairman. One can say that countries like Germany and France which have much lower direct tax rates get much better productivity, and the examples that have been referred to of the automotive industry are a direct example of that. One can show that the smaller firm sector in the UK, the number it employs, the number of new companies that are started in the UK at the moment, is half that of the US making a proper comparison on population grounds. I cannot prove it. One can only say that the circumstantial evidence seems to show that if you do this the chances of greater productivity and greater profitability and then better investment seem higher.

Sir Kenneth Bond: Do British managers show as much enterprise as their foreign counterparts and, as a second part of the question, in recent years have managers tended to play more safe than they have done in the past and, if so, why would that be?

—*A:* (*Sir Arthur Knight*) Here, chairman, one can only talk on the basis of personal observation and experience. I know of no general survey that one could make which would provide a satisfactory answer to that question, but as one who has spent may years actively engaged in running businesses in France, Germany, Italy and in the United States I have found no difference in quality between our people as individuals and those people as individuals with whom I have had to have dealings, either as employees of our own companies or as competitors. Has there been a change in recent years in the willingness to take risks? I am very struck in my own business with the determination that managers show now, still, to get on with their job and to take the risks that have to be taken and to fight the battles that have to be fought.

Chairman: May I ask your views on a point which has been made when I have visited a number of City institutions about ECI? There seemed a suggestion that ECI is too restricted in the sense that they are supposed to be finding equity for lame ducks, for the people who do not have a current track record which enables them to raise equity in other ways. Quite apart from one traumatic experience which ECI have had, do you feel they are too narrowly limited?

—*A:* (*Mr Holdsworth*) As a director of Equity Capital for Industry I know the problem. It was set up by the City a year ago so it is very early days. I believe you are going to take evidence from Lord Plowden of the ECI so I ought not to anticipate that. It is not intended to deal with lame ducks. It is intended to deal with special situations due to inflation and various other circumstances where companies cannot have rights issues or cannot use the normal City mechanism. People talk about the gap. If one defines the gap as every Tom, Dick and Harry wanting to turn coal into gold—or perhaps it is the other way round nowadays—getting money, or if everybody who is in business now has to stay in business ad infinitum, then there is a big gap, but there is a fairly long queue of people limping round from agency to agency looking for money. I do not think that Equity Capital for Industry is narrowly based at the moment. It is perhaps only the definition of size, and we are back to the small companies again. It is not in its intention, probably in its size criterion.

Chairman: Before we come to the small companies, could I raise two fairly fundamental questions. Compared with a few years ago we have seen the growth of two vast groups of lending institutions: insurance companies outstripping the normal source of supply; and now pension funds are leaping over them in terms of size. We all recognise that their overriding consideration must be for the pensioner, either next year or in 40 years' time. It is a fact, is it not, that they tend to make very large investments in a relatively small number of firms in each case? Indeed, the Coal Board said to me yesterday that they had to have far more staff because they do go into the smaller end of the business. Is this a source of worry to the CBI or its members, that so much of the investment power is now in the hands of people who are trammelled by their requirements and obligations and so tend to move only in big amounts and bigger companies?

—*A:* (*Sir Arthur Knight*) It is certainly not a source of worry, in the sense that they have large funds at their disposal and they have now become, for most of industry, that source of our long-term capital which makes us feel as we do in all the evidence we have given. One accepts that this introduces a bias, in that administratively they find that they cannot deal with a wide range of investments, and therefore, administratively, this means that the larger firms have an advantage perhaps greater than they used to have in terms of financing.

In terms of the power which is exercised, or could be exercised, this leads us on to a question which we will come back to later, if we may. But your question points much more perhaps to the specific problems which the situation creates for the small and medium-sized firms.

Q: Could we now come to the smaller firms, then. Is there anything you particularly want to highlight; or any general message for us?

—*A:* (*Mr Lyon*) If I may, I would like to point out that there is a great deal of difference even in small firms. There is a start-up situation two men with £20,000, and there are some small firms with 199 employees—we usually use 200 as the criterion. Some small firms are quite substantial in size. With, let us say, 200 employees, they could have a turnover of £2 million. So we have always to bear in mind that there are the two types of animal. You are probably most interested in the venture capital side, I do not know. But you would probably rather ask questions than for me to give a preamble.

Mr Brierley: There are four questions, chairman, which I think we ought to ask the CBI to comment upon, if only because we are later to get the AIB view and it would be interesting to compare whether the answers support or conflict with each other. The first question, Sir Arthur, is this: your evidence seems to point out the instinct of small firms to develop and grow from internally generated funds—retained earnings ploughed back—and certainly not to rely on excessive loan finance. This is mentioned both in this "Enterprise into the 1980s" which we have heard about, and also in paragraphs 115 and 116 of the main evidence. Is this a major issue in the minds of small firms—the lack of internally generated funds; and, if so, has the position worsened recently?

—*A:* (*Mr Bonas*) First, may I say that I agree that for small firms the importance of retained earnings is considerable. I think there has been more concern about it recently because of the uncertainties of the general business climate and the number of firms which have been seen to get into difficulties by being overextended. This has made smaller firms perhaps more cautious today than they would have been four or five years ago and therefore more interested in seeing that they retain more of their earnings. In this connection many small firms would want to point out the absurdity of the conflict in government legislation between dividend control on the one hand, and the apportionment rules for short-fall provisions which apply to the dividends of smaller or closed companies on the other. The apportionment provisions do not work clearly and predictably and it is not always possible for people running small companies to make forward plans with any sort of certainty as to what proportion of their earnings they will be able to retain. I think that the smaller companies in general would feel that it would be a great help if this area of uncertainty could be removed.

Q: Thank you. In your opinion, then, this is a serious problem with many small firms—the question of shortfall?

—*A:* (*Mr Lyon*) Yes, it is. And the question of stock appreciation relief is quite a factor which is always looming over their heads: they will have to find this money, or they might have to find it, very soon; they do not want to be over-extended.

Q: Changing the subject completely. Reading the evidence, I understand that the CBI is basically against subsidies of any kind except as a temporary stop-gap measure, until the obstacles are removed, as it were. Would you like to comment on that in two ways: (a) how you see those obstacles in the start-up situation; and (b) the financial factors which inhibit the growth from existing firms?

—*A:* (*Mr Methven*) One of the problems does appear to be the growth in the number of start-ups of new businesses that there have been, as compared with the USA. I think the problem is, first, that there is an information gap about finance, and I am sure that is quite clear to you. The second thing is the lack of private capital. A lot of businesses were started by, if I can put it this way, Aunt Agatha lending £5000 to her godson to start a garage business, and things like that. And because taxation, direct taxation, has been so heavy there is a lack of that sort of finance at the present time. It is not easy to apply it to normal commercial institutions, because the risks that Aunt Agatha may have taken may well have been non-commercial risks. We are pressing for substantial cuts in direct taxation in the UK. This should mean that the amount that people can accumulate privately should increase a bit, and one should see businesses started in that way. But it is going to be some time before that happens and we think that probably some sort of temporary facility is needed to overcome what we believe to be a problem. How might that be done? Well, sir, a number of countries have looked at it in a number of different ways: there is the SBA in the States; and the continent has done it in different ways. I think that, if it were to be a guarantee scheme, because small businesses are suspicious of government, all forms of government, it should be as little attached, or seen to be attached, to government as is possible.

Mr Mills: On that first point, whose responsibility is it for the lack of information?

—*A:* I think, if I can put it this way, it is both sides. First, I think that banks and other commercial institutions are deliberately developing their information services, both for big and small businesses. But that is a developing situation which most people feel has not been perfect in the past. The second thing is that the small businessman may well not know exactly where to go. The same sort of problem exists in Holland, Germany and America. The small businessman in the UK has certainly felt pretty overwhelmed by the amount of legislation, form-filling, and so on, that he has. So I would say that it is both sides. And this sort of committee is probably going to help with this sort of problem because it has brought it right out into the open.

Chairman: In view of your reference to the SBA, we have in this country almost a proliferation of bodies: COSIRA; the development fund recalled by Lloyd-George in the time of his tax on land values; and then, of course, there is the new branch of the Department of Industry; and a lot of others. Apart from policy questions like the 98 per cent withholding tax, and all that, do you feel that we have the right sort of set-up? Do you think we ought to be moulding ourselves a little more on the Americans; or have the CBI as yet not got a view?

—*A:* (*Mr Lyon*) Yes, we have a view. We do not want any more departments; we want to make the ones there are now work better. I am giving evidence to Mr Lever this afternoon. The small firms division of the Department of Industry has not been going very long; the experiment in the west country has only been going about six months. We think that until some of these innovations produce results, it is crazy to put something else on top. All these departments cost money, and in the Smaller Firms Council of the CBI the unanimous view is that the priority would be for taxation to be reduced: taxation and legislation. Whenever the government starts thinking of other departments, new departments, the members of the Council think of more legislation and more taxation. We think that there are enough departments now.

Lord Allen: Chairman, could I follow that question on taxation, if I may. I wonder whether Mr Lyon could tell us whether he has any thoughts about how a tax system could discriminate between those entrepreneurs, if you like, who take advantage of the tax concession for their business, and those who take advantage of it for other reasons? Do you have any thoughts on that?

—*A:* We have studied this over 10 years, whether there is a possibility of differentiating, and we have always come to the conclusion that there is no possibility at all. Who is going to say, "This is a worthwhile enterprise, and this one is not"? It is impossible. We find it impossible. If somebody would like to give us some ideas which we could evaluate we would be most grateful—and I mean that quite sincerely.

Q: I wondered if you had any, since you are going to give evidence elsewhere today.

—*A:* It is terribly difficult to differentiate between an industrial company and pseudo-industrial company.

Mr Murray: You are not arguing for specific discriminatory action, but for a general reduction in taxation, which hopefully would spin off into more activity in that particular area.

—*A:* As John Methven has said, income tax reductions at the higher level cost much less than at the standard rate, and to drop the whole of the investment income surcharge would cost a maximum of £170 million, which is only one-third of 1 point off the standard rate: that is the most it would cost. You might get a lot of tax exiles back: that is on the credit side. You would get tax exiles back and would probably show a profit on it. That means your top rate of tax in this country would come down from a maximum rate of 98 per cent to a maximum rate of 83 per cent. You cannot have investment without investors. And if we had even pop singers—these tax exiles—with some loose money around some of it might find its way into small businesses.

Q: It might; but why should they not put it into Courtaulds instead?

—*A:* They could put some into Courtaulds: we do not mind some of it going into Courtaulds, as long as some of it comes in our direction!

Mr Brierley: Chairman, I think you have already asked my third question, which related to the SBA and the SBICs. So I will move on to my last one . . .

—*A:* (*Mr Methven*) Could I just add one point on the question of whether it should be restricted to an SBA, or something like that, if a temporary facility is required. Our professional view is that we would prefer to see a state-backed guarantee operating through

GOWLAND
18 R

Date of application

21/11/78

On loan to

V.O.L

Recalled on

1. 23.11

2.

3.

Shelves checked on

1.

2.

3.

Replacement
ordered on

the private sector suppliers, rather than going to the SBA type because again we think that smaller businesses would be more inclined to go there than they would to another government facility.

Q: Mr Methven has already referred to this question of the information gap, which is mentioned in paragraphs 112 and 113 of the evidence. Clearly, this is an important thing: it has been brought out in many pieces of written evidence. Indeed, it has been referred to as bewildering in terms of the number of facilities which are available. Would you like to elaborate on (a) how you see the information services being improved to the point that they are effectively getting through to smaller firms, and (b) whether the banks themselves have a part to play in this?

—*A:* I think a lot is being done already. I think the thing that will help more than anything, quite honestly, is for there to be a lot less legislation; and also for government to say whether form-filling has to be voluntary or whether it is compulsory; and a general recognition that the vast majority of businesses in the UK are small businesses and not big businesses, and designing government legislation for that, rather than, if I may put it, for Sir Arthur's business, which is highly professional at all those sorts of things. It is generally reducing the administrative burden on the small firms rather than the big ones.

Sir John Prideaux: Inevitably there is the possibility that adequate bank finance is not available in the early stages and a great number of cases have been investigated, and are being investigated all the time, but it always comes down to the fact of viability; and viability of course is not an exact science. I was wondering if Sir Arthur, or any of his colleagues, could give any idea as to how viability could be more accurately and helpfully judged than is the case at the moment.

—*A:* (*Mr Lyon*) I think that is a question more for a psychologist! I am afraid on that one it does depend very much on the individuals—on the individual asking for the cash. I do not think that there is any formula which could be laid down for this. If he does not have a track record, it is the responsibility of the individual. I suppose you could go into his ordinary creditworthiness with his bank account or his mortgage repayments; but I cannot think of any other answer.

—(*Mr Holdsworth*): I do not think anybody would have backed the Wright brothers as an institution, in flying. It really requires some dedicated, trusting individual.

Chairman: Nor could anybody be found to back Whittle.

—*A:* (*Mr Bonas*) I just want to add one or two points where the banks could be more helpful. First, many small businesses are not aware of the criteria which the banks apply when deciding whether or not to lend. They do not know to what extent banks depend on security as against project evaluation. And I think banks could do a good deal more about making these criteria known. Quite clearly they have some difficulties when deciding what to do in this regard because they are at the one time supplying a service or a good, if you like, which is the loan, and, at the same time, they are applying some measure of financial discipline, especially to the smaller company. So they have a conflict there which is difficult to resolve. It would be wrong ever to say that there should be less discipline: the disciplines have to be there. What I think is important is that the disciplines should be very well understood, perhaps better understood than they are at the moment. This would make it much easier for the smaller firm to formulate its approach in a way which will be acceptable from the beginning.

The second point is that there has been some extension on the part of the banks in using industrial advisers, having them on their staffs, and I think we would welcome that. Where it has been done it has been thought to be very helpful indeed.

Q: Some of the evidence we have had suggests, particularly with small, highly technological firms, of which there are quite a number, that certainly the local bank manager does not have the amount of technological expertise either to advise or to evaluate. Is that a fairly general feeling?

—*A:* (*Mr Lyon*) We are advising the banks on this and they are taking it on board. It is terribly difficult to evaluate a project. For each of those that is a success there are probably five failures. Not every investment is a successful investment. But we come to this information gap, and there is a slight gap there. I would say, though, that as a result of your committee sitting the banks have been prodded and they are doing something.

Mr Mills: What representations have you, Mr Lyon, in the CBI, made to the clearing banks on that very point? Surely you are not just waiting for this committee?

—*A:* It is the other way round: it is on the shoulders of the clearing banks all the time, and we are telling them. I have been to see the chairmen of the four major clearing banks on this subject: they invited me to discuss it. They are quite willing to accept ideas and they have done so.

—(*Mr Methven*): Could I add two things to that, chairman. The way we have been trying to operate, certainly over the last year or so, is to produce discussion documents to highlight this sort of point. It is, of course, also dealt with in our evidence to your committee. Both have been widely published.

Dr Mitchell: May I ask whoever is appropriate to comment more on industry's own responsibility, particularly towards new firms. Industry generally has an interest in there being more new firms, although, in particular, you have an interest that there should not be more new firms, because they would be coming in to compete with you. So this is perhaps a difficult situation. However, if I may link this with your ideas about taxation: you attach very great importance to reducing taxation, which is, after all, a negative policy. You also want government guarantees, shall we say, to help small and new firms. Government guarantees, if they are going to be effective at all, cost something—and that means more taxation, not less.

On taxation generally, it is all very well to look back to the mythical, as I think they are, days of Aunt Agatha and all that, but in the present day I think Aunt Agatha is a myth, because she is now much better informed: she reads the *Daily Mail*—the *Money Mail.* As a result of this she does not put her money into her godson's enterprise; she puts it at the very least into unit trusts. It is a very difficult situation for new firms, is it not, from the personal relationship that is alleged to have happened in the good old days? It seems to me that industry itself has an interest in this and I would like to know more of how you see your role in relation especially to the creation of more new enterprises, or adapting the system to support new enterprises.

—*A:* (*Mr Lyon*) We think the existing institutions will probably learn: we are trying to teach them.

Q: But this is government support, though.

—*A:* If the question is, 'Should large industries help other industries', this is very interesting. A very expensive study has been done in the States by the MITT, costing at least $1 million; they studied this very subject. It was on the west coast of America where the electronic industries were starting up. They found that where companies were started by other large industries, by big brother, the failure rate was five times greater than where the individual entrepreneurs started up on their own. So you see that it is the motivation of the individual who has his own money in the business that is important.

You have said that guarantees will make additional taxation, which we do not want. So what we positively say is that if there are going to be guarantees they should go through existing institutions such as the banks, who are very responsible people; and we will improve their knowledge. That is the way it should be done. I do not think large industry can easily particularly spawn off small industries; I do not think this process works.

Mr Murray: Why do you think that state-backed guarantees should be limited to small firms as such? Small firms surely are not the only source of growth for the future: firms of all sizes have a part to play in this? The logic of providing state-backed guarantees for enabling potential development to grow should presumably be as applicable to larger firms, or to particular activities within larger firms, as to smaller firms as such. Is there not a place for both?

—A: (*Mr Methven*) I think there is a reason to distinguish. We have shown that we believe—and I believe a large number of other institutions believe—that there is no real shortage of finance for large firms: that is fundamental to what we have been saying. We can show—although I would accept that the evidence in "Enterprise into the Eighties" is not as firm as we would wish to put before you—that the number of starts of small businesses in the UK is less than in other major industrial nations. There appears to be a problem there. That is the reason why we have looked for finance for the smaller firms, because we do not believe there is a shortage for the big.

Could I come back to Dr Mitchell's question, which is a very profound one. There are a number of things going on in the UK, and this is common to a number of other industrial nations: that is, that industries are getting bigger in the UK, as they are in Germany, and so on. Each time that one has a depression in the economic cycle the number of small firms that are able to supply big firms appears to go down in the UK. This is largely anecdotal, from talking to people like Thorn Industries, that the number of small suppliers in Japan is greater than it is here. I do not think there is any conflict between the sort of big firm that I came from, ICI, and the small firms, because one is looking to them to do specialist jobs which very often the big firms cannot easily do. There are instances now—indeed the division of ICI from which I came is encouraging small suppliers because this helps them with their business.

Dr Mitchell: Encouraging them with money?

—A: If necessary. But more particularly at the moment, Dr Mitchell, with a proportion of their orders.

Chairman: And also advice?

—A: And advice, chairman. This is something quite new since I left the industry three years ago. There is a greater realisation of the problem.

The last thing I would say is that I hope you are wrong about Aunt Agatha—I do not mean it literally. All I would say is that the countries where there is more private capital still—and this is obviously relative—have a more thriving small firms sector than we do—and that needs some explaining.

Dr Mitchell: It is what comes between that is the trouble.

—A: I agree. We have not carried it as far as we would wish. But there is a problem. When you get, as you do in Germany, a father who wants to pass his business to his two sons, who pays one-sixth of the taxation that we pay in this country, then there are problems because we find, and it is anecdotal at the moment, that small firms do not want to expand in the way that is sensible for the UK, because the disincentives of the taxation system are extremely severe. That, I believe, is where we are more likely to see an up-turn in employment.

Dr Mitchell: I accept that. But that is not new business: that is transforming them.

Professor Bain: Could I finish on the grey area between small and large firms: thinking of firms with profits ranging from, say, £½ million a year to £3 million a year. Do you think that the facilities for supplying equity to rapidly growing small and medium-sized companies—companies that want to retain their independence, I stress—are satisfactory in regard to both availability and cost?

—A: (*Sir Arthur Knight*) It is always a problem when people want to retain their independence, and the area which has been described by Professor Bain is one in which the share system is being extended to over-the-counter trading and,

to that extent, equity for such companies is, in a modest way, more easy the moment they get a quote. But to retain independence in this tax system, and to grow beyond the size that Professor Bain has described, becomes almost an impossibility.

Chairman: Could I just say a word thanking you for the very valuable evidence you have given this morning, and say a word about publication. The committee decided from the outset that we intend to publish all evidence, but not to follow some of our predecessors in this field and wait until a final report was published a year or two later: we are doing it on a publish-as-you-go basis. You will see that the first evidence we received, from the Treasury and from the Department of Industry, was published fairly quickly afterwards; both the transcript of the oral evidence and the written evidence with it. In your case of course you have already published most of this. But for the sake of tidiness in informing the public, we would propose to publish your written evidence together with the oral evidence.

With regard to the oral evidence, as you will have seen a full transcript has been taken. We would like to send it to you to look at and to tidy anything up. Secondly, if there is any evidence you have given which was meant only for the ears of the committee and which you would like us to regard as confidential, if you would like to sideline that we will look at it with a view to dropping it. So we will leave the arrangements for the evidence between the secretary, your people and the CBI.

—A: Thank you, chairman. I would like to thank you and your colleagues for this reception. We realise that the picture we present as the CBI is necessarily somewhat generalised, and we would hope that you would be finding the time to take evidence from some of the individual firms.

Chairman: That is in our minds. But at the moment we have a full load of evidence taking us right up to Christmas and beyond. Thank you very much, sir.

(The witnesses withdrew.)

WRITTEN EVIDENCE BY THE TUC GENERAL COUNCIL

Introduction

1. The TUC welcomes the setting up of the Committee to Review the Functioning of Financial Institutions under the Chairmanship of Sir Harold Wilson. A thorough and systematic review of the financial institutions has been overdue for some years but the Wilson Committee's work is timely, particularly given that the Committee has decided to give priority attention to the provision of funds for industry and trade. The TUC welcomes this priority which accords with the priority issue as seen by trade unionists. The trade union approach is above all a practical one: an approach designed to ensure that financial institutions play their part in the long run development of the United Kingdom's productive industries on which in turn depends the overall success or failure of the economy.

2. The TUC recognises that a review of the financial institutions is a complex task and that it could therefore be argued that the Wilson Committee should not issue a report until the whole review is complete. On the other hand, the argument of this submission of evidence is that a first report on the priority issue is needed in its own right and also needs to be completed as quickly as possible. This is because the United Kingdom is rapidly approaching an economic cross roads and major strategic decisions on which road to follow will shortly have to be taken. It may be of course that the Wilson Committee will not be able to define the detail of any recommendations it might want to make during the course of 1977, but it should be able to define with some precision the principles which should guide the provision of funds for industry and trade. The theme of this TUC evidence concentrates on the investment challenge and presents as proposals rather than as a detailed blueprint, ways in which the financial institutions could help meet this challenge.

3. The evidence is in three main parts. The first part considers the investment challenge and sets out in broad terms the TUC's assessment of how this relates to the path which the economy should follow. The second part discusses the criteria for investment. The third part sets out some proposals for implementing these criteria and the consequences for the institutions.

I THE INVESTMENT CHALLENGE

The Importance of Offshore Oil

4. The urgent new factor that has to be taken into account in deciding upon a strategy for the UK economy is offshore oil. Offshore oil is not a bonanza which will automatically solve the UK balance of payments problem, but it would be wrong to downgrade its importance.

5. Estimates of the value of offshore oil are difficult to make with any precision, but the broad areas of magnitude appear to be as follows: by 1982 the yearly benefit to the Exchequer by way of royalties, tax receipts and BNOC revenues

will be of the order of £4 billion: also the yearly boost to profit incomes arising from offshore and related activities will be of the order of £1 billion. In addition to this direct increase in funds, offshore oil, by allowing a faster rate of economic growth, will indirectly increase the total amount of savings in the economy, unless of course the proportion of total income saved falls sharply. The evidence suggests that there is a long run trend growth of the proportion of income saved. Account must also be taken of the positive effect of the Social Security Pensions Act on the total amount of saving and, perhaps above all, of the positive effect on the flow of funds into the pension funds. By any standards these are dramatic changes in the financial scene.

6. The investment challenge is based on the fact that the benefits of offshore oil are finite. Therefore the key issue is how to use the surplus funds for investment in the regeneration of the UK economy. The objective would be that by the time the oil flow began to lessen the UK manufacturing and productive sector would have been built up so that it could meet and beat any international challenge. This is not to deny that more rapid progress should not be made in meeting the most pressing social priorities, such as national insurance pensions, but the strategy presented in this evidence allows the highest long run increase in general living standards on which a substantial increase in the living standards of the pensioners and other needy groups can be built.

The Decline of Manufacturing Industry

7. At one stage it might have been plausible to suggest that the UK was moving to a more mature economy whereby a small but nevertheless efficient manufacturing sector was providing the base for expanding services in both the public and private sector. However this description lacks plausibility given that the manufacturing sector's performance has been poor whether it is measured in terms of output, employment, investment or productivity. The public expenditure difficulties being faced at present result not so much from an over-rapid expansion of public services but an insufficiently rapid expansion of the manufacturing sector to provide a base for these services. It should be noted moreover that there is no hard evidence to prove that the public sector has "crowded out" the manufacturing sector in that the manufacturing sector would have grown any faster with a lower level of public expenditure in say the past twenty years.

8. The overall level of demand remains of central significance but the main difficulties of the UK economy do appear to be on the supply side. These supply side difficulties do not arise prima facie because the level of demand is "too high"; there has been a long run increase in import penetration by competitive manufactured goods which continued in 1975 despite the fact that it was a year of depressed economic activity. A number of independent studies have confirmed the fact that there is a bigger rise in manufactured imports for a given increase in income in the UK, than is comparably the case for our main competitors.

9. This basic problem has been extensively discussed at the National Economic Development Council and in the Economic Development Committees and Sector Working Parties. There is now considerable agreement that, while it is important not to forget price competition, non-price factors—such as design,

quality, reliability, technical progress, delivery, spares, supplies and after sales service and marketing—are crucial in explaining the poor response of UK manufacturing industry to demand either from home or abroad. Indeed there is a strong argument which suggests that the UK is locked in a vicious circle which traditional economic policy measures have not been able to break.

Investment

10. The UK economy has both a problem of an insufficient quantity of investment and of a poor quality of investment. These problems are in fact interlinked and it is misleading to suppose that they can be solved separately in practice. A low level of investment will be reflected in a stock of machinery which is less up to date and less likely to produce goods which compete in both price and non-price terms.

11. These interlinked problems have been made worse by traditional policy measures applied in isolation to more structural reforms. Three instances of this can be given. First, there is still a continued tendency for there to be an imbalance between increased investment abroad by UK companies and investment in UK manufacturing. This is particularly important given the UK's long tradition of overseas investment and more large multinational companies than most of our main competitors. While it is recognised that much of UK investment overseas is financed out of interest, profits and dividends earned abroad so involving no immediate exchange cost, there is nevertheless a substantial economic cost in projects which have been lost to the UK and initiated abroad. The book values of net assets abroad attributable to the UK grew from £3·4 billion in 1962 to £10·1 billion by 1974; growth of outward investment was particularly strong in Western Europe with the book value of investment growing from £455 million in 1962 to £2·8 billion in 1974. In contrast the book value of inward investment into the UK was £1·4 billion in 1962, of which £299 million was from Western European countries, and £6·6 billion in 1974, of which £1·86 billion was from Western Europe. One current example of the outward investment problem is in the petrochemicals industry, where there is considerable doubt whether "downstream investment" using offshore oil as a feedstock will be based in the UK or in other Western European countries. The consequence in terms of extra imports into the UK instead of exports from the UK is clear.

12. Apart from the drain of outward investment which traditional measures have not corrected, there are further factors which tend to perpetuate the investment problem. A second factor is that weaknesses on the balance of payments lead to policies which restrict aggregate demand; this in turn weakens investment demand and there is little evidence to suggest that manufacturing investment picks up to fill the gap left by restraints on either personal or public current spending. Furthermore, whatever view is taken about the relationship of profits and investment—and this is discussed in detail in Part II—a depressed level of activity associated with balance of payments difficulties is in turn associated with a depressed rate of return which is not likely to encourage investment.

Employment

13. Turning to the employment picture, the TUC is deeply concerned about the present high level of unemployment. This is in part a reflection of the world

recession, a problem the UK shares with most other countries in the Western world. However, there are certain special circumstances in the UK, the most notable of which is the decline in the proportion of the labour force employed in manufacturing which fell gradually between the mid-1950's and 1970, but which from 1970 onwards has fallen steeply, with only a temporary halt in 1973. There has been a steeper fall in the proportion of labour force in manufacturing in the UK than in any of our main competitors in the 1970's.

14. The argument is sometimes advanced that this fall in manufacturing employment is no cause for concern since it is a reflection of higher productivity. This might have been plausible in, say, 1973 when output was increasing fast, but since that time manufacturing output and employment have both *fallen* by about 5 per cent, leaving output per person *unchanged.* These in fact are deeply disturbing figures and show how productivity has been ratcheted down through policies of insufficient growth. The international evidence strongly suggests that the countries which have had the best productivity record are the ones which have expanded manufacturing output and employment the fastest.

15. A further factor on the employment side that has to be taken into account is the increasing size of the total labour force, mainly because of demographic factors. Between 1976 and 1979 the size of the labour force is expected to rise by 150,000 per annum and this trend is forecast to continue into the 1980's. Given the Government's public expenditure plans there is little prospect of the public sector providing any significant employment increase up to 1980.

Investment Prospects

16. The immediate prospects for investment in manufacturing are more favourable than they have been for some time. The Department of Industry forecasts that there will be a 10–15 per cent increase in real terms in 1977 compared with 1976, with the prospect of a 20 per cent increase in the 12 months up to mid-1978 compared with the 12 months up to mid-1977. However, even following these increases investment by mid-1978 will still not have reached the peak of 1970. In addition the trend growth in investment which was apparent in the 1950's and 1960's has halted. Taking the cyclical peaks of the economy as convenient measuring points investment grew from £1·4 billion in 1957 to £1·7 billion in 1961, to £1·8 billion in 1966, to £2·1 billion in 1970 (all figures in 1970 prices). Had this secular trend continued then investment might be expected to be £3 billion by 1977–78 compared with the present forecast of £2·1 billion.

Doubling Manufacturing Investment

17. The above information gives some idea of the magnitude of the problem. The objective should be not only to restore the trend rate of increase of manufacturing investment but to increase the long term trend. One might consider a scenario for the economy in which we *double* the amount of gross domestic fixed capital formation in manufacturing industry between 1978 and 1988; this is equivalent to an annual increase of 7–8 per cent. This should be against a background of high general economic growth, but there is no reason why the UK economy should not be on a 5 or 6 per cent growth rate in the 1980's given offshore oil. The difficulty will be not so much to achieve an initially fast rate of economic growth, but to sustain it. In other words the difficulty will be to

ensure that sufficient resources go into manufacturing investment to sustain this growth without running into bottlenecks and a rapidly increasing import bill.

18. While a doubling of investment may sound an ambitious target it is in fact a quite modest objective if the annual increase in investment is set against the overall growth of the economy. It should also be pointed out that the increase in net investment (ie once account has been taken of capital consumption) may be less than 100 per cent. Indeed there are good grounds for arguing that British industry does not scrap its plant and machinery soon enough and replace it by new equipment; that machine tools in the UK are older on average than those in Germany or Japan is a reflection of this. Nevertheless, despite the relatively modest nature of the target, there can be little ground for believing that present financial arrangements will ensure that finance is available to meet the target. The problem is not one that can be solved by the financial institutions alone; Government policies on the overall level of demand and investment policies by industry are also needed, but there can be no doubting the pivotal role of the financial institutions. The next section of this evidence discusses the investment criteria that need to be taken account of if we are to reach this target.

19. It should be pointed out that offshore oil and energy prospects will demand investment targets in other areas as well, for example, in insulation of buildings and conservation in general, the development of the coal and nuclear industry, the alternative energy sources, and the transport system. These are however very much in the domain of the public sector and so lie outside the strict terms of this evidence, but they are none the less vital in complementing the manufacturing investment target.

II CRITERIA FOR INVESTMENT

20. The criteria by which companies should take investment decisions and the criteria by which financial institutions should take decisions about financing companies pose complex problems. The view is often put that funds are always available for any profitable investment opportunity; if there is a financing problem then this is because an investment project is not profitable. On this view relative profitability can be measured by comparing the rate of return on the actual project with the rates of interest on the borrowed capital, and so an unprofitable project could be explained by either a high rate of interest or a low return on the project. Undoubtedly the Wilson Committee will read and hear many arguments in this vein, which have the purpose of suggesting a number of policy measures such as relaxation of dividend control, removal of price control, lower corporate taxation, lower interest rates through reduced public sector borrowing, in other words reduced public expenditure, and a variety of arguments to improve business confidence, such as reductions of higher rates of personal taxation and a promise not to introduce a wealth tax, planning agreements or industrial democracy legislation.

21. The Wilson Committee must not be misled by these arguments. The TUC would agree that there must be a relationship between the cost of a project and the return that is expected from it, but this is by no means a simple matter.

22. There are two distinct questions that have to be answered. First, do the financial institutions operating in the financial markets act to steer funds into those companies with the highest profitability? Secondly, is profitability the correct measure?

Does the Market Work?

23. The answer to the first question must be that there is no evidence that the market has operated in a way that ensures that the most profitable firms obtain finance in preference to the less profitable firms. This is a subject which has been studied on a number of occasions. For example, the Royal Commission on the Distribution of Income and Wealth in its second report on "Incomes from Companies and Its Distribution" examined whether dividends performed the function of allocating funds efficiently between companies. They found that "the statement that internal funds are not used as profitably as externally-generated funds could not be proved". They also concluded that the evidence suggests "that the profitability with which funds can be used is not the sole factor in determining the level of retentions".

24. A study was prepared for the Royal Commission by Mr Meeks and Professor Whittington on the Financing of Quoted Companies in the United Kingdom. They wrote that "the fact that those companies enjoying the highest rates of growth by equity issues were not unusually profitable raises some doubts about the allocative efficiency of the capital market: it might be expected that an efficient capital market would allocate more funds to the more profitable firms". Meeks and Whittington stress that problems of measurement and interpretation prevent them from drawing clear inferences on this issue.

25. In a lecture to the Institute of Fiscal Studies given in June 1974 Professor Whittington surveyed some of the conclusions of other studies in this field. He quotes one study entitled "Higgledy Piggledy Growth Again" by Rayner and Little which examined the predictive content of stock market prices. The Stock Market is based on the assumption that differences between share prices must be related to differences between the prospective earnings attributed by the market to the shares. They found that differences in historic yield ratios of shares did not effectively predict future trends in earnings. Rayner and Little concluded that "the yield structure of the market does not appear to perform a beneficial social purpose. It might as well be picked with a pin". In fairness Whittington believes that this is a somewhat strong statement, but his own conclusion is worth quoting: "Our conclusion on Quality (ie, that retained profits are used less efficiently than funds raised on the market) is that the issue is undecided, but the very fact that it *is* undecided after a considerable amount of expansive investigations, suggests that some writers on the subject have over-stressed the importance of capital market discipline".

26. A further point might be made about profitability. The financial institutions often claim that by going for the most profitable investments they are looking after the interests of those who have deposited money with them. In fact the institutions are making an unjustified elision of depositor interests and shareholder interests, as well as mixing this up with national and industrial economic interests. Pension funds are special in having a trustee status, though it is perhaps difficult to reconcile the opposition of pension funds to TUC proposals for greater democracy in this area with their claim that their paramount interest

is protecting pensioners and contributors. The position of the insurance companies and banks is quite different: while they are subject to various statutes, eg those governing fraudulent taking of deposits or regulations governing solvency or valuation of assets their main duty under existing company law is to look after the interests of their shareholders.

27. It would be quite wrong in the case of the banks for example to assume that there is a seamless web connecting the interests of clearing bank depositors and their shareholders as the trend of bank profits indicates this quite clearly. The 1976 profit increases for Lloyds, Barclays, Midland and Nat-West were 55 per cent, 40 per cent, 100 per cent and 81 per cent respectively. The banks have been blessed by the automatic endowment effect of high interest rates (the interest rate on current accounts remains zero, or a negative figure if account is taken of bank charges, while overdraft rates go up) and they only belatedly took action to adjust their charges in 1973 following considerable political and public pressure.

28. One of the classic statements on the imperfections of the Stock Market is contained in Chapter 12 of *The General Theory of Employment* by J M Keynes. It is this chapter which contains the famous quotation "When the capital development of a country becomes a by-product of the activities of a casino, the job is likely to be ill-done". As with all famous quotations it is usually misquoted or the author's original argument is mis-represented. The main body of the chapter is concerned with subject examined by Rayner and Little—the impossibility of a market allocating resources in a state of imperfect knowledge about the future. However Keynes was also concerned about the second question regarding profitability: whether it is the right indicator at all. He concluded, writing in 1936, "I expect to see the State, which is in a position to calculate the marginal efficiency of capital goods on long views and on the basis of the general social advantage, taking an ever greater responsibility for directly organising investment; since it seems likely that the fluctuations in the marginal efficiency of different types of capital, calculated on the principles I have described above, will be too great to be offset by any practicable changes in the rate of interest".

Profits and Investment

29. Profitability or profits are themselves insufficiently exact terms. There is first of all a difference between the share of the national income going to profits and the rate of return on capital employed. It is quite possible for the share of the national income going to wages to rise and therefore the profit share to fall without the rate of return falling, provided the economy is growing. Because the UK economy has grown so little arguments about the rate of return have tended to become arguments about the share of national income going to wages and profits. In the absence of economic expansion increases in the rate of return are regressive from an income distributional point of view.

30. There is a further difficulty in trying to assess whether the rate of return is a correct measure of the technical efficiency of the way economic resources are being used. Some economists would deny that it is possible to measure the rate of return on capital in any meaningful way. It is conventional wisdom that capital should be measured at replacement rather than historical cost to deal with inflation. This may be justified in that it ignores what technical progress has taken place since the original plant was built. It may well be that if the plant

were replaced, it would be replaced by one which is completely different in scale and layout. Qualifications such as these have to be borne in mind in assessing figures for the rate of return on capital employed.

31. Turning to the figures themselves they show that there has been a trend decline in the real post tax rate of return in the past 20 years or so, but that this was accompanied, up to about 1970 at least, by a similar decline in the post tax real cost of capital. From 1971 onwards the cost of capital rose again while the rate of return fell to under 2 per cent by 1974. Since that time the rate of return has recovered. Figures are not available beyond 1975, but 1976 and 1977 are likely to show some further improvement in the rate of return, whereas 1976 will have seen an increase in the cost of capital which is likely to be quickly reversed in 1977.

32. On an individual enterprise basis there is no reason why trade unions should not be interested in seeing their firms achieve the maximum return from their assets, provided this is in the context of a growing economy and that firms are not attempting to increase their share of the national income through inflationary price increases. Moreover there is a strong case for making the level of the rate of return, and the use to which this surplus is put, a matter for joint determination. Indeed it is legitimate to view such a surplus which is subsequently reinvested as current wages forgone in favour of higher real wages at a later date when the new investment comes on stream. A separate issue is whether a means can be found—as has been suggested in Sweden and Denmark—of giving workpeople a share in the capital growth of the nation, eg, through a workers' national capital fund.

33. Trade unions in individual companies have no objection to the use of the rate of return as a way of measuring the *relative* benefits of investment projects. Indeed the internal rate of return is a technique that is widely used in the UK public sector. However a useful technique of investment planning at company level should not be elevated to a supreme guiding light of policy at the national level, either in terms of the "qualifying" rate of return or in terms of allocation of funds between sectors. The 1974 Economic Review argued while the property boom was in full swing that although the rate of return on property was higher than the rate of return in investing in modernising industry, the long run efficiency of the economy is not helped by having old fashioned machines yet brand new half empty office blocks.

34. For the UK one strong reason why the rate of return is a poor guide is that the UK economy contains many multinational companies, either UK or foreign owned, and the rate of return in the UK branch or plant can be a function of the transfer pricing and trading activities of the group.

35. Given the structure of the mixed economy in the UK and the fact that a large number of workpeople have their savings in the form of life insurance policies or prospective occupational pensions, there must be some positive rate of return on investment. However, any move to a higher rate of return in the economy should be gradual and can only take place once a faster rate of growth is under way.

36. A new role for the financial institutions and new criteria are needed because their present policies based on the rate of return do not fit in with the investment target. Moreover because many of the funds for investment will come from the public sector new criteria will be needed for private sector cooperation with the public sector in the use of these funds. This new role for the financial institutions in the financing of new investment is not one they have traditionally performed. While the institutions are heavily involved in the total financing picture, the stock market is primarily an institution for the trading of existing securities and only secondarily a device for raising new money. As Meeks and Whittington argued in their study for the Royal Commission "New equity finance in total plays a minor role in the financing of the typical company compared with receipts from internal sources. Consequently, if increased equity issues were to be elicited by an increase in dividends upon the ending of dividend restraint, then the increase in issues would have to be very large if it were to permit a material proportionate rise in the investment of a typical company". International comparisons are fraught with difficulty in this area but according to official data assembled in the PEP Broadsheet "National Attitudes and the Financing of Industry" the stock market supplied less new equity finance, in relation to GNP, in the UK than in France, Germany, Japan, or the US over the period 1963 to 1973.

37. The author of the PEP booklet, Yao-Su Hu, concludes that "there is little evidence that, with Britain's slow economic growth, the financial system has failed to meet industry's demand. If a high rate of growth comes about, however, it may not be sustainable unless the system undergoes fundamental changes". The PEP broadsheet describes the historical background to the development of the financial institutions. England was already a great commercial and trading power before the industrial revolution and industrial enterprises were formed by wealthy individuals who could finance investment out of retained earnings. Because Britain was first in the field and had the advantages of the links of Empire there were no competitive pressures to invest. In contrast to Germany for example no financial system came into existence specifically to channel funds into industrial investment. The British stock market historically was more interested in the stocks of overseas Governments and railways than stocks of British companies. By 1933 Governments and railways still made up 80 per cent of the securities quoted in the Stock Exchange.

38. The specific criteria the TUC has in mind are that the institutions should direct funds to companies and projects with an adequate rate of return in the long run, to companies which are investing at home rather than abroad, and to projects which help maximise the growth rate of the UK economy and therefore help restore full employment. The criteria should be aimed at arresting the decline in the UK manufacturing sector in terms of output, employment and productivity, and providing for a competitive manufacturing sector by the end of the 1980's when the oil revenues will begin to diminish. Particular priority must be given to developing the regions of high unemployment, both the traditional regions and the new pockets of high unemployment in city centres. These criteria are not in conformity with those presently operated by the institutions, but they are not in conflict with their duties to meet their liabilities. The ability to pay an adequate level of pensions, with a given distribution of income, in 1997 or pay bonuses on life insurance policies will depend on the real growth in the economy in the next 20 years, not on immediate movements

in share prices or dividends. The third section of this memorandum presents possible ways in which these criteria can be formulated and ways in which the institutions can take account of them.

III IMPLEMENTING AGREED CRITERIA

39. The previous section has shown that the agreed criteria for investment to reach the investment target may well be different from the criteria presently adopted by the financial institutions. This section first set out the process, via the industrial strategy, through which investment opportunities can be identified. It then discusses the consequential changes for financial institutions and the structure within which they operate if the agreed criteria are to be implemented. It then considers how these criteria might be implemented in practice, first for the public sector institutions and secondly for the private sector institutions. Finally this section discusses what changes might be needed in the framework within which the institutions are operating.

The Industrial Strategy

40. In order to guide the institutions new impetus will have to be given to the industrial strategy to identify, in a way which it has failed to do up to now, specific investment projects in particular companies which meet the criteria outlined in paragraph 41. The TUC will be pressing for the Government for a more vigorous and active industrial strategy. There are a number of ways in which industrial strategy can reach down to the company level and the discussions within the 5 priority sectors may be one of them, but an essential ingredient in identifying domestic investment opportunities in the major companies must be planning agreements. It is only through planning agreements that the investment projects of major companies can be planned and monitored.

Consequences of the Strategy

41. Apart from improving the industrial input, the actual links between industry and the financial institutions also need to be improved. The previous section noted how the development of the UK financial and industrial sectors were not linked historically. Few countries differentiate so sharply between the industrial and financial sectors and the fact that we speak colloquially of "the City" as opposed to industry is symptomatic of this. The Wilson Committee could usefully undertake a study of the social and educational backgrounds of managers in industry and managers in financial institutions, with international comparisons if possible.

42. If a strategy is to mean anything at all it must involve a process whereby plans are thought through on a long term basis and action taken accordingly rather than a process by which action is taken in an ad hoc fashion in response to immediate events. Thus an important element in the industrial strategy is the setting of targets for the UK penetration of world markets, and of ceilings to limit import penetration into the UK market, with the consequential setting of investment and manpower plans.

43. Once a strategy has been agreed and adopted it is vital that all elements in economic society put their weight behind it. The UK has not been able to adequately mobilise resources in this way in the same way that our competitors

have. Two examples illustrate this. First the incursion of Japanese goods into the UK market,—notably motor cycles and televisions. It appears that the Japanese have followed a practice of predatory pricing whereby their industries run at very low profit margins in an attempt to break into and then dominate the market. Once market domination has been achieved—which may take some considerable time—then the price can be raised to allow a higher profit return, as by this time the competition has been eliminated.

44. A second example is the French experience whereby resources of the public and private financial and industrial sectors can be quickly mobilised to meet major national strategic objectives. Only belatedly are steps being taken to provide an export strategy for the UK telecommunications industry. Since 1965 SOFRECOM the specialist French telecommunications organisation—involving the PT and T, banks in the public and private sectors, and the major equipment manufacturers has ensured that a unified French effort can be mounted to win consultancy work, the subsequent export order, and provide finance. In fact competition for major projects is increasingly becoming a matter of competition between nations, but all too often UK firms are found competing amongst themselves, and even if they win the order they often find it difficult to obtain export finance. National attitudes are important; while the evidence is only impressionistic there are grounds for believing that if a French or Japanese firm wins a major export contract it does so for France or Japan rather than the firm, and that the financial institutions perceive a clear duty to assist the national interest. That perception does not seem to apply in the UK.

The Role of the Public Sector

45. The public sector institutions can most easily take account of longer term national strategic considerations and there are strong grounds for building up the existing public sector bodies, notably the NEB and the Scottish and Welsh Development Agencies. The oil revenues provide a means of giving these agencies a satisfactory degree of funding. When fully operational the NEB should probably be disposing of £1 billion a year and the SDA and WDA together a further £½ billion a year. They would thus be receiving over a quarter of the oil revenues, thus reflecting their role as the main interventionist agents in the industrial strategy. A special priority should be the development of new enterprises in areas of high unemployment.

46. The NEB, SDA and WDA will be operating on a long run commercial basis, but there will continue to be a need to give subsidised help selectively to industry through the Industry Act, under Sections 7 and 8. However, the general nature of state finance for investment through the tax system needs extensive reform. The TUC has refrained from calling for a fundamental change as it is clear that any change in the immediate future will be a destabilising measure. The Government should however give advance notice that the present system of tax allowances will end and that the fiscal incentive will operate through a new investment reserve fund. This will have the aim of smoothing out cycles in manufacturing investment through varying releases from the fund, which as in Sweden, will be geared also to meeting industrial strategy and regional policy objectives.

47. Investment allowances have been proved to be an inadequate and unselective form of incentive. They provide help only to the already profitable firms

which are paying tax and not to the potentially profitable firms but presently unprofitable firms which are paying no tax. They have been of little use in the past few years because of the general problem of tax exhaustion and they have contributed, though not nearly as much as stock appreciation relief, to the general problem of deferred tax liabilities.

Private Sector Institutions

48. Turning to the institutions in the private sector the trend increase in term lending by the banks should be encouraged. However, the dangers of borrowing short and lending long are real enough to prevent the banks being a major long term source of external finance.

49. The recent White Paper proposals on the supervision of Banking should help in preventing the emergence of unscrupulous secondary banks, and the Bank of England should be ready at an early stage to impose quantitative controls on bank lending to property and financial companies. A tighter rein on bank profits is needed but by direct action by the Price Commission on bank charges as well as through the supplementary special deposit scheme, which has the side effect of restricting the banks' overall operations.

50. The main suggestion the TUC wishes to make at this stage regarding the banks is that some means must be found of improving relations between banks and industry, particularly with small firms. These firms do not have the financial expertise of larger firms but they tend to deal with branch banks which may not have the expertise either. One example is in the field of export finance, where many small firms do not appear to understand the ECGD provisions and it may be that this has not been properly dealt with by their local bank manager. The proposition that exports should be invoiced in "hard" currencies and imports invoiced in "soft" currencies is a relatively simple one, but British industry does not appear to have been getting this advice from the banks. If they have, it is not apparent that detailed information on the forward exchange market deals needed when exports are invoiced in foreign currency is likely to be available from the local bank manager, though there is undoubtedly expertise in the head offices. The closer involvement of financial institutions of competitor countries, e.g. the banks in West Germany, in firms to which they help finance on a long term basis is a factor explaining better industrial performance in those countries compared to the UK.

51. It remains to be seen whether FFI will prove to be more successful than hitherto with a lower level of nominal interest rates. Many firms have undoubtedly been discouraged by FFI's high fixed term rates. While FFI may never reach the £1,000 million mark which was once envisaged, it could play a useful role.

52. One suggestion which the TUC would like the Wilson Committee to examine is whether medium term loans should be rediscountable at the Bank of England. This would involve a subsidy and the Committee would need to consider whether this should be for all classes of lending or certain categories, e.g. lending to manufacturing industry.

53. The main TUC proposal for the financial institutions is for a new lending facility to industry which would be jointly funded by the public and private

sectors. The public sector stake would be financed largely out of oil revenues, but also by the new savings medium mentioned in the following paragraph. The main institutions from the private sector would be the insurance companies and pension funds. The facility would in fact be a massive extension of Equity Capital for Industry, but it would be able to offer loan finance as well. It would be specifically aimed at financing projects and companies which would not qualify under present arrangements but which when taken in aggregate could provide an adequate rate of return in the long run. The spreading of risk would help the institutions to meet their pension commitments. A further area for discussion is whether the pension funds should not be moving away from a funded approach to one based on "pay-as-you-go" for example as operated in France. The new facility should, when operational, be of the order of £1 billion a year and at least half of this should be put up by the private sector institutions. Such a facility would remove much of the instability of the flow of new money into equities.

54. Little has been done in an imaginative way to encourage saving by ordinary people at fair rates of interest in a way that can be channelled directly into manufacturing industry. The FFI scheme is only for deposits of £1,000 or more. A new national savings scheme (perhaps called North Sea Oil Bonds) could be launched paying high rates of interest which only the institutional investors have been able to obtain up to now, which could be linked to the new lending facility.

The Institutional Framework

55. The proposals made in the previous paragraphs will require some general changes in the framework within which the institutions operate. The new lending facility will not be able to operate satisfactorily unless some means is found of giving it some central direction and of creating a two way channel of communication with the industrial strategy. Neither the new facility or individual institutions will be able to meet investment criteria without a systematic and formal framework.

56. A new standing committee on finance for investment should therefore be formed, again on a strict tripartite basis, with the operational task of transmitting to the institutions the priorities identified in the industrial strategy. The trade union and employer sides of the Committee would reflect both the industrial and financial sectors. The NEDC Committee on Finance for Investment under Sir Eric Roll's chairmanship has been keeping under review the provision of funds for investment, though its role has been a passive one. The new Committee which would replace it would have a more active role and would not be part of the NEDC machinery as such though it would need to have close links with it. It would be responsible to the Chancellor of the Exchequer and the Secretaries of State for Industry and Trade.

57. The exact powers of the standing committee are open for discussion. One option would be to imbue it with regular statutory powers of direction. Another option would be for its operation to be based on a voluntary approach, but with back up powers to be used if necessary. A further option would be for it to operate purely on a voluntary basis. There are arguments for and against all these options, much would depend on the attitude of the institutions to the committee and to the investment target which would be guiding its operations.

The standing committee would oversee the activities of the new lending facility and FFI as well as individual institutions in the private sector.

58. The standing committee would also have the task of overseeing Government decisions in the financial sphere. For example, it would receive an annual report on the activities of ECGD and issue advice on its operations. It should also be responsible for the operation of dividend control.

59. The new standing committee would have to develop clear lines of communication not only with Government Departments but also with the Bank of England. The TUC will be exploring in further evidence to the Wilson Committee ways in which the Bank of England's activities might be related more closely to an economic and industrial strategy which has been agreed on a tripartite basis. The TUC is not satisfied with the way in which the Bank combines the role of Government agent and the role of spokesman for the financial institutions, but we will wish to give this area further detailed examination.

Conclusion

60. This first evidence from the TUC has attempted to set out certain principles which might guide the Wilson Committee in its examination of the provision of funds for industry and trade. The TUC attaches considerable importance to the Committee forming an early view on this and publishing it as a basis for public discussion, followed later by a fuller report on the supervision, regulation and ownership of the financial institutions.

61. There can be no doubting of the need to focus attention urgently on what is going to be the major strategic problem for the UK economy: how to prevent and reverse in the 1980's the deindustrialisation of the United Kingdom.

May 6 1977

Committee to Review the Functioning of Financial Institutions

Note of a meeting held at the Guildhall, London, on Tuesday, 11 October 1977

PRESENT:

The Rt Hon Sir Harold Wilson, KG, OBE, FRS, MP (*Chairman*)
The Lord Allen of Fallowfield, CBE
Professor A D Bain
Mr G V Bayley, CBE
Sir Kenneth Bond
Mr Z Brierley, MBE
Mr K R Cork
Professor R Dahrendorf
Mr A Graham
Mr R E B Lloyd
Mr L A Mills
Dr J E Mitchell
The Rt Hon Lionel Murray, OBE
Sir David Orr
Sir John Prideaux

Mr B P Hudson (*Secretary*)

Witnesses:

Mr D Basnett
Mr B Callaghan
Mr D E Lea
Mr C H Urwin

on behalf of the Trades Union Congress

Note taken by CSD Reporter

Chairman: We are very happy to welcome you. Before we start discussing the subject before us I would like to have a word about the evidence. It is the policy of the committee to publish all oral evidence, and you will have seen that we published the Treasury and Department of Industry evidence shortly after they gave it. Although the TUC evidence has been published—I am happy to say that nearly all evidence to the committee has been published by those who wrote it—we should like to publish your written evidence with the oral evidence. We would propose to do this some time next month publishing the evidence of the CBI, TUC and the Association of Independent Businesses as a transcript of the whole day's hearings. Unlike our predecessors under Macmillan we prefer to publish more or less at the time and not issue two or three volumes two or three months after the final report. What you may find convenient is a full transcript of the evidence. This will be sent to you and, obviously, you are free to correct it if necessary. Should there be anything you say that you do not want published you can sideline it and it will be cut out. If you are agreeable we will deal with the evidence on that basis.

The committee have had the written evidence, of course, very full evidence, and we have all read it in preparation for today. Could I just suggest that we try to cover three main subjects which arise from the evidence: the first is the need for a big increase in manufacturing investment and the doubts expressed as to whether existing systems of finance will be adequate for that purpose; alternative criteria to the profit criterion in doing this; and thirdly the proposals you have made for change in financial institutions, and particularly the relations between the institutions and industry. Those are the main themes although they may well get mixed up one with another. I would like to begin by asking if there is anything in your evidence particularly which you would like to highlight to the committee across the table before we start detailed questions.

—*A:* (*Mr Basnett*) I wonder if I may make a short introductory statement. First of all, of course, thank you for receiving us. Thank you also for advising us of what is to happen to the oral evidence, and we welcome the suggestion that it should be published. We will try to address ourselves to the three points you raised. I think it might be useful, however, if I just made a few points in support of the evidence submitted. You will see from the evidence that we welcome the work of your committee because we believe it is of central importance to the major economic problems facing the country at this time. I need hardly say that we welcome the decision of the committee, announced after the September meeting, to issue a progress report.

When I turn to the TUC's evidence itself our starting point, of course, is the industrial strategy and the need to ensure that the benefits of North Sea oil are used principally to strengthen the UK's manufacturing base. Indeed we find it somewhat remarkable that these two related themes have received scant attention in the vast volume of submissions to this committee, but they are certainly central to whatever we have to say. We believe that fundamental decisions will soon have to be reached on the resources generated by North Sea oil. We know that those resources are, of course, finite and that when they run out Britain's wellbeing will depend on the performance of our manufacturing industry and its ability to compete in both price and non-price terms in the world market, and this is why we call for a doubling of the level of investment between 1978 and 1988 which implies an average increase of between 7 per cent and 8 per cent. The basis for this calculation is the 5 per cent growth rate which is needed to sustain full employment by the 1980s which we consider to be a most important social objective to be followed in this country. The McCracken report, which in many senses is highly conservative, sees no reason why the OECD economies should not resume growth rates in the 5 per cent range, and this is by no means unrealistic for us given that we have during this period the advantages of North Sea oil. We do not deny that consumption should increase but we are arguing that investment needs to be increased proportionately more and, while there may be differences—I am sure there are in your committee—on the methods of reaching this goal, we would hope that the broad goal of emphasising the need to increase proportionately investment would be accepted and that your committee would take a forward look, as the TUC has tried to do in its evidence, at how this goal might be achieved.

We do not, of course, say that there is one simple answer to our industrial problems but the experience of the 'fifties and 'sixties is constructive. This was a time when government policy was very much geared to reliance on the market mechanism with a dismantling of post-war controls, and when British industry was becoming exposed to international competition, after quite a few years of a closed market, with the European countries and Japan. The rate of return on capital was a lot higher than today but the UK manufacturing industry performance could not match that of our competitors and our overall growth rate lagged behind. In part this was due to the stop-go policies and, in that sense, North Sea oil means that we will be in a totally different situation on that subject.

We would not be satisfied, of course, if a major part of the new resources were to go into overseas investment. We already have a great deal of long-term investment overseas. It has not been a basis for a sound industrial economy at home in recent years and it is quite unacceptable, as you may have noticed by some protests made, to British workers to treat this island purely as a banking operation.

It seems to us that the central problem of the financial institutions is this: how do they on present arrangements take account of the needs of the industrial strategy to meet target shares of home and export markets? The basic work of the sector working parties is the setting of targets for shares of markets both at home and abroad, and the relationship to this strategy of the financial institutions seems to us of prime importance. Of course, we contrast the activities of the Japanese in this area and we know the relationship of their financial institutions to the strategy of their industry. The initial Japanese penetration of UK markets for durable consumer goods was achieved through Japanese companies running at very low profit margins, and we can see this happening in this country at the present time. In other words, to achieve certain levels of market shares, which was very clearly their strategy, may well mean sacrificing short-term profit levels in favour of long-term objectives. The TUC does not see how present financial arrangements with the institutions will readily provide finances for strategies of that order or of the order which is coming from the sector working parties.

Two of us—Harry Urwin and myself—are of course members of the National Enterprise Board, and one of the most important recommendations of our evidence is that there should be at least £1 billion funding for the NEB and £½ billion for the Scottish and Welsh development agencies. We hope there will be further questioning on this point but we do think that to be of substantial importance. However, we think the private sector institutions must play a part in the industrial strategy. The TUC recognises that by and large industry in Britain has been reliant on internal finance to a considerable degree, an average of 80 per cent or so. However there are two good reasons for looking at the financial institutions, in this case the pension funds and life companies which we emphasised in our evidence. We are talking about an increased flow of savings going into industry. The institutions account for about half of the market, that is the stock market. The performance of a firm's shares traded on the secondary market would influence its other financing operations and investment plans but the institutions have to be very conservative in their investment as, of course, their involvement in new issues shows. There are reasons to expect that the importance of these financial institutions will grow in real terms, not just in money terms. The evidence submitted by the National Association of Pension Funds shows that the net investment by pension funds accounts for nearly 5 per cent of total wages and salaries compared with 3 per cent 10 years ago. The total net investment each year of insurance companies and pension funds is now £5000 million and we can expect that figure to grow in real terms given the increased economic growth and given the new requirements on the occupational pension schemes.

What we are arguing in our evidence is that a modest proportion of these funds should by agreement be steered into a new lending facility with government backing which would be explicitly used to help provide finance for firms with projects which have long-term strategic importance. We hope that the committee will discuss this proposal in a Green Paper sense in its first report, which I mentioned at the beginning, in order to promote a wider discussion both on that and other parts of the evidence. I thought I would just say that at the beginning, Mr Chairman, to underline what we think are the important parts of our report.

Q: Thank you very much. I would like to begin by asking how far you discriminate in your thinking between the quantity of investment—and you have given quantitative figures of the requirement as you see it—as opposed to the quality. Would you like to say a word also about the basis on which you say that it is a doubling of investment which you have in mind? Why doubling between 1978 and 1988? How far and in what way do you feel that the system as it is today, the one we are looking into, is not going to deliver the necessary finance if the demand is there? In other words how far are you saying that it is our job, so to speak, to make recommendations for increasing the demand for capital and, if that is so, if I read you aright, why you feel that the existing institutions will not be able to produce the necessary finance to make that possible?

—A: Harry Urwin is a member of the Roll Committee and I would ask him to take the first part of that question.

—*(Mr Urwin):* Quality as against quantity: nationally it is where it is directed and how it is directed, and this is why we feel that you cannot just leave it to the people who are seeking to make the best capital value out of the use of funds. Naturally, we favour investment if it is properly managed; good management has got to go with the investment. What we see as needed and what we expect to get from capital employed in manufacturing industry is a substantial improvement in productivity to bring productivity up to the level of our main competitors. What is clear is that without investment we cannot possibly get the extra productivity. The countries that have done well in productivity improvements, like Germany and Japan, are where there has been a steady stream of investment to the industry under good management with right strategies and so on. This is the way we would see it going. Quite clearly you will not get the extra productivity in periods of recession. The natural reaction of the workforce is to spread the available work. Even in our own country with all the disappointments we see that during the periods of expansion productivity per man goes up in the manufacturing industries. Our weakness has been that we have not been able to sustain the growth pattern. For various factors it has been stopped. If we had been able to sustain the growth pattern no doubt the investment would have been more continuous and the productivity would have gone up. To summarise, the investment has got to go into the right areas, into the key areas, and it has to be properly managed. Without good management the investment would be wasted.

Q: We had the CBI before us this morning, and perhaps what you have just said is your answer—that productivity per man goes up as the economy expands and is naturally low at a time of stagnation. The point they were making—and you will have seen their evidence—is that compared with all our principal industrial rivals the productivity is much lower than them and, indeed, they put it in terms, without using the word, of over-manning factory by factory. What would be your comment on that?

—*A:* It depends what you mean by over-manning. If you say that in a given British factory there are more men and women working than in another factory, let us say of one of our competitor nations, that may well be true, but if you brought precisely the same equipment from the competitor nation into the British factory then this would change. For instance, if you compare the manning levels of the Ford Motor Company in the United Kingdom with the manning levels in British Leyland they are considerably lower in Ford than in British Leyland, but Ford have 2½ times the investment per man that British Leyland have with better selected equipment and the like. I have no doubt at all that if people in Ford left Ford and the same number of British Leyland workers went into the Ford factory you would get precisely the same output under Ford management with Ford equipment and so on.

Q: With the same number of workers?

—*A:* Yes. You need to examine selected cases, and we have done a number of samples of this kind. If you take, for instance, the level of productivity in British manufacturing industry it is not good but if you select a few firms like Cincinnati and others and compare them with anywhere else in the world they are very good, so it is the general level. One that has been examined most closely is Alfred Herbert which was market leader and had to be rescued by the government—a firm making machine tools when half the machine tools they themselves were using were more than 20 years old. Men were using cigarette packets to put in finely tuned machinery where they had to work to tens of a thousandth of an inch—no wonder they were in trouble. This was a market leader some years ago, and you can take this example many many times over in British industry.

Q: When you see the CBI evidence to be published with yours you will find that I was pressing them very hard on just that question, and there was distinct reference to Alfred Herbert. I would be grateful if you could give examples of, picking up a phrase from your written evidence, situations where the use of commercial criteria has directed resources to the wrong area. Were you thinking of property or over a wider area than that?

—*A:* I was in charge of our union in the Midlands for several years and, at one time, when we had visitors I used to take them on to the top of the building and point out the number of factories where they were making goods to go all over the world—the town of a thousand trades, we called it. Now you can take them on top of the same building and all you see is multi-storey office blocks owned by finance houses. This is the change that has come about. If those factories had been modernised and equipped well and so on, instead of those multi-storey office blocks, I think we would have had a different story to tell.

—(*Mr Basnett*): I wonder if I could add a word to that, chairman, because in your second question you asked us about quality, and in the third one why we do not think profit is a sufficient criterion for the investment, and this really relates to examples of where investment has gone in the wrong direction. I think there has been an examination of where the money went, a lot of it going abroad, a lot of it going into property speculation and very little going into manufacturing industry, so there was a lack of sense of direction. One issue that is important to us which I have mentioned is that we have an industrial strategy, which is a strategy over a number of years which we need to follow, and there is no connection between financial institutions and that strategy at the moment. One of the sector working parties has given a very clear indication that we should be concentrating on the activities of the petro-chemical industry. In fact it looks very much now as if the petro-chemical industry may go to the continent instead of remaining in this country and, of course, we would say at any time that for the development of such a strategy you will have to be able to take social judgements and moral judgements as well, so regional policies are part of that. You have to be able to direct investment into regions for reasons that are social and, of course, these strategies tend to be long-term. The comparison I tried to give between the way the financial institutions in Japan act in relation to strategies of Japanese industry, which in the first instance has concerned itself with market shares rather than with profitability, I think is an illustration of how they succeed in that relationship and we do not succeed, but these are reasons why we would argue that there needs to be some relationship established between financial institutions so that our strategies can be more closely followed.

Can I just make one statement about quality of investment which arises from a discussion of the National Economic Development Council yesterday which surprised some of us, and that is the constraints which are incurred which will affect growth at the moment. These constraints occur for a number of reasons but two reasons we were given were the obsolescence of our machinery and that machinery is there to make products which the rest of the world does not want. Investment has not been going in the correct direction. That was produced by the NED Office but relates to the quality of our investment.

Just one more word on productivity, if I may—again the Economic Development Committees have done a lot of work in this area and have comparative figures on labour problems. It has been suggested on a number of Economic Development Committees that we go to the countries concerned and find out the reasons for the difference in labour productivity. I was associated with one team comprised of management and trade unions, and they said it is not just labour; it is an issue of management, an issue of economy of scale, an issue of investment, an issue of the size of the market, an issue of the management structure. In other words it was a whole host of reasons rather than the simple reason that the CBI reach when they are talking about labour problems. Underlying everything was that the investment which occurred made labour productivity higher than ours.

Q: You referred to Japan. I do not know much about Japan but is it not a fact that financial institutions, which you said were very industrially orientated, are themselves the owners of a substantial slice of Japanese manufacturing industry? —*A:* I believe so, chairman. I believe there is an exchange of personnel between banks and industry.

—(*Mr Lea*): This is one of the more general questions we are raising. In Japan it is internalised in the sense that if the strategy is to go into certain areas there is no question about the finance being available. What we see as a gap in general terms at the moment is that if a sector working party comes up with a set of priorities one is confronted by different criteria in terms of the rate of return. We are not saying there is anything wrong with profitability as a test but it is not an unambiguous one, and how do you then relate that to the priorities of the industrial strategy? That is the question we are posing here. Prima facie the lack of any institutional link between the financial institutions and industry with industrial strategy as a nexus is something we hope you will look at in detail.

Q: Yes indeed, but going back to Japan I take it you are not proposing that our clearing banks, for example, should become owners of manufacturing industry to the extent they are in Japan?

—*A:* We are not specifically suggesting that, no, but we would think there was scope for a role for the clearing banks as well as the institutions in this new committee that we are proposing should be established, but the question of ownership is one which at this stage we are not proposing.

Sir David Orr: I think a couple of very important points have been raised by both Mr Basnett and Mr Urwin, and I would like to ask a couple of questions first of Mr Urwin. You made a point about old and obsolete equipment requiring different scales of manning than modern equipment, but I think you would agree that all the figures suggest that for a new investment which we make we get a lower output ratio from capital put in with new investment. I think the figures which are quoted show that, but there must be some reason for this. Do you think that it could be that management are buying the wrong equipment or installing the wrong equipment? Is that the main reason, or is it the reason that, having put in modern equipment, it is not efficiently manned? You have not mentioned in your paragraph 9 the question of over-manning. You bring in other factors which make us less competitive like design reliability, delivery, spares and so on, but surely in this question of not getting as much out of our new investment as our competitors get—and we are right at the bottom of the league on this—over-manning must be a major problem?

—*A:* (*Mr Urwin*) I take the point about sometimes the wrong equipment being bought. When I was involved in an inquiry into why certain companies needed rescuing this came up, as big investment had taken place earlier, but the shop stewards and union officials had pointed out to the company that some of the machines they were installing were not suitable for the work and that they would not stand the pace and the volume of production required. They were told they were completely wrong, and afterwards large amounts of this investment were wasted so that, as I said earlier, unless the investment is linked with the right kind of management you can get things wrong.

In November 1973 when the previous Conservative government was in, I went on a ministerial visit to America with the then minister of industry and visited a large number of firms, many of them with investments in Britain. We were pleading with the Americans to come and take over our industry, as on other occasions we have gone to Japan and pleaded with the Japanese to take it over. There is something seriously wrong when you get into that situation. Here we were talking to the various American companies who were making everything from food processing, pharmaceuticals, to floor coverings, anything you like—not just motors but a whole range of things—and almost without exception they said that their productivity levels were good in Britain compared with their other investments in other parts of the world, that their labour relations were good and so on. We did not get involved in motors but when you forget motors and look at all the other American investments in Britain their profitability and productivity were quite good, so what I am saying is that given the right sort of equipment and the right sort of management the British labour response is good.

Q: You have commented about the motor car industry. If we take Ford in the UK against Ford in Germany (and I believe Ford is a very efficient manufacturer), we hear that Ford need considerably more operatives in this country. It is certainly the case in my own industry even though we have very efficient operations, and I believe it is true also of the chemical industry and I think the chemical industry in this country is still an efficient industry, so I would have thought that the figures suggest the contrary. Can I ask Mr Basnett a question. You talked about profitability and you talked about profitability in the 'fifties and 'sixties, and investment correlation. Can I ask you, do you really believe that there is no connection between levels of profitability and levels of investment, and do you not think that the present really low level of real profitability must be a discouragement to investment?

—*A:* (*Mr Basnett*) The sector working parties have not identified low profitability as being a major reason for investment not taking place.

Q: But the charts show such a close correlation that there must be some connection.

—*A:* I am sorry, Sir David, but are you arguing that the charts on profitability . . .

Q: As profitability has come down, and it has come down steadily, if you look at the CBI chart you can see that investment levels have come down almost in parallel.

—*A:* (*Mr Lea*) We know there is a whole range of factors which determine our economic performance, and there has been a decline in the rate of return on capital, but certainly at the present time the major problem is capacity utilisation. If you are talking about incentive to invest, I do not know what happens in your own business but certainly in general it is the case that it is a major deterrent when you are not using your present plant for more than 80 per cent of capacity. In the 1980s the balance of payments constraint will be much less than it has been for the last 20 years and we can be reasonably assured that the 4 per cent to 5 per cent growth rate will not have to come to a halt because of the balance of payments deficit. We have our own chart here showing how output per person employed does relate to the growth of the economy, and it is as clear a chart as the chart which Sir David would wish to pose. I do not think we can say it is a black or white situation but in the 1980s what we are emphasising is that we are in a whole new ball game when we hope we will have a growth scenario when we believe that profitability in a secular as well as in a cyclical sense will be important. It has been very difficult in the last few years to distinguish what is cyclical and what is secular.

Q: You hope to see higher levels of profitability in the companies in which your members work?

—*A:* I think that is true.

Chairman: In what you were saying, Mr Urwin, you qualified it in relation to the motor car industry of which you have some experience, not only in your trade union capacity but in the inquiry. On the other hand you refer to Ford. It happens to be a fact that after comparison with Germany and France they are going to build their new plant in Britain.

—*A:* (*Mr Urwin*) That is right. As a matter of fact I was going to suggest that Sir David read the claim we submitted to Ford, where we supplied a lot of information that shows how research and development costs which have been incurred in Germany can be paid for in Britain, and things of that kind. I would suggest also that with the transfer of models, which means that some of the higher-volume models are being made in Britain now and some of the lower-volume models in Germany, you might see a transformation in the next year.

Q: Based on productivity?

—*A:* Based on productivity, yes, given the same equipment, given the same methods. Can I say this: I have tramped many miles in German factories and talked to the people and so on, and the first time I went into a German car factory I stood up on the gantry with the production manager and it looked to be going efficiently. Everybody seemed to be moving, and I said, "Everybody is at the double in this factory". He said, "You pick any one individual out and look at him and see him or her working and see if they are working over-hard", and nobody was. People were properly organised. Methods were right. Management was right. People were riding round on bicycles in the factory. If you tried to ride round a British factory on a bicycle the tyres would be cut to pieces before you got 10 yards. These were the differences. You cannot just put people into factories in that sort of condition and expect them to respond in that way but there are plenty of examples we can show you where the British reaction is as good as anyone else's.

Lord Allen: I wonder, chairman, if I could put a question to Mr Urwin following his reply to Sir David Orr. He illustrated firms in his experience who were buying the wrong machinery and the wrong equipment. Was there in your experience, or is there now any evidence to show that machinery has been bought as a result of consultations with the workforce beforehand?

—*A:* These are the problems. This is why, when I was involved in the inquiry into British Leyland, when they asked what were the new joint committees to do, they said, "First of all before you lay down the plant and equipment the company should come with their plans to the workers and say, 'Do you see anything wrong with those?".' Having got their response and they agree that they are the right kind of machines and so on for the job, they are more likely to make them work efficiently, but I can tell you of a factory in the midlands, quite a well-known company, where there are machines now uncrated that have been there for a long long time because probably they were not the right kind of machines.

Dr Mitchell: Could I ask Mr Basnett or colleagues to elaborate a bit more on the relationship of financial institutions to the industrial strategy. The industrial strategy as I see it from my end consists mainly of sorting out key sectors—I think we have beyond 30 now—and then putting a certain amount of finance in order of priority into certain industries. There is the non-ferrous foundry scheme and there is a list of others. The non-ferrous foundry scheme is perhaps a good example because the social input of that is fairly obvious. One of the reasons they are in trouble is pollution legislation, is it not, and the finance required for that? This has been found under the Industry Act with some success, I think. That is fine. This is straight government support and the money comes from the government and it is administered by the regional office in association, of course, with finance institutions because many of the schemes have money put in by the banks or by other institutions as a joint scheme. This sort of thing also happens with the selective investment scheme and with the accelerated project scheme that was the predecessor. Government money was put in in the usual way and administered by a government department and, very often, it attracts money from the institutions. I am told that outside the assisted areas at the moment most of the money going in to industry is in fact relief grants which, of course, means association between financial institutions rather in the way, I imagine, you want. It seems to me that this is already beginning. The industrial strategy already exists and there are the section schemes although the order of magnitude may be wrong. We may need a lot more schemes and the amount of money put in to them may need to be increased, but could you go on from there and explain in a bit more detail where you want to go in terms of relationship between the government putting money in in the usual way through government departments and associating financial institutions somehow more with this?

—*A:* Chairman, the two schemes that were introduced by government—first the accelerated projects scheme and then the selective investment scheme—in both cases had particular projects identified, and the companies were persuaded to bring them forward. It had always been a real issue, whether they would not have come forward anyway. There is always a danger you are giving public money away unnecessarily. Nevertheless important projects have been brought forward and something like £750 million worth of investment has been made as a result of the use of about £100 million or £80 million worth of grants and the like, and this is continuing with the selective investment scheme. At least you can identify where the money is going and the effect this will have on the balance of payments and the effect this will have on employment and things of that kind. To that extent it is good. If you have the Department of Industry sponsoring this kind of scheme and at the same time you have the National Enterprise Board seeking to play a part in industry, naturally an employer is going to look towards the selective investment scheme rather than the National Enterprise Board, so there can be some conflict of interest here. I believe the time is now opportune for these organisations to be brought together to see what is the best way.

Q: It is a consolidation exercise you are after basically?

—*A:* Yes, but first of all an examination, an examination of where there is unnecessary overlapping or where you may be drawing the wrong kind of investment, because naturally people will go for the cheapest.

Chairman: When you say bring them both together, do you mean ultimately integrate them or do you just mean getting them together in a room and sorting things out?

—*A:* To start by examination of the various schemes with the intention of bringing about a greater co-ordination of the work and maybe integration, I do not know, but that would be anticipating too far. Certainly what I am afraid of is that you start a number of separate organisations which become self-perpetuating bureaucracies and do not like to be merged together and co-ordinated, which is certainly not in the national interest.

Dr Mitchell: Do you consider this consolidation to be regional consolidation or industrial consolidation?

—*A:* I see it as a co-ordination at the centre and a development towards regional organisations. For instance, the National Enterprise Board started off on the basis that we have the Scottish Development Agency and the Welsh Development Agency but we do not want any English regional agency—a couple of English directors were sufficient. Now they are coming round to the point of view that the Scottish Development Agency is probably doing better than relying on regional directors and are moving towards committees in the various English regions.

Sir Kenneth Bond: I was a little bit confused about the first part of our discussion. Harry Urwin was saying, and I can follow this, that if you used funds and made investments productivity would follow, and one can see that one could achieve lower unit costs, better value for the customer and the ability to sell more goods in competition with the rest of the world, but then David Basnett said that the productivity was more, if anything, the fault of management. If it is not really a question of investment I am just wondering whether in fact one really ought to be concentrating much more on whose fault productivity is and solving that before one uses funds for more investment.

—*(Mr Basnett):* I think you are raising again the problem that was raised initially. What I said in fact was to relate the experience of the tripartite team that went to the United States, and I did identify there the question of scale of investment so it is as important to the difficulties of productivity and other issues as well as the issue of the structure of management. There is a whole spectrum of reasons which lead to the differences in productivity. I really do not think basically there is any difference between Harry Urwin and myself on this but there are other reasons to be taken into account. Could I just say this in principle: there is a problem in this area and trade unions would not say that there is no problem, but at one end of the spectrum the comparisons have been drawn by Sir David for firms where productivity is lower than abroad. There are other examples where it is higher and there are examples where it is very close to our competitors, and those are in the newer industries, the processing industries. Indeed if you break down most industries you find the processing parts of the industry are more comparable than taking the industry in total or some of our older industries, and when we do make comparisons of productivity we tend to do it as a generalisation whereas if you look at different parts of British industry some of them are good whereas some of them are bad. The main substance of our argument is that the main problem is the quantity and quality of investment and how that relates to our industrial strategy and how it relates to using the advantages of North Sea oil to create a manufacturing base. There is a problem there. We think the problem should be looked at.

Q: If you had more investment and you did not achieve the productivity to go with it what would then happen?

—*A:* If you did not achieve productivity the simple answer is to sack the management! Any management is going to very carefully examine its investment programme before it starts. I think Lord Allen's question is relevant in this. Where there have been examples of investment having been carried out in full consultation with the work people concerned the productivity has usually been very good. You do get problems where you get changes due to mergers or where you get investments where there has not been consultation and where there may be resistance, but if the companies concerned work more closely with the unions higher productivity usually results.

Professor Dahrendorf: Chairman, I am still puzzled about the main issue we are discussing here and I would like to ask a question about that, but not without at least mentioning that I think one would be grateful if we could hear a word about another point and that is that we are always talking about manufacturing industry and the creation of wealth. I would be very interested to know what the view of Mr Basnett and his colleagues is about the wealth-creating effect on the financial institutions themselves, the uses of the financial institutions in the economy of the country. That is a minor point. The major point on which I am still puzzled is this: assuming that investment is the main problem of British manufacturing what evidence is there that the availability of funds is the main issue in relation to investment, and what reason is there to believe that the only way in which funds could be made available for further investment would be by government action? Assuming for the moment that we are not in fact talking about capacity utilisation and such things, why is it that availability of funds through government channels or public channels should make a lot of difference? What is the argument against those who say that the market is perfectly capable of taking care of it?

—*A:* For the evidence I will ask Mr Lea, but I drew attention at the beginning to what had happened in the immediate post-war years, and the fact that our financial institutions have great savings in this country through occupational pension schemes which are used very conservatively. What we are arguing here is that this needs to be directed in the direction of the long-term industrial strategy that needs to be followed, and so far there is no evidence that this is occurring through the normal industrial markets.

—(*Mr Lea*): As regards the problem of evidence on a question like this, obviously by definition there are no statistics on the shortfall of supply of funds. I do not know of anybody who collects statistics of projects which could have been carried out if the funds had been available at a different price, and I think I would suggest that there is a fallacy built into the way in which the question is posed. It is rather like any other commodity—tomatoes or anything else. You are talking about the supply and demand in complete isolation one from the other. Quite clearly in some senses it is the price which equates supply and demand, and there are no statistics by definition as to what projects could have got off the ground at a different rate. Taking the analogy of the public sector we have at the moment a discount rate of 10 per cent which went up, I believe, from 8 per cent and, in that respect, you have projects lined up below 10 per cent that do not get off the ground because 10 per cent is the qualifying rate, so that you could, I suppose, look up a list. I do not know who has such a list but there is obviously a list you could draw up in principle of projects that do not meet that qualifying rate. Obviously if you define the qualifying rate as 10 per cent and then say all the projects qualifying at 10 per cent have the funds available, by definition there is no shortage of funds, and I am saying the key to the apparent conundrum is that you do not get any statistics because of the way in which you pose the question. If one were looking at what projects could be got off the ground which would be remunerative if one had a different discount rate or if, for example, at the present time because of the way in which we are trying to look 20 years ahead, you might think that the rate of return or the rate of interest is too high to make projects with a 15 to 20-year timescale appear to be remunerative.

Mr Murray: You are talking about future hopes for profitability but you are also talking about immediate or fairly short-term investment and investment in the hope that profitability will come. How do you bridge this particular gap of expectation? How do you cover this uncertainty which, for example, came through very clearly in the CBI evidence this morning?

—*A:* At the moment the problem of capacity utilisation is one where you have to get over the confidence problem.

We are not trying to be dogmatic but we hope that your committee will be able to pick up some of the suggestions in our paper, whether in terms of a countercyclical investment reserve fund whereby you can make funds available more cheaply at a time of low returns and stagnation, or whether one should be concerned more with the longer term problem. Quite clearly, to use the classic phrase about pushing on a piece of string, you have a separate problem of how to get things moving at the moment from the conceptual longer term problem which was just being posed. I think that the pump priming type of operation on a short-term basis means that there is a role for some intervention against the natural play of market forces at a time when you know that the funds are available, you know that there is plenty of money available at the moment, but you cannot get the demand side off the ground. I think at that moment in time there is a case for some type of countercyclical arrangement, whether it is purely fiscal or whether it is institutional, or a combination of the two.

Mr Mills: Just to follow Professor Dahrendorf's point, through you, Mr Chairman, could the TUC give an indication of where the NEB has intervened in cases where the market has failed to provide appropriate funds?

—*A:* (*Mr Basnett*) One can name companies. Sinclair Electronics have developed a very small television set which could not get money on the money market. It has been lent money and it is developing. But the major area where the NEB wants to act is in support of the industrial strategy. Currently what it is looking at is the bottleneck industries and what it can do to restructure those industries and expand them. But there is no way that we can see that that could occur without the NEB conducting these examinations and trying to produce the restructuring and the expansion of the industries concerned. The fact is that if you look at every upturn in industry that there has been since the war, on each occasion it is exactly the same industries that have caused the bottlenecks, and nothing has been done. The only way we can see it being done is through an institution like the NEB.

—(*Mr Urwin*): I think this is the key point. We are told that the banks are stocked with money. Why does industry not get it? This has been the worrying feature for a long time. I was talking to the chairman of a group of medium-sized firms the other day and he said that until a few months ago he had always found it extremely difficult to borrow long-term money from the City and in consequence they had to rely largely on generating their own profits to be able to expand, which meant that they expanded much more slowly than they normally would have done. I have no reason to believe that his views were any different from those of thousands of other medium-sized and small-sized companies: they have difficulty in borrowing the sort of money on the long-term arrangement that they need. Unfortunately since the war the big companies in Britain have been largely looking at how they can make profits by contraction rather than by expansion, how they can bring four or five companies together and cut off the least profitable 20 per cent, rather than thinking in terms of expansion. These are the problems that we have, and this is why the small entrepreneurs with their new ideas, like this electronics business, this new television set, and so on, the sort of people who would like to keep it to themselves, who would like to develop as private industry, come in the end to the NEB and say, "Will you please help us on this because otherwise we will go under?"—and they have a very good idea. It is the small firms and the medium-sized firms expanding that can develop the economy just as quickly as the big firms. So if the big firms are thinking only in terms of profitability through contraction rather than profitability through expansion, then there has to be some State intervention.

Professor Bain: Could we go to the questions of co-ordination and the criteria for financial investment? Our present system is that the financial institutions and the companies in which they invest decide where they are going to lend or invest using commercial criteria. That is essentially with the anticipated rate of return on their funds. We all know that the anticipated rate of return on funds, if the system was unaffected by any outside forces, might not correspond with the greatest national advantage. So the system we have is one in which the government intervenes through tax policy, through regional policy, through exchange control, and through selective assistance schemes of various kinds, to ensure that the criteria in the market correspond to what the government sees as the national advantage. That goes for the industrial strategy too. The Ferrous Foundry Scheme is an example of this. In paragraph 33 of the TUC paper you imply that this system works satisfactorily for the individual company, even though that company may span a wide range of activities or industries. But you assert that other criteria should be used by financial institutions and you go on to develop them in paragraph 38, which I will come to later. I wonder if first you could explain why it is that you draw this distinction between the investment decisions of the individual company where commercial criteria are said to be satisfactory and the investment decisions of the institutions where they are not satisfactory, given that both of them have an equal anticipated rate of return and the rates ruling in the market are acting as a co-ordinating mechanism within the system.

—*A:* (*Mr Lea*) I think what we had in mind in the first sentence of paragraph 33 was something a little more straightforward than Professor Bain is inferring. Clearly it is one thing to say that if you want to put up a new bean canning factory and there are three different places you can put it, that is not something that we would say would be for the outside agency to judge between given the availability of regional grants and other regional incentives. I think that is rather different from the use of the Industry Act, etc., to introduce other criteria. Under the Clothing Scheme, or something like that, one is covering a whole industry. In other cases there are one or two major firms that one is dealing with. I think that the problem of structure is a different type of problem from the problem of selecting an investment within a particular company, and quite clearly it raises separate considerations. I do not think that the first sentence of paragraph 33 should be read to mean that we think that there is no problem about the way in which companies carry out their investment appraisal: it simply says that we have no objection to the use of the rate of return as a way of measuring the relative benefits. It is precisely because the interface between a company and the general common weal is where we think there is a role for State intervention that we draw that distinction. So when we pick up the present use of the Industry Act and the role of the NEB, and so on, we are essentially talking about wider considerations in society and not trying to talk in principle about the internal position.

Q: Do you think that the relative rate of return is a good measure within the company?

—*A:* I think that there are problems of short term and long term here as well. But I see less problems about the use of the rate of return within a company than I would do between industries embracing other problems of industrial structure.

Q: Even within companies it is possible for the government to influence the direction of investment, as indeed it does. Take, for example, in regional policy, regional development grants. It can discriminate fairly closely between different types of machine tool investment, for example through the section 8 Machine Tool Scheme. Is there anything wrong with this way of co-ordinating the system to get the investment in the direction that one wants it?

—*A:* I am sorry, I think we are talking at cross purposes. Perhaps the point I was making is one where we are misunderstanding each other. Clearly, the Industry Act would discriminate in the use of funds by company X between use A and use B, but that is not the same as intervening in the direct management of company X; that is a different sort of consideration. Here one is in a different argument about the nature of company law and who should be on the board of the company. I am quite prepared to discuss that question, but I think that is a different sort of question.

Q: I am not trying to follow that one. I am trying to see why it is that you think that the institutions should be directed to some extent in their investment pattern, when the government has means and has used means to carry out the industrial strategy, to discriminate between particular classes of activity, to try to eliminate particular bottlenecks—all the things that you have been telling us the government should be trying to do—through the market system without direct intervention in companies in the past. What I am trying to see is why it is that you are suggesting that this should not be done for investment by institutions in the future, why you should not leave it to the companies to follow these criteria. The government set the criteria, or influence them, the companies come along and say, "Since there is a section 8 scheme it is profitable for us to invest in machine tools", go to the financial market, get the funds from there without anybody telling financial institution X that it has to lend to company Y or invest in company Y. In other words, what is wrong with the structure of the existing system that you have to bring in an organisation to co-ordinate rather than leaving the rates of return available in the market to do the job for you automatically?

—*A:* With great respect I think that it is somewhat misconceived to describe the Industry Act and other ways of discrimination as the market system and to suggest that we are now going over to something quite different. In some respects we are talking about generalising and extending some of the instruments available, but I think that to introduce a dichotomy between the market system on the one side and some type of intervention on the other side is not a correct way of looking at the problem. After all, it is not the market system which defined the powers of the NEB: these are powers defined by parliament and they are guidelines for the NEB. That is not the market system. That is a system introduced through the political process. I think we would be extending that in some ways, but not to the exclusion of the market forces, because clearly on the demand side it is still working in a market economy and certainly in the world economy it is very much a market economy.

—(*Mr Urwin*)*:* I would have thought, chairman, that Professor Bain was making our case for us. The very fact that section 8 of the 1972 Act has been used first of all for the sectoral schemes, then to assist companies in the national interest as well as those that needed rescue, showed the value of some sort of selective investment approach identifying the areas where you need it. In these wider sectoral schemes, like the Non-Ferrous Scheme, the Clothing Scheme, the Ferrous Foundry Scheme, the Machine Tool Scheme, and all the others, you have identified it and shown precisely what you want the money for and how you want it using and whether it is being done under proper management or not. We are saying that these are successful, everyone is commending them, they are doing the job that they were intended to do, but on such a small scale as not really to make the impact which is needed in order to assist British industry. We are looking for ways in which this can be widened and broadened and for ways to get it moving.

—(*Mr Basnett*)*:* Could I underline that? I think the whole import of our submission is that private institutions' money should be related to industrial strategy. There is a limit to which this money can be used for this purpose. We said in our evidence that the financial institutions tend to act in a conservative manner. But it is a fact that our manufacturing basis of industrial strategy has been eroded and there is a very real need for the use of money in relation to that strategy and in relation to other economic and social strategies. For instance, what would have happened to Leyland and Rolls Royce if the government had not intervened? The collapse of those firms would have been quite dramatic. You can say the government can do that. But there is a limit to which it can. The NEB has had to take them over and is reviving and resuscitating those firms. But it needs money, and it needs continuing money, and the resources of the government in this area are not sufficient to deal with the whole range of problems that faces British industry at the moment.

Q: What I am trying to see is why it is that you say that the present mechanisms cannot be extended if need be. If one can identify any other general characteristics where there should be some special consideration given, the government could have a section 8 scheme for it. I think this can be done. Why is the TUC saying that we should not be going at it in that way, we should be going at it in some other way?

—*A:* (*Mr Urwin*) If £100 million worth of government money used under section 8 can bring about £750 million worth of investment, if you add £1000 million available for these schemes—not exactly the same but various schemes of this kind—then you could start to get British industry moving.

Q: If your supposition that this would apply on the same scale was correct, then obviously you would get that much more investment, though I think it is debatable whether you could pump-prime to that extent.

—*A:* With respect, I did not say precisely the same schemes—variations of them.

Q: Could I move on to the particular criteria that you suggest? In paragraph 38 you suggest that there are three criteria that the TUC has in mind. The first is that there should be an adequate rate of return in the long run. Mr Basnett, you said something about the conservatism of the institutions in the new issue market. I am wondering whether this implies that you think that the institutions take too short term a view, and if it does what is the evidence for it?

—*A:* (*Mr Basnett*) I will ask Mr Lea to give the evidence. It has been our view for a long time, and indeed there are a number of statements to the effect that commercial institutions do take a short-term view.

—(*Mr Lea*)*:* The evidence so far as I am concerned is that I have never met in any circumstances a group of people, pension funds or insurance companies, who have said other than this, that they have to be very conservative, they have to worry about risks, they have to think of the interests of their policyholders, which incidentally overwhelmingly nowadays in the pension funds are trade union members investing their savings in one way or another. The problem they are faced with, when we talk to them about industrial strategy they say, "There is nothing we can do. We are constrained by our articles of association, etc, in the way we approach this." We are saying that if we could give them a guarantee they might be very happy to participate voluntarily in partnership with the government in a scheme whereby they could be a little more adventurous in this sort of way. We are not claiming that this is holy writ, but that is the proposition which we are asking you to examine.

Q: So the proposition, if I have it right, is that you are suggesting that the government should guarantee the rate of return on a certain part of the funds provided by the institutions?

—*A:* That is right.

Q: At gilt-edged rates, presumably?

—*A:* We say that there would need to be some actuarial consideration of what would be a reasonable minimum guaranteed rate given that it was open-ended at the top. If the Treasury were putting in £500 million a year and the institutions were putting in £500 million a year one cannot say off the top of one's head what would be the guaranteed rate of return, but something on those lines.

Q: Is there any reason in principle why the government should not simply issue an extra £500 million of gilts and provide the funds themselves?

—*A:* No, because this would not in any sense involve the institutions in the way in which we think there is a need and a desire for them to be involved. Indeed on the part of the trade union members' pension funds I think the proposition would be that if this was spread across the industry with this guarantee open-ended at the top this would be very different from a gilt-edged market.

Q: So from what you are saying it is not only a question of getting the funds going the right place but you have a separate objective, which is in some way to get the institutions involved?

—*A:* That is right.

Q: And that is a separate objective, nothing to do with providing the funds?

—*A:* With great respect, as the institutions are now we say in the total equity market of £50 billion, responsible for £25 billion to £30 billion, and it will be growing at £3 billion or £4 billion a year. If we are talking about more than half of the equity market being in the institutions and this being savings of people it is surely highly relevant to the total operation of the savings mechanism in our society how we relate that flow of savings to the demands of industry. So I do not see that this is separate in any way from the problem of the industrial strategy.

Q: I agree that it is relevant, but I am not sure that one has to do it that way. Could I take you to your second criterion, where you are suggesting that funds should be provided to companies which are investing at home rather than abroad. Is there evidence that the financial institutions have been putting up money for companies to invest abroad in recent years?

—*A:* (*Mr Callaghan*) We know that the figures show that most investment by UK companies abroad is financed abroad. Apart from the case where firms can meet what I think is called a super criterion under exchange control it is financed abroad. I think this is brought in as a limiting factor. I think we are well aware of the facts. But we see it as important, certainly in terms of the use of the North Sea oil revenues, that as a general objective we should try to secure as much of this investment for home as abroad.

Q: Is it really an argument against liberalising exchange controls?

—*A:* It is indeed.

Q: Are you suggesting that the super criterion is too lax?

—*A:* No, we are not suggesting that. We are suggesting that it would be a mistake to relax the existing exchange controls. We have expressed concern on this and to some extent we have been reassured by the government that there is no 'flight of capital' out of the country.

Q: We are looking here at specific criteria, and the fact that this is not operational, because what you are saying is that there is no evidence that in the past the financial institutions have been putting too much money into this activity.

—*A:* No, we do not make that criticism, and it is quite clear from our evidence that we are not making such a simple point. However, we are implying, and stating it now, that it would be wrong to relax exchange controls at the present time.

Q: The third criterion is that they should be projects which help maximise the growth rate of the UK economy. I wondered what measure, other than the expected profitability, which is the measure that the government says is the best single measure, you were suggesting should be used as a criterion of contribution to expected growth?

—*A:* (*Mr Lea*) I think that the employment consequences of the industrial strategy are in mind in paragraph 38, but we have in fact covered a lot of this ground in the last half hour. I do not think we would stick on there being three headings. In broad terms I think that the third one is trying to draw attention to the sort of problems that we have been discussing so far. If one thinks about the use of funds in the last boom, it was quite clear—and this was to do with the Paper on competition and credit control and all the rest of it—we did not think that this was directed in any way at the long-term growth prospects of the British economy. But I do not think one can answer that question fully without going over a lot of the ground that we have already been considering.

Q: Could I ask one final question on this? Can you give us some indication of what sort of calculations would be made in deciding whether an institution should be asked to support a particular project and who would take the decision?

—A: This is the question of what would be the modus operandi of this new agency. We are not being dogmatic about either its composition or its modus operandi. What we would assume is that the people taking the decisions would be the management team but there would be a policy council, just like on the NEB there is a policy council, and then people who have the responsibility of day-to-day management of the NEB's operations. Whether incidentally these people taking these decisions would include the people from the other agencies, such as the NEB, and people from the trade union movement, and so on, is for consideration. But I think you are raising the question here as to how this could be got off the ground. We put the emphasis on its being a voluntary arrangement in the sense that we would hope that once your committee had introduced the discussion to a wider public, and maybe come up with a firm set of recommendations in the final report, that the institutions would see that this was very much an idea that they ought to participate in and enter into talks about the preparatory committee before the whole thing is got off the ground. So I think it would be a gradual process and it would be premature for us to try to dot all the i's and cross all the t's this afternoon.

Mr Lloyd: Clearly, the TUC would not be putting forward recommendations for a new mechanism unless they felt a clear need for it, although I think David Lea did answer Professor Dahrendorf by saying that he was not certain that there was any statistical basis that he could put forward.

—A: I said I was certain that there was not a statistical basis by the nature of the case.

Q: Could we just explore that a little further? In paragraph 17 you postulate a doubling of the manufacturing investment, which is quite modest, 7 per cent to 8 per cent per annum in real terms, and in the same paragraph you say that that would ride along with an economy growing, again in real terms, at 5 per cent or 6 per cent each year. Given that quite modest rate of growth in the economy and not overmuch investment either, why do you feel that the normal sources of finance would not be forthcoming? I know this is going over old ground, but we must understand you better.

—A: At the risk of being repetitive I may say that first of all the relationship between the growth of GNP and the growth of manufacturing investment is something of the ratio that we have described. We are not claiming that we have got that absolutely right and your researchers may produce a different answer. But that is not the main burden of your question. The main burden of your question is whether or not we need some new instrument to meet the financing of 7 per cent to 8 per cent growth. I would point out that a doubling over this 10-year period does involve the order of £7 billion or £8 billion extra by the end of the decade on top of the average net capital appreciation at the moment. So I think the question is not so much whether we can have this 4 per cent, 5 per cent or 6 per cent growth rate in the 1980s but whether the flows of savings and industrial financing will be of a different order than they were in the 1970s. The answer is unequivocally yes, it is going to be a very much bigger operation of financing than has been true in the 1970s.

The second question is, is it prima facie necessary if we are going to be looking strategically long term at the needs of the economy, when the oil runs out or runs down towards the end of the century? What happens if we do, long term, think of the type of structures that are going to be needed? Prima facie the answer is that one has to find some way of ensuring that there is a link between the savings flow, which is increasingly going to be institutional, and the demand for funds.

The final point I would make is that of course at any point in time, given the cost of money, and so on, you can demonstrate that there is no shortage of funds because of the problem about how the price is determined. What we are saying is that we believe that some closer relationship between the institutions and the demand for funds in this new growth scenario is going to be highly desirable if we are going to have a strategic view of the economy. If a strategic view of the economy means anything at all it means that there are going to be recommendations coming out of the sector working parties, and so on. There seems to be no difference between us that under the Industry Act and other like legislation schemes affecting particular companies are a welcome development in our economy. What we are suggesting is that this same set of principles needs to be generalised and co-ordinated in some way, which I think is one of the major tasks that you have before you.

Q: Chairman, how does the TUC reconcile that assertion of a gap with the findings of the Roll Committee in March of this year, which were tabled, as I remember it, at NEDC, under which they drew up three scenarios—and David Basnett and you will recall all three—and they said that even in the extreme case of a 25 per cent per annum increase in investment in the late 1970s, far higher than you are postulating, financing constraints are unlikely to become an early or serious problem even should the development of investment become that favourable.

—*A:* Because we are talking about the 1980s, we are not talking about 1977 or 1978. I do not think that the Roll Committee—and I am surprised that Mr Lloyd should pose the question in this way—were suggesting that you can have 25 per cent compound over 10 years and not have a problem. We are talking about the problem of doubling over 10 years. They were talking about the next couple of years. There is no contradiction between what we are saying and what the Roll Committee are saying.

Mr Murray: You seem to me to be talking about a pattern of investment as well, not merely a gap caused by the difference between the size of the pool of savings and the demand for investment. You are saying that there needs to be an explicit view taken in some quarter about the right pattern derived from wherever it may be, and that this too needs to be incorporated into the total decisions, and that it will not be incorporated unless there is a new institution of the sort you are describing.

—*A:* Yes. It is becoming apparent in the discussions on industrial strategy that the major problem that has been reached is of linking the sector level, the findings of the sector working parties with what is going to happen in the particular companies. This linkage is the major problem now confronting us. Unless we are going to define industrial strategy as a lot of talk and no action there must be some translation of the recommendations of the industrial strategy into investment priorities, and so on. So there is a systematic pattern which will have to emerge and it will have to have some impact on the investment decisions of particular companies. The financial part of the jigsaw puzzle of the industrial strategy is what we think is your essential role to investigate and recommend on and we have been trying to address our minds to that problem in our evidence.

Mr Mills: What is the view of the TUC as to the extent to which the financial institutions are currently fully alive to the implications of the industrial strategy?

—*A:* Very little indeed. I make the point about the institutions, they are not claiming otherwise. I think they would say that they have no standing in the matter in very broad terms. Although there might be some relationship in particular cases with some schemes under the Industry Act, in general terms to the tune of a big proportion of the savings flow coming through the financial institutions I do not think they would claim that there was any overt or explicit relationship with the industrial strategy, because there is no such instrument available.

—(*Mr Basnett*): Could I add that no senior trade union official need ever be short of a lunch. Insurance companies will always invite him to lunch to explain why they have to behave in the short-term way that they do. That is the way they justify themselves. We see no evidence of any connection between the financial institutions and the industrial strategy. I did illustrate before that there were examples of identification of investment opportunities through the industrial strategy that have brought no response from NEB and financial institutions. When we talked about 25 per cent per annum, the Roll Committee was of course talking merely about the year 1977/78, whereas we are talking about the 1980s. But not only that, our manufacturing base has a strategy which is designed to build it up again. We are concerned too that the oil revenues should be used to a higher proportion to build up our manufacturing base beyond the 1980s. The lack of help from the financial institutions is something which has concerned us.

Mr Murray: So you are saying that the financial institutions should be brought into the industrial consensus, they should feel part of this activity, rather than stand aside and mechanically produce the amounts of money in response to certain criteria, that they should be conscious of the whole gamut of things that the industrial strategy is involved in. Is that what you are arguing?

—A: Yes, in two senses: in the sense of the contribution they can make and in the sense of the response made to the consensus which is already emerging within industry and because of the consensus which the industrial strategy does represent.

Mr Lloyd: Of course at the moment the industrial strategy is dealing with sector requirements in the 1970s and 1980s. Do you seriously believe, any of you, that at the level of the firm finance will not be forthcoming in the normal way, because that again is in contrast with the situation which has obtained with lesser growth rates in the 1970s where finance has been shown in evidence after evidence to us to be available for any viable projects?

—A: We are conscious that finance is not available in certain areas of high technology where we have intervened. I would again say that some of the sector working parties have identified opportunities which have just not been followed.

Q: By the financial institutions or by the firms in the sectors?

—A: I do not know who is responsible in those instances, but it may be the firms. If you look at the petrochemical industry you will see that they are international. It may well be that they have taken a deliberate decision to go to Europe instead of this country. But I would have thought that the involvement of the financial institutions on the evidence of the sector working parties would have shown a long-term profitability in which they may have wished to involve themselves.

Mr Bayley: Could I start with the criteria for investment somewhere in the area that Professor Bain was questioning and then move on to the TUC proposals for a change in facility? As to the criteria for investment, could I direct the TUC witnesses to paragraph 26 in their evidence, where at the end of the paragraph in relation to insurance companies they talk about "their main duty under existing company law is to look after the interests of their shareholders". They must have overlooked the legislation that specifically governs the operations of insurance companies, which places a primary duty on those companies to safeguard policyholders' security and their expectations. In any event we should just remind ourselves that something like 35 per cent of life assurance is mutual, that is co-operative, and therefore has no shareholders anyway. As for the rest, shareholders' interests are specifically subordinated under the legislation to policyholders' interests, and indeed the Department of Trade is charged with the specific duty of monitoring the arrangements for seeing that that happens. That is the observation. Coming towards the question, I do not think any of that matters anyway, because I was pleased to see in paragraph 35 that the TUC believes that the savings of workpeople for life assurance and pensions are entitled to a positive rate of return. You do mean there, do you not, a positive real rate of return?

—*A:* Yes.

Q: Moving then to paragraph 38, and this is where we come very close to what Professor Bain was questioning you about, the insurance companies and the pension funds have recently published their evidence to this committee, and it enters into a good deal of detail of what their investment objectives are and what the management of their funds is trying to achieve. I would like to ask Mr Basnett if he would develop a little more in what way he reads those objectives as differing from his own as expressed in paragraph 38. I have in front of me both the NAPF evidence and the insurance companies' evidence. It says here: "The insurance companies will seek to determine a basic investment policy which is likely to offer the maximum overall return over the medium to long term." After referring to the way it is influenced by the legislation I was talking about it goes on lower down to say: "The cost of acquiring and selling assets also militates against a rapid turnover, reinforcing the objective of selecting investment on a medium to long-term view." This evidence which is in front of us is very much at odds with what you were just saying about the short-term view. Could Mr Basnett elaborate?

—*A:* Our overall argument is simply this, that we are concerned that our manufacturing base over the last few years has not been growing. Pension funds have to look to their overall return, have to look at the cost of acquiring something, which means that they go in for long-term investments. This leads them in many cases to go into property, and one pension fund is investing in paintings, whereas at the same time, as the industrial strategy has identified, there is a rundown of our manufacturing industry from lack of investment. It seems to me that if the situation in this country is being eroded it is in the interests of the pension funds and the financial institutions to help to restore industry and to help to make better wealth creation than they have done in the past. That underlies a large part of our argument.

Q: Thank you. I am trying to see as clearly as I can the distinction which you are drawing between what they are stating are their investment objectives at the present time and in what manner your own objectives differ from that. I think you were saying just now that you recognise that they have to get the maximum rate of return for their own constituents. How does that differ?

—*A:* (*Mr Lea*) Could I pick up the point about how our analysis would relate to how we would propose to deal with the problem, because I think it gives you a better picture in answering your question than this rather abstract talk about criteria? There is this ongoing series of reports and recommendations under the industrial strategy. I do not think we need to apologise for reiterating this, because it is an ongoing process whereby one gets particular problems and proposals made in particular situations and particular industries. This is not a question of at any point in time the government or the National Economic Development Council writing down three criteria to use as a yardstick for the savings of the institutions or any other savings flow in the country. We are, however, saying that we think that there will be an increasing number of projects which need to be backed arising from the proposals made under the industrial strategy. We are talking about a modest sum. I do not know whether there is a touch of irony in Mr Lloyd's use of the term 'modest' in connection with a 7 per cent rate of growth of investment or a 5 per cent growth rate of GNP. It is not modest in terms of the 1970s: it is ambitious, but it ought not to be ambitious in relation to the 1980s. £1 billion per annum is not these days a big number. Our national income is £100 billion a year. So that is 1 per cent in those terms. We are talking about this equal participation as an illustration of what we would be saying on the part of the institutions and the Treasury. When one looks at the relationship of this to the flow of funds in the institutions, and we say take a figure of 10 per cent, one would be looking at this frankly by way of being a new departure in some ways and in that sense experimental, but handling a very modest sum. I keep emphasising when we read comments on our evidence that £1 billion is not a very big sum to be talking about. It is obviously big in relation to any one institution, but it is not big in relation to the flows of savings in the economy. So we would be saying that the criteria would be built up as one went along, it would be an ongoing process, and it would be worked out in conjunction with the institutions themselves, not just by the government or by the TUC or by some external agency: the institutions would participate in it. Anecdotal evidence builds up to a powerful body of evidence if everybody says the same thing every time you meet them, which is that there is a sense in which at the moment there is no overt link possible with the industrial strategy. I think the best way that we can answer your question in relation to criteria is to say that in practical terms they would evolve as they went along by being linked with the industrial strategy which will throw up problems and proposals each year as it goes by.

Sir David Orr: When Mr Lea says that the members of the pension funds would welcome this connection with the industrial strategy could I ask how widely he has consulted on that?

—A: I cannot tell you how many people as a percentage of the total number of people in the institutions, but I have never met people in the institutions to discuss this sort of problem who have not said that they fully recognise the need for an industrial strategy. They feel that it is not possible as things are at the moment for there to be any overt connection between themselves and the industrial strategy because they have to adopt an investment policy which as it is at the moment in terms of spreading risk, and so on, there can be no way in which they can decide to invest funds to meet criteria which might be decided by some external agency. Whether it is in terms of participating in a jumbo project in the Middle East or in terms of building a channel tunnel, when one says that therefore there is prima facie a need for some discussion as to how the flow of savings can relate to an industrial strategy I have never found the answer to be other than an affirmative one.

Chairman: Is the TUC case not really a two-stage process—first, that there should be a new industrial strategy, that there should be an investment programme increased by £1000 million a year in the 1980s, and that requires a clear decision that there should be a strategy first, but that they are suggesting that since there is not such a strategy operating or in prospect institutions are at fault for not financing it? Do we not have to create the demand first before we see how the demand can be met by the financial institutions, be they the main City institutions, the banks, and so on, or be they the insurance companies, pension funds, and the rest? If this is so, is it not the case that the decision on industrial strategy which you are urging on the committee is really a decision for government? The government has the say in regard to its involvement with NEDC and the working parties, the government have to embrace this policy as a first stage, after which the government could then go, no doubt with full TUC support, to the financial institutions and say, "This is our strategy. We want another £1000 million put up. What can you, the financial institutions, what can you, the banks, and the others, do in order to meet it?" In other words, is not the whole argument that it is not the financial institutions who are failing to adopt the industrial strategy, but that the industrial strategy has not been accepted, whether by government or by anyone else concerned, or by industry, to ensure that the demand is there, and then to ask the institutions how they would propose to meet it as a second stage? Is that not the real issue?

—A: I think that is certainly a fair way of putting the sequence of events, but . . .

Chairman: If the banks say, "We would not meet it if the government approached us", then they are perhaps putting themselves at risk of serious criticism by the committee. But as I understand it the banks have not said, "We will not meet it", they have just said, "We cannot initiate it".

Mr Lloyd: Chairman, could I follow that? It seems to me that when David

Lea said that he did not think the financial institutions were able to adopt and relate to the industrial strategy one ought to define terms within the document on industrial strategy, which had frankly a lot for everyone in it, and among the things in it, as I remember it, was that all parties would aim to increase the real profitability of industry; that was one of the things. Surely if industry is made more profitable in real terms then it could bring forward propositions—and this is the way it would work in practice. It would not work with a great lump sum. It would work firm by firm. Taking David Basnett's example of the downstream petrochemical complex, that company, feeling more content with real profitability as the basis of its calculations, would ask for the money, and I cannot see why it should not get it on the basis of all the evidence we have had from everybody else. So of course financial institutions do and will relate to the industrial strategy in that pragmatic way. I think what we have heard this afternoon is a sort of edifice or structure built in a sense for no particular reason in terms of the practicalities, because I do not believe that things have been turned down, except for the one example that we have heard about, the petrochemical firm.

Chairman: Could I supplement that? The suggestion is that the financial institutions have not done this, or are not doing it, but is it not a fact that if somebody—for example, the government or the members of the CBI—said that this is the industrial strategy, then the bankers around this table and their colleagues would be sitting there with open arms waiting for it licking their chops and generally looking forward to a situation where somebody was really going to borrow the money with the necessary security?

Mr Lloyd: It is a fact that the various funds which have been prepared, one which was popularly called some time ago the Lever Plan, have been very much smaller than the sums which have quite rightly been talked about. But there were not many demands on it.

Mr Murray: Is another bit of the jigsaw to what the chairman has put up that in fact we have a new kind of scenario and it is new in three different ways? First, we have the new role of the institutions as such. They have a role now thrust on them perforce by the development of pension schemes, insurance, and so on, which it seems to me with the greatest respect they are still not fully coming to terms with. So first of all there is the new role of the institutions. Secondly, there is the prospect of a much bigger flow of savings in the 1980s than they have traditionally been used to handle in the 1970s. Thirdly, there is this question of how you involve them, and I think Mr Lloyd is quite right on this. Do you just say, "There you are, there is the City of London, go to the City and ask for this and tell them all about it"? Or do you invite the institutions into the party in a way which would not only apprize them of the needs of the strategy but also bring in their experience, their knowledge and their wisdom? Is this not in fact a new scene for the institutions which they have not really come to terms with yet, and do you not want to create a system of which they are part and feel part of the total activity, not something rather isolated, rather remote? Is it not making them part of the whole consultative and determinative process that we are talking about here?

—*A:* (*Mr Basnett*) The answer is Yes—it would have been interesting if I had said No! There is obviously another relationship between the institutions if they are involved in the industrial strategy, which is important, and they become part of the consensus, whereas at the moment they are quite separate from the development of that strategy in the sense of influencing it or being influenced by it.

—(*Mr Lea*): I think there is a technical sense in which there is another area, as I said in response to Professor Bain. We would have to look at this concept of being able to have some guaranteed rate of return on this tranche of money to give the confidence to the institutions and to see how one went with this type of approach which was at the same time open-ended in terms of the rate of return. I think this could usefully be explored.

As a final point, I am sure we want to reiterate that we are sure that you are not going to try and reach finality in your first report on this, but we would hope that some of our suggestions could be looked at with a degree of imagination because, as has been said, the scenario of the 1980s, which is taken to be your timescale minimum, is going to be a very different scenario from that of the 1970s. Therefore many of the questions are going to be novel questions requiring novel answers. It is obviously a multi-policy problem. There are problems in other areas of the economy, such as the problem of organisation and how it relates to productivity. But to say that that has to be dealt with before this is almost passing the buck to somebody else. I think this particular problem is certainly going to be one which is there if one looks at the scenario of the 1980s and we hope that you will help to ventilate some of these ideas in a general sense in your first report.

Chairman: I think what we have to do is to establish the demand and then see how it can be met, as I say, with a government guarantee of the new strategy expenditure, in the same way as they guaranteed a certain amount of money to the NEB—not enough, some of you said earlier in the arguments you put foward. If they do that then we can see how it is going to be met. I remember—and I think Mr Basnett is just old enough to remember this—that when I made my first speech at the Labour Party conference as leader in 1963 I was dealing with an argument about technology when the then government had said, "We have all the technologists we need". I said, "of course you have all the technologists you need if you do not order any technologists. We have as many bullfighters as we need." Is that not the argument we are having today? The institutions are perfectly right in saying, "We have not seen any problems that we cannot meet. The money is there once the demand becomes articulate in terms of the individual firms or in terms of the spending authority that will then pass the money on to the individual projects, and when that happens we will be ready." As I say, we shall be actively welcoming it, because we shall have the money.

The only other question I want to ask relates to something which has been mentioned a number of times this afternoon, and indeed in other evidence that we have received, and that is about the insurance companies and the pension funds. If one compares the position that this committee faces and the country faces compared with our predecessors, Radcliffe and Macmillan, there are many big changes in the world, floating exchange rates, eurocurrency, and all the rest of it. But one of the big domestic changes is the growth of the relative importance of the financial institutions. We have had the upsurge of the insurance companies. I saw some figures the other day of how much they can provide compared with what it was 15 or so years ago. And of course insurance companies have now been passed in the race by the pension funds. I think it was Mr Basnett who said that the pension funds have got their own rules. The pension funds' first duty in the articles of association, put in by their constitutional terms of reference and by the law and everything else, have to give thought to one priority above all others—namely, finding the money for the pensioner of next year or 10 years or 40 years hence. The fact that in the course of doing it they are also the biggest source of investment capital in the country these days means that they are potentially very great lenders to industry. We are coming to this when we are taking evidence about small businesses. Unfortunately it suits them to invest their money in very large tranches, very large amounts. When I had lunch yesterday with the Coal Board's pension fund they mentioned this. They said they need far more staff to invest in small firms. So where you have pension funds with an overriding responsibility this does change the situation. Again, I would have thought that if you want the pension funds to subscribe to a £1000 million a year increase in the nation's capital investment in reorganising industry, then almost certainly the government would guarantee them, so that they know that they are not putting their future pensioners at risk.

Here, if I read your evidence correctly —and this is not something that has been made much of in other evidence—you propose that the pension funds should go on a pay-as-you-go basis?

—*A:* (*Mr Basnett*) Yes. That suggestion is made for examination.

Q: In a sense this is almost heresy. The pension funds are sitting very pretty. They are so powerful that they do not know how powerful they are. They could very well be, for example, transforming the nature of our society more than any government would ever dare to do even if it had a large majority in parliament. I found the Coal Board pension fund extending nationalisation quite considerably with nobody to argue about it as far as I can see. I wonder whether one of the things we must investigate is the complete change, not in our terms of reference but in the ambience of examining the role of the pension funds. This is something, as you have said, that is an important question requiring investigation perhaps when we have further evidence.

—*A:* Yes, Sir Harold. I am quite sure that I could not have put the situation better myself. The growth of the pension funds is most central to this. I think we used the phrase that we prefer to see new machinery instead of empty office blocks.

—(*Mr Urwin*)*:* Or leave some of the perfectly good shopping centres and stop knocking them down and putting others up; there always seems to be plenty of money around for that.

Chairman: Thank you very much indeed, gentlemen.

(The witnesses withdrew)

WRITTEN EVIDENCE BY THE ASSOCIATION OF INDEPENDENT BUSINESSES

1. We wish to thank the Committee of Inquiry for its invitation to submit evidence about arrangements for channelling savings in the economy into industry and trade.

2. We appreciate that a healthy economy needs efficient organisations of various sizes, but our particular knowledge is of the businesses which we represent. Our evidence will, therefore, deal with finance for quoted public companies and government controlled activities only where this may have some effect on unquoted businesses. Otherwise we have confined ourselves to considering unincorporated firms and unquoted companies.

3. The first part of our evidence defines the businesses which we represent. The second part explains what motivates the people running them. The third part discusses methods of obtaining finance. The fourth part contains recommendations for increasing the amount of money risked in industrial and commercial enterprises.

I INDEPENDENT BUSINESSES DEFINED

4. During the last ten years there have been various definitions used to distinguish smaller businesses from larger ones. Many of these, like the ones given to the Committee of Inquiry on Small Firms (The Bolton Committee), owe little to logic and much to the way in which Government Departments usually collect statistics. For example, the limit of £50,000 annual turnover in retailing can by no stretch of the imagination be thought equivalent to the limit of 200 employees in manufacturing, whether one considers capital or number of employees. (See Report of the Committee of Inquiry on Small Firms, Cmnd. 4811, Table 1.I).

5. In our Association's evidence to the Bolton Committee (November 1969) we stated that any statistical description would be quite arbitrary. However, we pointed out that a clear distinction could be made between businesses which were quoted on a stock exchange (or could rely on support by the state out of taxes) and businesses which were unquoted.

6. A quotation transforms a company because:

(i) it obtains a whole new source of finance and no longer has to rely on ploughed back profits for expansion;

(ii) at the first quotation, or soon afterwards, the top managers of the business cease to have a crucial financial interest in its success (as opposed to an interest in maximising their own drawings);

(iii) the company should become obliged to publish information about its doings in return for inviting the general public to participate financially;

(iv) the effect of having marketable shares means that a public company is so often liable to a takeover: this can force companies into high distribution in order to maintain their share values so reducing retained profits below what might otherwise be prudent.

7. At no other point does a business change its nature radically.

8. We have always maintained therefore that the distinction between quoted and unquoted businesses should always be borne in mind when drafting legislation concerning companies, taxation, and many other business matters. This distinction is reflected in our membership which includes independent businesses of all sizes, from single man businesses to some employing about 2,000 people.

9. You may like to note that in 1966 independent businesses employed 39 per cent of the working population compared with 37 per cent in quoted public companies. (The Private Company To-Day—Merrett & Lehr).

II THE MOTIVATION OF OWNER/MANAGERS

10. There are various motives which drive a man to start his own business or perhaps expand an existing business. These include:

(i) A desire to prove one's own ideas and one's own abilities;

(ii) A wish to be independent;

(iii) A desire to feel that one can make a real contribution to society personally by running one's own company;

(iv) The chance to secure a bigger reward than would be possible in a "safe" job.

11. In some degree all of these factors will be present. However, if people are to start any new businesses it must be possible for them to save enough capital to do so while they are reasonably young. It is equally important that success should be sufficiently rewarded to justify the work involved and the risking of one's savings.

12. Because of the foregoing we believe that there are certain essential conditions for a healthy independent business sector. These conditions are:

(i) That a thrifty person with an average income from employment should be able to save enough to start a business of his own before he is too old.

(ii) That a man running a reasonably successful small or medium-sized business should be able to earn and draw an income similar to what he might earn elsewhere and still be able to retain sufficient profit after tax to maintain the business's real value at the very least.

(iii) That the owner/managers of medium-sized businesses should be able to arrange for the continuance of those businesses, distinct and intact, after their retirement or death without having to render their families destitute, without having had to reduce their standard of living appreciably below that of people bearing similar responsibilities in public companies, and without having had to prejudice the expansion of the business during their working life.

(iv) That those who risk their savings in an enterprise, whether a new or an existing one, should not fear that they will lose control of that enterprise if it reaches some arbitrary size determined by the legislature.

(v) That the burdens placed on businesses by the legislature will not continue increasing to the point where all scope for initiative is removed.

13. The smaller firm sector has been shrinking for several years because the number of new businesses starting has been lower, often considerably lower, than the number of businesses ceasing to trade. The reason is that most of the conditions above have *not* been satisfied. That they should be satisfied is of much greater importance than the possibility of improving the availability of institutional finance.

III THE FINANCING OF INDEPENDENT BUSINESSES

General

14. The initial source of finance for smaller businesses is that provided by the people actually managing them and by their friends. Thereafter the principal source is usually ploughed-back profits.

15. When a man, or a group of men, starts a business he is almost always expected to put up part of the initial capital himself. In many cases he provides the only starting capital. As businesses grow, most of them need to borrow from time to time. Such loans will probably be short term because a prudent man knows that with a fairly new business he cannot see far enough ahead to undertake even a medium term commitment. What is more he is loath to risk losing control of the business he is building up and is anyway conscious that inability to repay loans leads to bankruptcy. Therefore he expects to repay loans out of retained profits. (It is only if the owners of a business intend to seek a stock exchange quotation that they are likely to incur debts which they do not hope to repay out of profits eventually.)

16. As a business grows, its trade is likely to become more stable so that it will be reasonable to borrow medium term and at the same time possible to persuade lenders to undertake a medium-term risk because of the business's record. However, the borrower still expects to repay loans, though with an expanding business it is quite possible that a loan made for one purpose will be followed by, or even overlap, another made for a different purpose.

17. The extent of borrowing is, to a large measure, controlled by the unquoted company's profit record so that it is the profit which determines the rate of growth.

18. Your committee will be aware that the vast majority of independent businesses remain in the small or small to medium categories and the owners would never wish or be able to seek a quotation. Such businesses are, of course, vital to the economy. They carry out numerous manufacturing processes and services which large organisations cannot undertake efficiently, if at all. They provide employment for many skilled people and could, if encouraged, create additional valuable and satisfying jobs since they tend to be in labour intensive sectors. (Large organisations tend to be capital intensive so that when trade improves they do not take on extra workers but buy more sophisticated

machines.). In addition they provide the climate and the background from which some will grow to become the big firms of tomorrow (what the Bolton Committee called "the fliers"—Cmnd 4811, para. 8.7) and replace those which become moribund.

Earlier Reports on External Finance

19. The Bolton Report, published in 1971, is the authoritative source of information on small firms in Britain. On the subject of finance it said that small firms have suffered and still suffer a number of genuine disabilities, by comparison with larger firms, in seeking finance from external sources:

(i) The periodic "squeezes" and official ceilings on bank lending tend to hit small firms harder than large firms.

(ii) Some institutional facilities (e.g. the Stock Exchange) available to large firms are not available to small firms.

(iii) Small borrowers must generally pay higher rates of interest than large borrowers.

(iv) Many small firms lack knowledge about sources of finance.

(v) Many small firms are prejudiced against borrowing.

20. However, the Bolton Report said that most of these disabilities reflect the higher cost of lending in small amounts or the higher risk of lending to small borrowers. It did not therefore recommend the creation of a new institution for the provision of finance to small firms, nor did it support the provision of finance at subsidised rates. It did recommend setting up Small Firms Advisory Bureaux to help to bridge the information gap.

21. Long before the Bolton Report, we had the Macmillan Report in 1931 which identified the phenomenon which became known as the "Macmillan Gap", i.e. the lack of provision for small and medium sized firms of long-term capital in amounts too small for public issues. This led to the setting up of various institutions specialising in the financing of small firms, notably Charterhouse Industrial Development, Credit for Industry, and Leadenhall Securities. But these institutions could tackle only part of the problem. So in 1945 the major clearing banks, with support from the Bank of England, set up the Industrial and Commercial Finance Corporation (ICFC) which became and remains by far the most important institutional provider of long term capital to small and medium enterprises in Britain.

22. Then in 1959 the Radcliffe Report recommended that the clearing banks should offer long term loan facilities as well as overdrafts for short-term credit. It also recommended setting up an institution to finance technical innovation. Both recommendations were put into effect and there was a rapid expansion of the number of bodies providing finance for small firms.

23. Nowadays there is a bewildering number of sources and types of finance, ranging from ICFC, the merchant banks, finance houses providing instalment finance and hire purchase, leasing companies, factoring services, venture capital organisations and, of course, the clearing banks which now offer a full range of facilities from overdrafts to long-term loans as well as factoring, hire purchase, leasing etc. In addition, there are such bodies as the Council for Small Industries in Rural Areas offering loans at low rates of interest.

24. Nevertheless, there are still some shortcomings in financial aid for small and medium enterprises in Britain.

The Attitude of Banks

25. Despite the recent developments in the range of services offered by the banks and other financial institutions, small firms in Britain are at a disadvantage compared with their counterparts in many other countries. In Britain, the proportion of the total assets financed by the banks is much lower than in other countries. This is true of large firms as well as small.

26. It is said that the banks in other countries have played a bigger part in financing industry and commerce because these countries have not had such a well developed capital market as the British Stock Exchange. Whatever the reason, there is little doubt that the banks in Britain have been much less involved than those in other countries in financing small firms.

27. The Bolton Report showed that, on average, in the balance sheets of both large and small firms, a little over half of the total assets were financed by the owners' capital in the form of ordinary and preference shares, capital and revenue reserves, owners' loans and future tax reserves. About another quarter of the assets were financed by creditors. The banks financed less than 10 per cent of the total assets.

28. Thus, in Britain, if an entrepreneur wants to start or expand a business, he will normally be expected to finance at least half of the assets from his own or the company's resources. Few financial institutions will consider providing funds which put them in the position of financing a bigger proportion of the assets than the entrepreneur himself. The few that do would insist on taking a share of the equity in addition to some fixed interest loans and they probably want to appoint one of their staff or a nominee as a director of the company. By contrast, in some European countries, an entrepreneur can obtain support or expand a business in which he, himself, may be financing only 30 per cent or even 20 per cent of the total assets.

29. British banks are not unwilling to lend. Indeed, in recent years there has been no shortage of funds, thanks to high interest rates. But one of the factors restricting the amount of lending is that British banks insist on adequate security for long-term and medium-term loans, and even sometimes for overdrafts. The entrepreneur is expected to provide sound security in the form of either "personal guarantees" or fixed or floating charges on the assets of the company. We cannot entirely blame the banks for their attitude; they are protecting their depositors. They believe that the banks should not borrow short-term and lend long-term.

30. This obsession with security has meant that the British small firms are at a severe disadvantage compared with their European counterparts. It seems that the British banking system has been too conservative in its approach.

31. We think that the British banks could relax their rigid rules about security and the ratio of long-term lending to short-term borrowing. This need not be dangerous. After all, most banks in other countries seem to have survived profitably with more liberal lending policies. Even in Britain, we have some very

sound financial institutions which break the cardinal rule about borrowing short-term and lending long-term. They are the Building Societies which finance private housing. Their depositors can withdraw funds at very short notice, often within a few days or months. Yet they lend large sums repayable over 20-25 years. Admittedly they have full security by a mortgage on the dwelling but they rarely experience massive withdrawals of their funds. They also operate on lower margins than most banks and other financial institutions.

32. But even more important is the fact that, according to the Bolton Report, small firms were net lenders of funds to the banking system. In 1964 the total cash in hand at bank was about double the collective overdraft. By 1968 the ratio was lower but still positive. There are no recent figures and it may be that an up-to-date survey would show a lower ratio. Even so, it can be said that the banks, perhaps unintentionally, have transferred funds from small to large firms.

33. We acknowledge that smaller businesses sometimes believe that there is unreasonable discrimination against them because they do not take into account factors such as the following:

(a) The administration and professional costs in arranging and administering loans for a small sum is probably little different to that incurred for a larger loan. These overhead costs in arranging small borrowings are, therefore, inevitably heavy in relation to the amount borrowed.

(b) A lender of money must have at least some security.

(c) A lender of money is reasonable in seeking information about how the money is to be repaid.

(d) Lending in an age of inflation must prompt a lender to ask for a high rate of interest.

How small businesses approach borrowing

34. The intending borrower, in nearly all cases, seeks his money from the source where he has already an established personal relationship. In most cases, therefore, this leads the borrower to approach his bank manager initially. Failing this, the borrower will probably make an approach through either his accounting or legal advisers. It is unlikely that he will contact new sources until he has exhausted these possibilities since in the minds of many smaller companies the financial institutions of the City are suspect.

35. We quote below one professional adviser who has a wide experience of small businesses:

"The primary source of finance for the smaller business is retained profits. Borrowing, when used, normally falls into two main categories:

(i) "Borrowing in respect of fixed assets, e.g. property, plant, machinery, etc. In this case, there are a variety of sources available, such as:

(a) In the case of property, insurance companies will often make a loan for a fixed term, secured on the property, and secured on a life endowment policy taken out in the names of one or more directors. The main problem in making the approach is knowing which insurance company may, or may not, have funds available, since the availability of such loans seems to change in a very short time. Certain financial institutions, other than insurance companies, can also be approached. Private mortgages are now a thing of the past.

(b) In the case of plant and machinery, there are often various methods of financing, such as leasing, or hire purchase.

(c) In the case of motor cars, office equipment, and so forth, there is also the possibility of leasing or contract hiring, both of which avoid finding finance for the use of such items.

(ii) "The other main type of assets on which borrowing may be made are the current assets, or trading assets, such as stock, work-in-progress and debtors. Joint stock banks will normally advance money as working capital against such security and, additionally, factoring of debts can be used, although, by and large, this is found somewhat confusing initially by smaller companies and leads to extra paperwork.

The decisions on investing can arise from a multiplicity of reasons. It could be that there are surplus funds but that it is uncertain how these can best be employed.

It could be that it is doubtful if profits can be maintained without diversification into new products, or further mechanization. It could be that the company finds it is pricing itself out of the market with manufacture and, therefore, must take drastic steps to improve its efficiency by way of more efficient machinery. It could be that it is regarded that additional sales volume must be achieved, and this could lead to the opening of further shops, or branches, in the UK or overseas, etc. etc.

By and large, I find that the smaller businesses rarely have reason to compare alternative projects. Should such occasion arise, then it is more likely that the choice between alternative projects will be based just as much on management availability, availability of machines, know-how availability, etc., and probably, to a much lesser degree, on an attempt to use any sophisticated means, such as discounted cash flow, in determining the purely financial aspects of the problem. The smaller businesses feel that discounted cash flow is fraught with too many estimates anyway to be of any great value.

The fundamental approach to the investment from a financial point of view is likely to be the basis of what additional profit there will be against the interest on the new money to be locked up and the depreciation of new assets acquired. This rule of thumb method is likely to achieve reasonable assessment without bringing in any further imponderables.

Undoubtedly, the impact of inflation and high interest rates is slowly being brought home to the smaller businesses as a result of which borrowing is now being far more heavily scrutinized to see that the high interest charge will not exceed the additional profit. On the other hand, the smaller businesses are now fully aware that it is better to use someone else's money to depreciate with inflation, and to acquire with it an asset which might at least keep pace with inflation, e.g., property.

As a result of this, therefore, smaller businesses are now more likely to acquire their own assets if they possibly can even by borrowing to a limited extent".

The Problem of the Expanding Business

36. After their early years the vast majority of businesses grow only slowly. They may well have reached the optimum size for their activity but continue to perform a valuable part in the economy. Unless financial problems are created

by some outside cause (e.g. the levying of Capital Transfer Tax) such businesses will normally, though not always easily, find a means of meeting their borrowing requirements.

37. The problems of borrowing arise most acutely for Bolton's "fliers"—the businesses which expand faster than normal. Such businesses, being successful, are generally obliged to expand and increase their sales. Consequently they need additional "medium" and even "long-term" working capital to finance work in progress and additional sales.

38. Broadly speaking the working capital required by manufacturing businesses to finance the increase in stock and work in progress, the increase in trade debts over trade credits, and the extra plant which may be needed to increase sales is about 30 per cent of the anticipated sales increase. (This does not take into account the capital cost of extra factory space.) Once they begin to expand they are likely to continue expanding for a number of years, and so it will be necessary for them to borrow more and more working capital each year. This cannot be repaid unless the business ceases to expand, or is bought up by some conglomerate, or can carry on expanding until it becomes large enough "to go public", which may take 20 or 30 years.

39. As we mentioned above, the independent business almost always turns first to its bank when seeking a loan. We have reason to believe, however, that the banking system will not be in a position to meet the needs of independent businesses for medium and long-term loans (defined as five and ten years respectively) when the nation's economy begins to recover. The clearing banks proclaim that they are in a position to meet such a need. Rather than attempting to argue with them we urge the Committee to seek the opinion of the Bank of England on this matter.

40. There are of course various institutions which offer loan capital to independent businesses in consideration for participating in the equity—but independent businessmen in England are reluctant to part with any substantial portion of their equity because, rightly or wrongly, they fear that if their business prospers the institution may use its equity holding to displace the founder of the business. This fear is regrettable because it poisons the relationship between entrepreneurs and institutions. (A factor indicated in para. 34.)

41. It is very interesting to note that the anxiety referred to above does not seem to exist in the USA. Accordingly we urge the Committee to study the facilities which exist in the US for financing independent businesses, in the hope that some similar facilities could be made available in the UK.

42. The essential point is that in the US a financial ladder has been developed up which a small business can climb.

(a) The first rung in the ladder is the "seed capital". It must be contributed by the founder of the business with the help of his family and friends. The founder takes the first risk and must demonstrate that he is capable of putting his heart and soul into the business. This is the same in the UK.

(b) As the business begins to grow and requires more working capital, the second rung in the financial ladder is provided, either by private investors, or by bank loans, or by Small Business Investment Companies (SBIC's).

An SBIC is an Investment Company formed by private individuals for the express purpose of investing in smaller businesses. If they comply with the regulations laid down by the US Small Business Administration, they may then borrow from the banks $3 for every $1 of the equity capital lent by the SBIC. The loan capital provided by the banks in this manner is guaranteed by the Federal Government through the SBA.

It should be noted that the whole concept of the SBIC's was introduced under the Eisenhower administration in 1953 in order to overcome conditions which were strikingly similar to those which exist in the UK today: banks appeared to be overflowing with cash, yet private businesses found it difficult to borrow from them.

The fact that the Federal Government was willing to guarantee loan capital acted as a catalyst. It stimulated the banks to lend money without SBA guarantees. The result is that the US banks now, quite rightly, assert that the loans they make to independent businesses directly far exceed those made with SBA guarantees. This merely proves that the SBIC scheme was remarkably successful in achieving the purpose for which it was created.

(c) The third rung in the US financial ladder is reached when an independent business requires a further amount of capital. The banks or the SBIC, which have been helping the Company, will at this stage probably bring in an institution, which will provide substantial loan capital in consideration for a portion of the equity.

(d) The fourth rung is reached if the institution and other backers of the Company arrange for its shares to be offered to the public through the Stock Exchange "over the counter" market. This has two advantages. Firstly the existence of the "over the counter" market re-assures institutions that they will not have to tie up indefinitely the money they lend to independent businesses. Secondly, the founder of the business is willing to part with even more than 50 per cent of the equity in his business because he is confident that he will soon go public and it will be spread over a large number of shareholders.

(e) An Independent US Company reaches the last rung in the ladder when it is earning a net profit of about $400,000 a year and obtains a quotation on the big board of the US Stock Exchange. This again is similar to the UK.

43. We cannot emphasise too strongly three essential differences between the US and the UK.

(i) In the US there is a clear financial ladder up which independent businesses can climb.

(ii) Governmental backing for borrowing by businesses creates a situation in which loans are more readily available to them.

(iii) A better established "over the counter" market can allow the founder of a business to part with a substantial portion of his equity without fearing that he will suddenly be ousted from his company by some ambitious individual sponsored by a financier.

IV RECOMMENDATIONS

44. The decline of vitality of the independent business sector has been caused by a political climate which has been unsympathetic towards it. This climate has allowed the development of a tax system which tends to stifle enterprise and which is particularly onerous for small and medium-sized firms. Recently conditions have been made worse by other legislation which owner/managers consider to be as unnecessary as it is debilitating when applied to their businesses.

45. The decline of the sector has not been due to a general inability to borrow. Indeed, businesses with proven management and reasonably sound projects can usually borrow from banks and other institutions for limited periods without difficulty.

46. The measures which we recommend are intended, therefore, to encourage foremost private investment in independent businesses. The best way to achieve a healthy and competitive economy is to ensure that sufficient individuals shall again be in a position to provide risk capital. The first six recommendations are made with that in mind.

47. The remaining recommendations affect means of obtaining outside finance. They would apply in a limited number of situations but could be very important for the future of the economy.

Income Tax Rates

48. The high rates of tax on above average income are a disincentive to entrepreneurial effort in this country. The scale here rises more steeply than in almost every other western country: the top rates are higher. We recommend that the top rate in the UK should be similar to that in, say, France or W. Germany.

49. Any change in the top rates should be accompanied by relief from tax on lower incomes, in particular the bottom rate should be considerably lower than the present standard rate. Such alterations might necessitate an increase in VAT or other indirect taxes. A shift from direct to indirect taxation, however, creates a choice between saving and spending. We do not think this is the place to advance detailed argument on this subject but should like to refer your Committee to the section on income tax, in the enclosed paper, produced by this Association jointly with four others last Autumn.*

Contributions to Pension Funds

50. One of the principal ways in which individual savings are channelled into industry and trade is through pensions funds. This method seems likely to increase. The prima facie attraction of this method of saving is that, within broad limits, it is paid out of pre-tax income. It is of course one of many examples where relief is obtainable from very high rates of direct taxation provided that the income is applied to purposes approved by Parliament.

---

*not reprinted here

51. There are two disadvantages of making this form of saving more advantageous than others. The first is that almost all such savings finish in government stocks, property and holdings (equity or fixed interest) in quoted public companies. The result is that an increasing portion of the nation's capital becomes invested in organisations which may have passed the peak of their efficiency and in activities which may be in decline. The second is that such savings cannot be removed by the contributor for alternative investment until he is of pensionable age. A person who decides in the middle of working life to start on his own is likely to be severely handicapped if his savings have been paid into a pension fund and so are not redeemable.

52. Ideally no form of saving should receive fiscal preference over other forms. If there were reductions in the rates of income tax, as we recommend above, then the attraction of tax reliefs would be lessened and people would be more willing to make individual investments instead of making contributions to pension funds. Such investments would be readily realisable and could be switched to provide the initial capital or additional capital for a small business. We urge your committee, therefore, to look, not only at the rates of income tax, but at ways in which all savings might receive similar tax relief.

Corporation Tax—Rate

53. Although the basic rate of Corporation Tax is high, businesses able to take advantage of the available reliefs can reduce their liability enormously. Most large companies employ full-time taxation experts (some of them former tax inspectors) to help them to take advantage of every legitimate way of reducing their tax liability. Small firms cannot afford such expensive advisers. The more complex the system of reliefs becomes, therefore, the more small firms are placed at a disadvantage.

54. If Corporation Tax was fixed at no more than 15 per cent (with a classic, not an imputation system) and allowances (such as those on capital investment and on increases in stock and work-in-progress) were abolished, the system would be more equitable; small firms in general would benefit; and there would be little change in revenue.

Corporation Tax—Shortfall Provisions

55. The shortfall provisions, which compel "close" companies in certain circumstances to distribute profit instead of ploughing it back, can exacerbate the financial problems of a business. When there are fluctuations in the economy, it is prudent to create reserves in good years to weather the poor years. By their nature smaller businesses find it more difficult than larger ones to budget accurately so a buffer against bad trading conditions is vital for them. How their reserves are created is of no relevance.

56. As the shortfall provisions can exacerbate the financial problems of companies and there seems to be no sound reason for them, we believe that their repeal would benefit the independent business sector.

Capital Gains Tax

57. Inflation has made Capital Gains Tax a tax on capital rather than on gains. Thus it discourages savings and the conversion of savings and so reduces the

likelihood of private investment in new businesses and existing businesses. In any case the tax reduces the amount of capital realised; consequently some businesses are forced into borrowing from institutions.

Taxes on Capital affecting Existing Businesses

58. To an owner/manager over fifty years old there is little incentive to expand a business if the increased value would exacerbate the tax problems which would be caused by his death or by his attempts to pass on the business at retirement. We think it essential therefore that there should be radical reform of Capital Gains Tax and Capital Transfer Tax. (Please see the sector on capital taxes in the enclosed joint paper).*

Banks' Lending Policy

59. The clearing banks could help by undertaking a more liberal lending policy as suggested above. It is unlikely that this would happen spontaneously or on the recommendations of your committee alone. Therefore we propose a method by which the government could bring about a change of attitude by introducing a system of guaranteeing loans.

Government Guaranteed Loans

60. We believe that it would be a great help for the Government to introduce a scheme similar to the SBIC scheme in the USA. For example, it would be easy to set up an organisation like the Export Credit Guarantee Department for the purpose of guaranteeing medium and long-term loans by banks to independent businesses.

61. It seems reasonable to argue that if the UK Government is willing, in effect, to guarantee bank loans to foreigners in order that they may buy British goods, it should also be willing to guarantee bank loans to the independent British manufacturers who make these goods or to British merchants who sell them abroad or at home.

62. The existence of the ECGD scheme has encouraged banks to lend money to exporters without demanding Government guarantees. We believe that the same thing would happen if a similar scheme were introduced by the Government to guarantee bank loans to independent businesses.

63. The idea of the British Government's guaranteeing bank loans through a body similar to the ECGD was first published by our Association in July 1974 and has since been publicly endorsed by Lord Seebohm and Sir Charles Villiers.

An "Over the Counter" Market

64. It could benefit some companies which were not yet earning (and might never earn) sufficient profits to obtain an official quotation under existing Stock Exchange rules if there was an "over the counter" market in their shares, which operated as easily as that in the United States. This could help those companies which needed to sell off a little equity but were afraid that all of it would fall into the hands of one institutional lender.

65. As people would want a reasonable net return on investments in relatively

*see footnote on page 119

unknown businesses such a market would of course have greater success if the rates of income tax and investment income surcharge were reduced.

* * *

66. We appreciate that some arguments in this memorandum may not have been as fully developed as your committee would like so we should be pleased to submit supplementary evidence orally or in writing.

Committee to Review the Functioning of Financial Institutions

Note of a meeting held at the Guildhall, London on Tuesday, 11 October 1977

PRESENT:

The Rt Hon Sir Harold Wilson, KG, OBE, FRS, MP (*Chairman*)
The Lord Allen of Fallowfield, CBE
Professor A D Bain
Mr G V Bayley, CBE
Sir Kenneth Bond
Mr Z Brierley, MBE
Mr K R Cork
Professor R Dahrendorf
Mr A Graham
Mr R E B Lloyd
Mr L A Mills
Dr J E Mitchell
The Rt Hon Lionel Murray, OBE
Sir David Orr
Sir John Prideaux

Mr B P Hudson (*Secretary*)

Witnesses:

Mr P D de Laszlo
Mr C J Dauris
Mr J E Critchley
Mr E G Wood

on behalf of the Association of Independent Businesses

Note taken by CSD Reporter

Chairman: Gentlemen, may I welcome you on behalf of the committee. You will be aware that at the press conference I had after our last all-day meeting when we reviewed the progress of our future plans I made it clear that the problems of small businesses were very much in our minds and that we would need to take their evidence, and you are among the first from whom we have taken evidence. Could I just say a word about the way we propose to handle evidence, which I hope will be convenient to you. We have, of course, the written evidence which has been carefully studied and has been read by all of us, and the committee naturally want to publish all evidence, written and oral. In your case, as with most others I am happy to say, the evidence has been published by yourselves. We do encourage this and we are glad this has happened though we shall want naturally to publish it as part of our transactions. Unlike our predecessors, the Radcliffe Committee, however, we do not propose to wait for the publication of evidence on behalf of the committee right at the end of the day after our final report. We are trying to publish evidence as we go along, and I am referring to oral evidence as well as written. As with the Treasury and the Department of Industry, who gave evidence to us last month, we shall take a full transcript and then send that to you so that you can make any reasonable corrections which may be necessary. You can tidy it up but also, if there is anything in the evidence, for example, referring to an individual firm or something which should be kept confidential in the interests of that firm or for any other reason, when you get the transcript if you would sideline that, marking it in your view unsuitable for publication, we will take full account of that in our editing before final printing. Our proposal would be to continue in the way we started last month, and that is that after each day of taking evidence we will publish all the evidence taken on that day, so today this will comprise the evidence of the CBI, the TUC and yourselves. Subject to printing timetables and the time we require to look at the transcript we hope to be publishing this around the end of next month. I hope that is agreeable to you.

As I say, we have had your evidence. We have also had evidence on the problems of small businesses from more than one source and, as I say, you can assume that we have read it. I would like to begin by asking whether there is any particular point in it you would like to highlight in the oral evidence and then, when you have done that, I think we should try to put the questions into five main areas: the role of small businesses in the economy—small though they are called they employ about 30 per cent of the working population; secondly, the alleged information gap—some of your members do not quite know where to go; thirdly, any problems in the provision of loan finance; fourthly, problems in the provision of equity finance; and fifthly, the contribution of specialist agencies in respect of small businesses, of which there seem to be quite a number. We would like to hear your views on these, so could I first ask you if there is anything you would like to highlight in your evidence?

—*A:* (*Mr Dauris*) The only point we would make is one we have tried to emphasise in our written evidence, that we consider that the problems of institutional finance are marginal. What most small businessmen see as their problems are, firstly, internal finance, something they would generate themselves as profit, because almost all of them want to retain their independence, and, secondly, the provision of private finance because we think that institutional finance can never fill every gap because, by its very nature, it is institutionalised. A committee can never look at a man and see that he has a flair which an individual, perhaps, might take to if he is willing to risk his capital. If, therefore, the taxation system is such that the internal finance can be generated and provide finance then we think there would be the incentive to grow, and the institutional finance could be a help towards that.

Q: I do not know if the five areas I mentioned make sense to you but, if so—and please feel free to range over all five at once if you wish—the first is the role of small businesses in the economy.

—*A:* We would be happy to take them in the order you have given them. Mr Wood will start on that, if he may.

—(*Mr Wood*)*:* On the importance of small businesses to the economy one could go on for a long time but I would like to stress just two aspects. One is in terms of employment and the other is in terms of their contribution to the economy and to the wealth of the nation. There are roughly 1¼ million small businesses in Britain and they employ between them at least 5 million people. In our current situation we have 1½ million people unemployed so if every small business in Britain could take on one additional person tomorrow we would not have an unemployment problem. That, I think, is the major virtue we ought to stress about the small business in the current situation. It is by its nature labour intensive usually rather than capital intensive, and many of them I think would be in a position to expand given the opportunities. The other point in relation to the contribution to the economy is, as you have already said, that 30 per cent of the nation's wealth in the private sector is generated from the smaller businesses, and we would like to see this proportion being increased by encouraging more small businesses to grow.

Unfortunately the small business in Britain has been in a state of decline for at least 50 years. Those of you who have seen the Bolton report will know more about that. What we still do not know at the moment is the extent of the latest decline. We do know that more and more businesses are going out of business—small businesses. I am sorry to say that the latest official figures that we have available about, for instance, the manufacturing sector relate to the year 1972, and we would like to have some more official figures about the number of small enterprises in, for instance, manufacturing, but if we take that sector there are roughly 72,000 manufacturing enterprises in Britain and, of these, 90 per cent—over 70,000 of them—are small by the Bolton definition of fewer than 200 employees. The reasons why they are in decline are many and various, and I would like to stress that we believe it is not simply finance alone. There are many other factors at work but, obviously, you wish to dwell mainly on finance factors.

It is very difficult to answer your question, to what extent has their growth been hampered by the lack of both internal and external finance, because of all the other factors at work; but if we just take those two, on internal finance I will repeat and stress what our chairman here has said, that we believe that small firms need to be able to retain more of the profit they are generating, not simply profit but other parts of the wealth they create. For instance, the impact of the increasing national insurance contribution over recent years has affected small businesses more than large businesses, and it is a point which should not be overlooked. On external finance, again I would like to stress the need for more external finance not of an institutional nature but external finance more from private sources and from sources where the people concerned and the people providing the money are prepared to take the risk along with the businessman, rather than insisting on the businessman taking the majority of the risk by insisting on security for the loan. That would start the thing moving along. Other people on the panel here may wish to add to that.

Q: In paragraph 13 you say that the small firm sector has been shrinking. Can you expand on that? You have figures on this, have you?

—*A:* Yes. Again I quote from the Bolton report that in the manufacturing sector—and I have to quote manufacturing because this is the sector we do have most information about—roughly in 1924 to 1925 nearly 50 per cent of the people employed in the manufacturing industry were in firms employing less than 200 people. By 1968 or so that figure was down to below 30 per cent. Similar shrinkage has taken place in the retailing sectors and other sectors. It is not so much that small firms have declined but they have not expanded in tune with the rest of the economy.

One major point I would like to make is that Britain has the lowest portion of employment in the small firm sector of any industrialised nation, lower even than America which is often thought to be wholly big business. We have the lowest proportion. Japan has a very much higher proportion. So has every other European country. We have the lowest proportion so there is the extent of the decline that has taken place in Britain. Our small firm sector has not expanded similarly to the rest of the economy.

Chairman: Are there any questions from my colleagues on this first area?

Mr Murray: So what you are dealing with here is that this is a secular decline, in fact. You are hoping to arrest this and possibly turn it around but there are underlying tendencies to reduce the number of small firms.

—*A:* Yes. There have been tendencies, of course, in all countries for this trend to take place for reasons to do partly with technology, although technology is not in fact the major reason. A study that has been done fairly recently by the National Institute of Economic and Social Research shows that if you look at Britain and America the proportion of people employed in large factories and large plants has remained virtually unchanged since about the year 1910. It is actually round about 10 per cent or 11 per cent but the proportion of people employed in large businesses as opposed to large factories has, of course, increased because of mergers, takeovers and all the factors that go to make the large business stronger in some respects in terms of marketing, management know-how and so on, and access to finance is a particular point; but there are other special reasons that work in Britain which are to do not just with finance but with a whole host of other things—social attitudes, for instance, towards the small businessman, the influence of the education sector. There are very many factors.

Q: What happens to small firms? Do they just fade away? Do they disappear or are they gobbled up by the big firms?

—*A:* Small firms are always in a fluid state. There are many small firms coming in and many small firms dying. It is an organic situation and it is a very good thing, we believe, that a business does not actually have the right to stay in business for ever. If its quality or its service decline then we need to shift resources of manpower and capital into other types of sectors. What has been happening in Britain is that not enough new businesses have been generated as compared, for instance, to other countries. In Germany, the USA and Japan there has been a far bigger increase in the number of new businesses started, not all of which survive. Half of the ones that start go out of business within 10 years anyway, and that is perhaps the test of whether they are capable of surviving, but if you bear in mind that every big business today was a small business at some time what we are in danger of in Britain is not fostering enough seedcorn. You can only grow into an oak by starting as an acorn and there is a need in Britain to have more acorns to grow some future large businesses from.

Dr Mitchell: Could I just clear up these statistics? I take the point about acorns and seedcorn, I am sure, but with the one million enterprises employing 5 million people you are going right down to part-time retail establishments, are you not?

—*A:* That is true. I would like to emphasise that as far as our association is concerned we are predominantly concerned with the independent company as opposed to the self-employed tradesman.

Q: So that there is secular decline, sure, problems sure, but part of the decline you are quoting is the change in the retail sector—supermarkets and all that sort of thing—which is very much customer orientated because these are the people who can reduce their margins and reduce their prices, so that is part of the inevitable pressure?

—*A:* Oh yes, it is inevitable pressure, but the figures I quoted were from manufacturing rather than retail, and the same decline has taken place in the manufacturing sector.

Q: Which is a different problem. The point I am making is that we have these two problems. One is small businesses as such which goes right down to the part-time pin money enterprise almost, or the fated to be unsuccessful enterprises that open up and close down all over the place. That is part of it, and the other part is the companies right down to the small end in industry proper.

—*A:* Yes. You have hit on a very important point. There is no such thing as a typical small business, there is such an enormous variety, but I think it might be useful if we could speak mainly in the context not of the tradesman or the corner shop but in relation to our members who are mainly independent companies in the sense of being unquoted companies.

Lord Allen: From what you have just said, that there is a need for more finance but not the necessity for finance coming from the institutional source, do you frown on the institutional source as small businesses?

—*A:* No, we do not frown on them but we do believe that there are limitations to what the institutions can do for the small business and the small businessman himself because, by nature, he is independent. That is why he is an independent businessman. It is his nature as much as anything, but if he can expand his business from internal resources, from retained profit, he will be much more enthusiastic about expanding his business than if he has to constantly go to institutions.

Q: I ask that because it may be said that the source from which you generate your capital, externally not institutional, may in this day and age not be prepared to supply that capital because they may see some greater risk now than they saw yesterday, so to speak. If that is the case I am wondering what you feel about the role of the Stock Exchange which seems to favour the big companies and certainly not the small to medium companies. Do you have a view about whether your small businesses are capable of looking in that direction?

—*A:* It is a point we were going to deal with later in our evidence but if you would like to deal with it now we can do so. I think Patrick de Laszlo is better equipped to comment about the role of the Stock Exchange and what it can and cannot do.

—(*Mr de Laszlo*): The Stock Exchange, as you point out, because of the nature of its own rules plus the Companies Act, is likely to be suited only to a fairly large company but, in practice today, it is probably going to take something like £1 million profit per annum before it will obtain a quotation, but there is quite a large gap in between—a company, say, making £300,000 to £400,000 a year—on which we have made a suggestion.

Q: Before you go on, may I say that I was interested in putting the question the way I did because I gathered from the comment made by Mr Wood that you were rather taking the institutional source as something you did not really want to be associated with. One is looking at the present system at the present time with a view to the future.

—*A:* (*Mr Dauris*) I think most people running their own businesses are suspicious of institutions, as indeed of management consultants and many others. As Mr Wood said, they do want to retain their independence, but they can look on institutional finance usually as a means to get them over a hurdle, as a temporary measure and not something permanent.

Q: But their independence today may contribute towards their liquidation, may it not?

—*A:* It can do.

—(*Mr Wood*)*:* Equally, getting heavily involved with institutions can contribute to that decline. One of the points about the small businessman, again quoting the Bolton report, is that many of them are proud of the fact that, as they put it, "We have never had to go to the bank", meaning that they have never had to borrow money from the bank. My view of that is that it is a short-sighted attitude and that in fact a good businessman should want to borrow money from a bank in the right proportions, but one of the factors again about the small business is that, as far as we know on the evidence that was available, small firms on balance are actually net lenders as firms to the banking institutions. If you take the total overdrafts of small businesses and the total amount they have in their current accounts and strike one against the other, you find in fact that small businesses are actually lending money to the banks. That was the case when the study was made. Whether it is the case now I would very much doubt in view of the change in finance.

Q: It is almost impossible to ignore the role of the small businesses when, as you said, they employ one-fifth of the total labour force in this country.

—*A:* (*Mr de Laszlo*) I am a small businessman amongst other things. Can I make a vital point, and it is that a small man wants equity capital. He is frightened of loan capital save for a short period, as has just been suggested to you. What he needs is a person who is going to take a risk and receive a good dividend some time in the future or in good years, but he is always acutely conscious of the fact that there are bad years ahead and in a bad year he may not be able to pay a dividend. That is if he has equity capital. However, if he is wholly dependent on loan capital he is required to pay interest and this threat that he has to pay interest to the institution means that institutional capital is not a thing he is pleased to have because it is not equity capital, and so one of the great pleas we would like to make, which we are united in wishing to stress, is that small independent businesses require more equity capital, and it is this that they find the most difficult to get. It is true that you have brought out the point, as we have too, saying that in the present climate since we cannot get the equity capital, having regard to what we regard as excessive taxation, then of course we must turn to the banks and institutions reluctantly, and that brings us to this question of the stepping-stone in the ladder by which you get your money, which would be the point which you mentioned—the over-the-counter market or more access to the public for funds.

If I may enlarge on that, this is entirely derived from my study of what goes on in America where I find a conspicuous difference of attitude. The small businessman in England is nervous about allowing any one partner or one organisation to have a large slice of his equity. If you seek a large loan from an institution in England they are inclined to ask for a slice of your equity, 30 per cent of your equity. This makes the man nervous.

Whether he is right or wrong to be nervous does not matter. He feels then that he is much more in the hands of that institution. In America the position is different. In America a business starts in the same way as it does here with seed capital provided entirely as risk capital; the next tranche of capital is probably equity capital from individuals who are willing to risk their capital; and then you have the banks and then you have the institutions coming in. This is a very important point. The institutions and the banks are willing to tie up their money because they know they are not going to tie it up for a long period. They know that the chances of recovering their money within a reasonable time are much greater than they are in England because a relatively small business can go to the public in America whereas in England you have to be a very large business to go to the public.

Q: If you are going to move gradually towards acceptance of institutional money, maybe reluctantly, what reforms would you like to see in the existing financial institutions?

—*A:* This is taking it out of order but we are very happy to do so. There are two suggestions we have made. One is that one should look at least at what happens in America where they were faced with a very similar situation to the situation we are faced with today. They were faced with this situation when Eisenhower became president and he pledged himself to deal with this very problem. The institutions and the banks declared that they were overflowing with money and happy to finance independent businesses. Independent businesses complained that they could not get at this money which, after all, is the crux of this discussion today. Why? What happened was that Eisenhower asked the Federal Reserve to look into the matter, and it was exceedingly interesting. The Federal Reserve reported that having regard to the principles on which the banking system was run the banks could not tie up a substantial proportion of their resources in medium- and long-term loans for independent businesses. That report created considerable concern and the Federal Reserve was asked to go into the thing again, and they wrote a thing like three telephone books being a complete analysis of independent businesses and the financial system of America. They came to the same conclusion, that the banking system could not supply the needs of the expanding independent businesses without some help from the government. That is what it amounts to.

If I may move from that there is a point here which I would like to bring in, if I may, Sir Harold. I remember writing to you as chairman of the Small Businesses Association to offer you our good wishes when you last became Prime Minister, and adding two points. One point was this particular point! We said we recognised the difficulties you would have in reducing taxation for independent businesses though we hoped you would do it, and went on to say that if you could not do that your government might consider allowing increases in stock to be written off against tax in the year in which they were incurred—I think I can use those simple words to describe what I said—which happily occurred later on.

I also made the point that I feared that if there were an upturn in the economy the banking system would not be able to meet the needs of independent businesses. In your reply you used a phrase which was exceedingly interesting, that you had been advised that clearing banks had adequate resources to meet all the needs of credit-worthy independent businesses. I was merely trained as a simple economist and my training led me to believe that this was unlikely to be the case. I would ask you, since you are taking this committee and dealing with this whole subject, specifically to ask the Bank of England whether they believe that the clearing banks do have resources to meet the needs of credit-worthy independent businesses, medium- and long-term. I would rather not quote the Bank of England. I would prefer you specifically to ask them.

Chairman: They will be coming before us shortly.

—*A:* Yes. They will recognise the question perhaps! The Americans, if I may quote them, came to the conclusion that the banking system could not meet this need because it tied up money for too long, and the Americans in their case had a great debate on setting up a national state bank, but the conclusion they came to was that they would empower their Small Business Administration to guarantee loans from banks to independent businesses, preferably in those conditions where more equity capital had been put in ahead of the loan capital, and in fact we wrote a pamphlet which contains a fairly accurate account of what was done in America to solve this problem.

We have then said in our report that if you do not care to turn to the American system the alternative would be to use or develop in England something similar to the export credit guarantee system. If it is reasonable to guarantee loans to foreigners to enable them to buy Jaguar cars—because that is what it amounts to —it must be reasonable to guarantee loans to manufacturers of products in England so that they may be exported. That is the basic concept. There is a vital point which I tried to make in this pamphlet about America, which was that with the export credit guarantee system and the government loan guarantee system to independent businesses in America it is noticeable that the amount which is actually guaranteed in both cases was only a small percentage of the whole amount which was loaned. Taking America, because the government was willing to guarantee loans from banks to independent businesses then that became an instruction to the banks to lend, and the banks went out and said, "You need not have all the trouble of getting a government guarantee, we will lend you this money".

Mr Murray: I am sorry to interrupt you but you say it was a small percentage. Can you give me any idea of the order of magnitude?

—A: I do not know accurately but it is of the order of 25 per cent in America, probably less. There is a difference of opinion because the institutions will proudly tell you in America, "The Small Business Administration is very small. We do the job", but they only do the job because if they do not supply the money then the small businesses get the loan anyhow through the Small Business Administration. We then put forward this concept which might be applicable to England, and I note with some interest that Lord Seebohm with whom I discussed the idea, who at first pooh-poohed it I think, later was quoted as saying that he felt something of that nature was needed in England in order that the banking system might be in a position to make loans.

Q: Of the 25 per cent—and I fully take your point about removing the need—can you give us any idea of the amount which was actually lost by the SBA? Was there in fact a figure?

—A: Very very small. I can quote you again this paper. The Small Business Administration itself claims that if the whole machine were wound up today their loss would be trivial, of the order of 4 per cent or 5 per cent of the money which they handle, and one must bear in mind that they are not only responsible for administering the small businesses but they are also landed with something they do not care for which is what they describe as crisis aid—that is funds which are handed out in emergencies, disaster funds in fact which are given away. They also have a very special problem in America—when they started they were accused of advancing an unreasonable proportion of their money to the white population and not enough to the ethnic groups. Then immediately they had to start lending money to the ethnic groups. It did not work in the first instance but they are proud of the fact that about a year later they got the ethnic leaders together and they managed to remedy that situation, so they have special problems but even then they claim that with the huge sums involved the losses are really trivial bearing in mind the additional tax ploughed into the state as a result of their success. We do commend to you to at least pay some attention to what has happened in America in this particular connection with this particular problem.

Mr Brierley: Chairman, this morning I asked the CBI four specific questions, and you have by ranging across a number of questions covered two of them certainly, but I would like to structure the questions a little more specifically on the remaining two aspects, if I may. Mr Wood earlier on pointed out the importance to the economy of the small firms and the advantages of an expansion of the sector, and I do not disagree with that one little bit, but you mentioned "given the opportunity". My first question is, did you perhaps mean incentive instead of opportunity? If I may just carry on to give you an idea whilst you are thinking about the answer to that one—unless you want to answer it right away—are you in fact saying that there are disincentives and that some of these disincentives are of a non-financial nature?

—*A:* (*Mr Wood*) I am saying just that. There are many disincentives which unfortunately have increased in recent years which make it difficult not only for people to start in business but also for people who are in business to want to go on expanding or even keeping the business going.

Q: May I now lead on from that to the specific question that I put to the CBI, because I would like to compare your answers with what the CBI said. This is the question I put to them: could you then comment upon what you see as the main obstacles, be they financial or non-financial, because I think we are concerned with the well being of the small firms not necessarily with one aspect of it, in two situations? Firstly the start-up situation, the setting-up of new companies, and secondly the obstacles and factors that you see which inhibit or prevent the growth of existing firms—both in respect of financial and non-financial. I think you might have to take those separately. It is a big subject, I appreciate.

—*A:* There are many things here but I can start by mentioning two or three. In the start-up situation we used to have a situation in Britain where a man who had perhaps worked in employment for someone else until he was around the age of 40 plus could, by diligence and by saving, accumulate sufficient money to start a business of his own. That has become increasingly difficult nowadays. The amount of money that people can save and the effect of inflation, of course, on that saving has made it more difficult, and the fact that now businesses tend to need more money in order to start with. You cannot now start a business so readily by buying, say, a few secondhand sewing machines. That is one factor.

The other factor which affects existing businesses, of course, can be summed up in one word—legislation. The effect of legislation over the last 15 years on the desire of the small businessman to stay in business to cope with all the problems which legislation has raised for him has reduced his ardour to go on to make a profit which, when he has made it, will be taxed away anyway.

Q: The mass of legislation to which he is going to be subject?

—*A:* Yes.

—(*Mr Critchley*): Can I add something there? I feel that this is a far more vital question than finance, personally. Unless you have worked in a small business you do not realise the unending volume of legislation—the Employment Protection Act, the Health and Safety Act, development land tax, national insurance, new pension schemes and so on. All these things are no doubt highly desirable in an affluent society. All these things can be coped with where you have professional experts to deal with them in cases like ICI, but how can a man who is managing director, sales director, production director, chief accountant and everything all rolled into one? He cannot possibly cope with this mass of stuff, and my advice to all these people is to throw the lot into the wastepaper basket. Either you have to run your business or you have to give up running your business and read all this bumff, and then you will not understand it! There seems to me a terrible thing here. One is imposing on ICI exactly the same legislation as you are imposing on a chap with 10 employees, and there must somehow be a dividing line between this. It is quite impossible. Everybody is frustrated and fed up, and if you look at the fiscal side of it what is the point of trying to build up the business if you know that capital transfer tax will smash it up in the end? There is really not any point. This dispirits the people. Then, when you look at all this talk about wanting finance for business, why does the legislation drain it out of the business not merely by the rate of corporation tax but shortfall? If you accumulate too much cash in your business you are forced to distribute it. What are you going to put aside for a rainy day? You cannot do it and you are draining the cash out when you want to leave it in as a reserve.

Take development land tax: I will give you a specific example if you like—a garage which has a British Leyland franchise. As you know British Leyland are rationalising their franchises, which really means that they are taking away the livelihood of people at a second's notice and saying, "You cannot sell Leyland cars". There is an empty garage. What do you do with it? Nobody will buy a garage so the only thing to do is to sell the garage as a supermarket store—bang development land tax, bang capital gains tax, a quarter of your proceeds disappear and you are left with far less to try and invest in another business. So it is good luck to your committee, but I think there are far more important things to be put right first! People are dispirited.

Q: I have a feeling that I opened up the floodgates there and all the pent-up frustration came through in those last comments but, in effect, are you saying that small companies should be exempt from some of this legislation, or are you in fact saying that because they are subject to it some allowance should be made—is it in taxation or whatever you may suggest—to compensate for smaller firms being put to this disproportionate disadvantage?

—*A:* You have quite rightly said, what are the constructive suggestions. I think basically we have no desire to see small firms feather-bedded fiscally. At least I have not. They have either got to stand on their feet or go out. I know this does not apply to big companies—if you cannot stand on your feet you are kept standing! I happen to come from Oxford and I dread to think of all the tax I pay to support the people who cannot stand on their feet, but suffice it to say that if it were in any way possible try and keep some of this detailed legislation off the smaller firms. To take each Act individually I think would be very difficult, but perhaps you could somehow exempt firms with less than 20 employees from a lot of this stuff. I do not know how you can. I am not being very helpful, I am afraid, but I am not asking for fiscal benefits.

—*(Mr Dauris):* The points which Mr Critchley mentioned I think fall into various categories. There is some legislation which we do not think should apply to small businesses, as we have suggested, and others which we would certainly like to deal with in a much more radical way. Capital transfer tax, which we mentioned, would certainly be one, and the Employment Protection Act would be another. This tends unfortunately to protect people who are in jobs at the expense of people who are not employed, because it is a severe disincentive to many small firms to take on additional employees. If I could explain that, if one has, say, a new project which will cause one's business to expand then there is a certain risk involved. If it fails then the cost of that failure will be increased if one has to sack the employees who were taken on, but probably those very employees would be very happy to take on a job even with a risk because they are among the unemployed. It does deter many smaller firms from expanding, and we do know this from talking to our members.

Mr Brierley: Chairman, unless anybody wants to ask a question on that broad subject I have another one.

Mr Mills: Chairman, it is not directly in relation to that but it is in relation to the wider remit of the committee and the finance of the institutions in relation to small businesses. Hearing carefully all you say about your attitude to institutions, you do make in your evidence a number of specific criticisms about the availability of different forms of finance—the lack of information, whether it is loan finance, equity finance and so forth—and one particular point you make in paragraph 23, which I think is quite right, is the bewildering number of sources and types of finance, and you specify some of them. In the next paragraph you say, "Nevertheless, in spite of all those different types and sources of finance there are still some shortcomings both for small and medium-sized enterprises". The first question I would like to ask, chairman, is, would it not assist if there were some co-ordination, some cohesion, between the different, what you call rather bewildering number of sources and types of finance? Would it not help from your point of view if there were some coordinated financial centre which could provide finance?

—*A:* This could be probably a well-trained chartered accountant who was one's adviser. As Mr Critchley is an accountant perhaps you would like to ask him.

Q: I mean not from your point of view but from the supplier of funds? Rather than have a bewildering number of suppliers of funds would it not help if there were some co-ordination between the different institutions that exist?

—*A:* (*Mr Critchley*) I personally feel that if a person wants money he will find it unless, as Mr de Laszlo says, there is a boom where the money runs out. Therefore we come on to the problem of how do you set about finding it and, as I see it, normally a person will go always to people he knows, and therefore the first approach is to his bank manager probably. His bank manager ought, if he cannot get it, put him on to somebody else. If he does not go to the bank manager he may well go to his accountant because, again, he is frightened of the faceless institutions and he prefers to go to the people he knows. Therefore the accountant ought to be able to find it for him or put him in touch with sources where he can get it. I personally feel that there is not a gap here. If a person wants money he goes to the people he knows and they will put him in touch with the sources to get the money. I always felt it was a little unfortunate in the 1967 Companies Act that up to that date virtually the auditor could be a director of the company—a private company, a small one—but that after that date he could not. If you had the accountant on the board he was much more readily available for advice, and if you paid him £300 or £400 a year the firm would make certain they got their money's worth and rang him up day and night, weekends and all! Now the accountant cannot do that so the firm never likes to ring up the accountant because they reckon it will cost £4! You have lost that personal contact. What I am trying to say is that I think the money is there and the money can be found if a person is keen to find it.

Q: I was rather going on the basis that should there not be some more co-ordination between the suppliers of funds to you? You instance the different types of institutions, and one can see how this is bewildering, and obviously it would be better if there were some co-ordination of financial supply.

—*A:* (*Mr Wood*) One thing none of us would like to see is some central body which was the sole source of finance for small firms; in fact, not even a central body because small firms are themselves competitive and they welcome some competition amongst their suppliers of finance as amongst other suppliers. We do not think that the information gap is as important as it is made out to be. There is a lot of talk about the information gap. Undoubtedly, because of the fact that, as I said earlier, there is no such thing as a typical small business you can always find the businessman who, for some reason, has not approached a source of finance which could have been available to him and which he could have made use of. COSIRA, for instance, is a very good source of finance for certain types of businesses. Not all businesses know about it, but we think the number missing this opportunity is relatively small in relation to the sheer cost of trying to make known to small firms the many sources of finance. What has been proved over and over again about information services and government aid and so on is that over and over again the small businessman, despite all the money you spend on advertising and so on, is unaware of sources of government aid. He is only interested in it at the point he wants the money and it is at that point, as Mr

Critchley says, that he goes to his bank. You have to bear in mind that banks have changed. At one time banks only provided overdrafts and short-term finance. Now most of the high street banks can provide a complete range of services—factoring, leasing, hiring, almost anything—and therefore we feel that if the man does not get the money out of his high street bank, if he is really determined he will find it by some means or other. By asking his accountant, by asking other people he will find the information he needs. We would be against setting up some sort of government service whose sole job was to acquaint small businessmen with sources of finance.

Q: Just to follow that particular point, if I may, chairman, you have referred at some length to the attitude of banks and, again, make some fairly severe criticism. In paragraph 30 you refer to the obsession with security that banks have, and you say that British small firms are at a severe disadvantage compared with their European counterparts. Do you make that criticism generally of the clearing banks? That is the first question and, secondly, does that criticism relate to the central lending decisions of the banks? Would you like to see more local autonomy in deciding whether to lend money? Do you think they are over-centralised at the moment, or what other criteria other than the ones you criticise here would you like to see the banks adopting in deciding whether to lend you money or not?

—*A:* It is a very big question but if I can start on that one, the point about security is simply this: that if the directors of a large company need some more finance from an institution it is highly unlikely that that financial institution will ask for the deeds of the house of the individual directors of that large company, whereas in the small business that is very likely to happen. After the security the business itself can offer in the way of land and buildings, the next thing is that the small businessman himself needs to place possibly in jeopardy the house that he lives in at the risk of his family. At some stage, if the business goes down he loses not only his livelihood but his life savings. That is true, of course, not just in this country but in others, but the major difference between British banks and banking organisations in other countries—not all European countries but certainly some and certainly Japan, for instance—is that the banks are much more heavily involved with industry and commerce, not just in the small firms but also in the big firm sector as well, to the point in fact that by British standards if you look at Japanese balance sheets most of them in this country would be regarded as teetering on the brink of insolvency, but they seem to thrive because they are quite happy for the banks to be in league with them. If I can quote a specific example, I was in Norway last year talking about small businesses, and I was pleasantly surprised to find that in Norway at any rate a small businessman who wants to start a business and has some security to offer can get from a bank a much bigger proportionate advance in the way of either overdraft or a long-term loan than you would expect to get in Britain. In Britain the normal rule is that a bank expects the businessman to finance roughly half of the total assets that are required—total assets in terms of fixed assets and current assets in terms of stocks. Once the figure falls below 50 per cent I am not saying the bank will not lend to him; they will and there are many examples of that but they are more reluctant to lend to him. They would like to see the figure around 50 per cent. In other European countries banks are in rather deeper than that.

Q: And you would like to see that here?

—*A:* Subject to the fact that some small businesses welcome that, others do not. We come back to the guarantee point earlier on, that if you are going to ask the small businessman not only to put up the 50 per cent but, in the process of that, hand over the deeds of his house as well, with a floating charge on all the assets, you are really not just asking him to lay his own business risk on the line but his personal risk, because you have to bear in mind that he is potentially losing not only his livelihood but any pension he might have tied up in terms of capital rather than pension fund, so it is a much bigger risk for the businessman.

Lord Allen: If the conditions laid down by the institutions are, shall we say, too rigorous for the small business, what kind of protection do you envisage for the investor?

—*A:* This is the central point, of course, is it not? We are not blaming the banks for their attitude because the bank, after all, has to protect the interest of its depositors. The bank is taking money off on a short-term basis and lending it out at risk to various organisations including the small company, and the bank therefore has to protect the interest of its own depositors. We could not expect banks to considerably relax their rules, and that is one of the reasons why we have stressed this suggestion of the guarantee system similar to the one which operates in the USA.

Mr Murray: You want the taxpayer to take the risk?

—*A:* No, Mr Murray. I must come in there. If I take Mr de Laszlo's point, the risk is to the tune of 4 per cent or 5 per cent. That is the risk. What the government in effect is doing in terms of guarantee is no more than it is doing currently with export credit guarantees.

Mr Mills: Were you not just saying that you did not expect the banks to relax some of their fairly rigorous criteria, but the analogies you are quoting of banks in Norway being more involved and lending more with far less security surely suggests that you would like British banks to be more flexible, less rigorous and more involved on a par with the analogy you give?

—*A:* (*Mr Dauris*) A large number of borrowing projects which are vital we believe to be satisfied if the loan is a short-term one. I do not think there is much shortage of short-term money. There is a certain shortage of medium-term money and probably of long-term, but one medium-term loan can become another medium-term loan so that probably does not really matter. There are a limited number of cases where a medium-term loan might be obtained in other countries where it does seem to be turned down here unless there is a tremendous amount of security given—as Mr Wood implied, more than would be required elsewhere—and one advantage of some form of government back-up or guarantee of a bank loan in such cases might be to save the need for directors' personal guarantees.

Mr Murray: Could I make one point here. I was not implying that the taxpayer should not in fact take the risk. If taxpayers collectively take the view that they want to see small businesses survive and thrive they may well say that it is a risk they should take, so I am not implying one way or the other.

—*A:* It is not much of a risk, if I may say so, because the tax will more than recover the losses.

Q: I would not want you to read anything into what I said one side or the other.

—*A:* No, I did not.

Mr Mills: Another alternative to the government underwriting loans to the extent you describe, of course, would be for the banks to be a little more venturesome.

—*A:* If the system was in existence we think probably the banks would be just a little more liberal in their lending policy, and this might well cover the point at that stage.

Mr de Laszlo: The questions you are asking always imply that, of course, the only proper solution is to go to institutions and banks. We must admit that we feel united about this. We feel that the proper solution is to get equity risk capital, that is to say that I ought to risk my savings in helping a man to start a business, and I will be keenly interested in following what he is doing, watching him and helping him. Any institutional money is in quite a different position and should really only come in when the buisness is on its feet and is expanding and requires money for a relatively short term, so the real nub of the problem at the moment is that you cannot get risk capital.

Mr Brierley: Can I follow that one for a moment, and I have to put the question direct to you: are you in fact putting this proposal forward as an alternative to a reduction in taxation, because reduction in taxation would largely provide the equity capital for small firms, would it not?

—*A:* That is the very point I am making. Reduction in taxation we think is the only fundamental solution, a reduction in taxation so that it is worthwhile for a man to risk his capital by investing—not lending but actually taking an equity interest in independent businesses.

Q: And if that were done there would be no need for the sort of suggestion you are putting forward now?

—*A:* (*Mr Dauris*) There might be a marginal situation of wanting a medium-term loan for perhaps a small- to medium-sized company, but it is a very marginal point, if I may say so.

Q: In the committee's mind I want to get the priorities clear. You are saying in effect that it is a lack of equity capital, largely caused by taxation and, if you like, the lack of retained earnings, profits and what-have-you which causes you to put forward a suggestion such as this in the circumstances now prevailing?

—*A:* (*Mr de Laszlo*) Can I answer that fully, since you have asked the question fully, and I use America as a parallel. There equity capital is much more freely available because the rate of taxation is lower; if you do not pay too much tax you do not mind risking your money for the chance of making a profit. So that is the first stage. But even then, when the business begins to succeed and is expanding rapidly they will need institutional capital, because in the circumstances now prevailing equity capital may not be so easily directly available. So you get the individuals coming in with the seed capital, the individuals assisting again with equity capital, then loan capital for a period, then back again into the market for equity capital.

Q: But I put it to you that if you have gone through those early stages even the British system as it presently prevails would not be lacking in bringing forward the funds.

—*A:* We never get through those stages. Most independent businesses never reach the size where they can go to the market. That is the difference.

Mr Lloyd: Could we just pursue that point? Do you not think that possibly even with a relaxation of personal taxation the portfolio investor, as opposed to the worker owner, might not prefer to keep money in a diversified spread of risks by saving though an institution? Are you sufficiently sure that the relaxation of personal taxation would bring the portfolio investor into the independent business?

—*A:* (*Mr Wood*) It depends how far you relax it. Let us face the fact that there are no longer as many Aunt Agathas around as there were. So unless you not only relax taxation but also change a lot of other things to change the distribution of income we believe it is not possible to go back to the situation of 50 years ago or even further back. I could quote the example of the wealthy Mr Rolls who supported the impecunious Mr Royce, who happened to have a bright idea, who eventually built the engine for the Spitfire. Where would Mr Royce have been without Mr Rolls? He would have had to find somebody to back him and it is very doubtful whether the institutions would have backed him in the early stages.

Q: But you obviously hope to encourage some Mr Royces. Thereafter there would be a residue where you would have to get the institutional investor in, in the form of a venture capitalist, or whoever he would be. You do not rule that out as a possibility?

—*A:* No. I think we want to see both things. We want to see relaxation of taxation and some further way in which the banks can, where the businessman wants it, make funds available to him without his having to go as deeply into his security.

Q: Yet on page 40 you say that there is evidence that institutional equity holders displace the founder of the business. My question there is, is it likely to happen where the institutional holder is in the minority of the equity?

—*A:* (*Mr de Laszlo*) Yes.

Q: It does happen, does it?

—*A:* I am afraid it does. Let us say an institution comes in and takes 30 per cent of your equity, it is still quite a big slice and it exercises great influence. There are two factors. First, you are always paying interest on the money and in bad years you cannot meet the interest. Secondly, there is the fear of the institution in a bad time saying, "You are not really the man, we think it is necessary to put somebody in", and they have a very large loan. So the institution that is prepared to lend you £100,000 in consideration of having 30 per cent of your equity has a great deal of power, power which the small man who started the business is very fearful of allowing anybody to have. The contrast in America is that the American independent businessman is prepared to part with a larger amount of his equity because he knows that the institution does not intend to hold on to that for more than a few years; very soon they will pass it over to the market. He will part with 60 per cent of his money divided over 100 or 200 people, who are portfolio investors, if you like, who will take a small portion of that portfolio and who are willing to invest it in this kind of a risk. They have not really got the facility for doing so in England.

Sir David Orr: Mine is a different question, chairman. I preface it by saying that I am greatly in favour of a healthy and vigorous small-scale sector. But in the evidence at paragraph 38 there is rather the suggestion that it is the worst that could happen to anybody that they would be merged or join a larger company. Are there not occasions when it would be in the interests of not only yourself but of your employees and of the economy in general? Are there not instances where merging and joining a larger parent wholly would be of great advantage because not only would it provide the finance but open up much larger overseas markets, and so on, which you yourselves could not contemplate?

—*A:* (*Mr Dauris*) Quite possibly, but then that would be an ordinary business decision taken for purely commercial reasons. What has frightened people from it is that it has so often been forced on businesses for reasons of tax, for example inability to pay in the past estate duty, now capital gains tax and capital transfer tax. In other words, the decisions are not made for the best commercial reasons. If they were we would be in favour of them.

Q: Are those enforced decisions increasing or decreasing? Are there more voluntary decisions to merge evolving now?

—*A:* I do not think there were that number of voluntary ones, because the people running the businesses normally want to retain their own independence.

Q: Even though they may see a bigger opportunity for their firm and their employees by going into the bigger pond?

—*A:* If they did I think they probably would merge. But Mr Wood made a point earlier that a lot of the benefits of size have tended to be much overrated in recent years. They have been justified on grounds of technology, that increasing plant size could make for greater efficiency, but in fact have been used to justify mergers of numerous separate plants where there can be no benefit from technology.

Q: But you admit that there will be many where the marketing opportunity will be beneficial?

—*A:* (*Mr Wood*) We are back to the point I made earlier about there being no such thing as the typical small business. Several studies have been made of the effects of mergers and takeovers on businesses. It is like the old saying that facts can be found to meet any opinions. Some of these studies demonstrate that clearly on balance mergers and takeovers have not improved the performance of the businesses and some of the studies contradict this evidence. So you pay your money and take your choice. There are some businesses where it is right from a business point of view to make that decision to merge. But what has happened over the last 30 years or so—you remember the days when the Financial Times was full of advertisements:

"Wanted—companies with tax losses of £50,000". Businesses were being merged not for good reasons but simply for fiscal reasons. Right, that has stopped. But there are still other reasons, mainly to do with estate duty, nowadays capital transfer tax, where businesses are selling out not for good sound business reasons but for other reasons.

Mr Murray: Profitability is only one consideration in the mind of the independent fellow who wants to run his own show. Even if he thought he might make some more money in a big concern it is important to him to run his own show, and making a bigger profit would not necessarily be an incentive to merge?

—*A:* People who have had experience of this kind of merger where a small firm is taken over by a big one have found by observation that the business changes its nature very much, that the employees of the big firm are forced upon it and the employees of the small firm do not fit in and they drift away. Many people in that situation who have had employees with them for a long time would be loath to sell out to a big firm for that reason even if they were taking a large amount of money out of it themselves.

Q: Money is not everything?

—*A:* No.

Q: There are factors other than profitability?

—*A:* Yes. Obviously you want to keep up a good standard of living if you are running a business. But, as you say, money is not everything.

Professor Bain: On selling out to large firms, Mr Dauris said that this was often necessary because for one reason or another you had to get some capital out of the firm. Is it the case, as has been put to me, that you get a much better price for your equity if you sell the whole business than if you try to bring in some organisation like EDITH or ICFC as minority shareholders?

—*A:* (*Mr de Laszlo*) Yes, most certainly. If it is a question of taking money out of the firm, perhaps because you are getting older or maybe you are ill, then you will have to sell the whole business as a rule.

Q: You get a much better price for your equity?

—*A:* (*Mr Critchley*) There is no question of it.

Q: What sort of margin is it?

—*A:* The differential?

Q: Yes.

—*A:* I would have thought that if you sold out your business you should get roughly the asset value or, say, five times the profit, whichever is the greater. But if you are selling part of it you will only get for that part what return will be made for the investment made in it. If you go to ICFC or any of these and want them to put in a certain amount of shares they will, so to speak, give you the price when you have told them how much you are going to pay on those shares.

Q: Does this mean that the terms on which ICFC and other providers of development capital are prepared to put up equity are unduly harsh?

—*A:* (*Mr de Laszlo*) In the context of your first question, it is not a matter of harshness. I think the function of ICFC is to provide capital for the expansion of the business, not to buy out the business.

Q: Let us talk about EDITH, then. Is it unduly harsh, do you think?

—*A:* (*Mr Critchley*) A private company there is probably in a complete cleftstick. With EDITH you are trying to get some money out so that you have money available for the death duties, or less than the death duties. If therefore you get a very high price for your shares and are prepared to pay a good yield, should you die the rest of your shares will carry a very high tax and you really will be clobbered. So do you try to get as high a price as you can and risk dying too soon, or do you take a lower price in the hope that if you do die you will not bust the business? I have great respect for ICFC. I have no connection with them. I have used them on several occasions. They have a reputation in the provinces. In the provinces everybody is frightened of the people in the City, the rolled umbrella and the bowler hat, the wheeler-dealers of money. But ICFC have an air of respectability in the provinces closer to a bank manager.

Q: That brings me to my next question. You were suggesting that the banks were obsessed by security. Would you say that ICFC as the major providers of medium and long term loan capital to the small companies were unduly concerned about security?

—*A:* I think they are pretty cautious and fairly expensive, but I would rather have them and not be mucked about than have somebody else somewhat more fluid and not quite know what they might be up to.

Q: So you feel that by and large their terms are fair?

—*A:* (*Mr Dauris*) Going to the ICFC needs a fairly large sum in practice.

Q: £5000.

—*A:* Probably £30,000 minimum in practice, and they prefer £100,000.

Q: They say they still do deal with the £5000s.

—*A:* (*Mr Critchley*) Indeed the costs will be just as high to borrow £5000 as to borrow £50,000; so it is relatively very expensive to borrow a very small sum, because there are all the investigations, and so forth.

Q: Again on the question of security, I understand that until a few years ago it was not possible, or easy, to get a floating charge in Scotland, which has been common practice in England for a long time. Do you have any experience of this or of the difference in lending standards of banks in the two parts of the United Kingdom?

—*A:* (*Mr Wood*) I do not have experience of the Scottish banks. We do have members in Scotland and if you want an answer to that specific question I have no doubt that we could get it for you.

Q: My final question on the development capital companies is this. We understand that as a result of the increase in the minimum size of company that can have a flotation the development capital companies now have to look for a dividend yield when they provide capital, whereas formerly they were looking more for capital gain from bringing a company to the market. Has this change caused any major problems for the larger of your members who might have been considering a flotation, and if it has is there a role for new institutions that look to capital gain rather than income in the short term?

—*A:* (*Mr de Laszlo*) I am not absolutely sure what you are speaking about. You are not speaking about a company becoming a public company, are you?

Q: I am thinking about a company at the stage that it is going to a merchant bank which plans to nurse it for a few years and then bring it to the market. Going back four or five years the merchant bank would not be looking for a high dividend yield while it was nursing the company but would expect to get its return from the capital gain when it brought the company to the market. With the increase in the minimum size of flotation it now takes longer to bring a company to the market and it is much less sure that it will ever be able to do so. So the institutions, who have to pay interest on their deposits and remunerate their own capital, are forced to look for income in the short term rather than the prospect of capital gain. Has this caused problems for the larger of your members, and if so should something be done about it?

—*A:* (*Mr Dauris*) I do not know whether we can answer that question. We think that even the largest of our members are probably not looking for a flotation in the foreseeable future. There may be one or two who could, but they do not seem willing to do so. The fear of borrowing from merchant banks for most of our members is that they fear that the merchant bank is only interested in floating the company and most of them, as we said earlier, want to retain control. Possibly those looking for a flotation have not joined us.

Mr Wood: To widen the answer beyond our members and talk about this in general, there is no doubt whatever that in recent years fewer companies have been going through this process. But I do not think that is entirely to do with the factors you mention. It is also to do with the Stock Exchange prices, that companies could not see any immediate future possibility of getting a Stock Exchange quotation, so they held back. But that is a separate issue.

Chairman: What are your views on the over-the-counter market?

—*A:* (*Mr de Laszlo*) I have advocated it very much, because I have seen the advantage that it has been in America. It has been an advantage to the independent businessman, because he wants to control his business—he is the creator of it and he wants to control it. He does not mind parting with a large percentage of the equity, 60 per cent or more, provided it is spread out over a large number of people, but he dreads the institution which has even 30 per cent of his equity, because they have too big a block. The over-the-counter market is a solution to this and it is certainly remarkably successful in America. There is difficulty in understanding why there is so much resistance to it in England. I have raised it with the Stock Exchange. All sorts of reasons are given. They all differ, there is no common reason, they are all rather tenuous and confused reasons.

Q: Have they not changed the rules slightly recently?

—*A:* No. They allege that today there is in effect no over-the-counter market—there are a few cases, I believe. But the answer is No. I have discussed this with them quite recently and their reply was, "No, we will do nothing to encourage it".

Q: The Department of Trade are drafting a new Companies Act. Have you been in touch with them about this?

—*A:* No.

Q: We are partly held up by legislation here.

—*A:* (*Mr Dauris*) There is nothing to stop a technically public company, say one with 50 shareholders or more, from offering its shares where it wants. What they would want to do is limit the size of the parcel of shares so that one individual or institution could not get hold of a large number. That even now, I believe, could be limited within the articles of the company. The problem probably comes in creating the market where they could be fairly easily bought and sold. There are public companies which are unquoted but have a fairly spread shareholding, and where often if a small shareholding is offered for sale the directors are the only people who are interested in investing in it.

Mr Lloyd: Could I ask Mr de Laszlo how he would propose that the over-the-counter market here would be supervised, controlled?

—*A:* (*Mr de Laszlo*) I doubt whether it requires a very great deal of supervision. I think the best thing to do would be to copy what they do in America.

Q: The SEC do it in America.

—*A:* Yes, the SEC. I have great regard for them; they are quite excellent. Here we have a slightly more mysterious system, which is the Stock Exchange itself controlling itself; so I am not altogether sure what the rules are.

Mr Mills: There is no SEC in this country.

—*A:* No. There being no SEC in this country it depends on the Stock Exchange. What happens in America is that it is a syndicate of brokers, as I am sure you know, and they form a market outside the Stock Exchange—that is to say, outside the public quotation of the Stock Exchange. But they are doing a great deal of business and it is a most valuable service not only to the individual but also to the institution. It does not want to lock up its money too long, it sees it has an expanding business and it realises that it can get out when the business may be making £50,000 or £100,000 a year, whereas in England they cannot get their capital out unless the business is making £400,000 a year.

Mr Lloyd: I do not follow why you make such a distinction in your own mind between that system and the new relaxation that there is under rule 163 (2) of the

Stock Exchange, where they are allowing that to take place, but under Stock Exchange supervision.

Chairman: That is what I was referring to.

—*A:* There is no objection as to how it should be done as long as it is achieved.

Mr Lloyd: So over-the-counter market is in small letters, there are various types of over-the-counter market and you would like to see one, or two?

—*A:* (*Mr Dauris*) Could I say that it would probably be of fairly marginal significance, the number of companies likely to be affected. We believe there are something like 2400 companies in America quoted in the over-the-counter market. It would probably be around 400 or 500 here. But they would be companies of a particular size and possibly ones which were growing to become very large ones. So we think it would fill a small but important gap.

Dr Mitchell: Could I raise the question of new firms, that one of the reasons for the decline is that new firms do not come in to replace the ones that are dying? I would like you to comment on that. The other point is a thought that has been put to me, which is that in the industrial sector itself one is very familiar with small and medium sized companies feeling happier and getting on better dealing with other small and medium sized companies. Would that be true to any extent of the relations between small industrial companies and small financial institutions possibly or those that are more locally controlled?

—*A:* (*Mr Wood*) To deal with the second one first, I am not quite sure what you mean by small financial institutions.

Q: Financial institutions have also been concentrated, so we are getting nearer to the all-purpose financial conglomerate. Is that development against the interests of small firms as such? Is this one of the historical reasons that small businesses are disappearing?

—*A:* It is a factor, although it is difficult to quantify it. In the past in my part of the country you could shop around the various banks but now they are all the same bank. If one turns you down you only have another four choices, whereas you used to have a lot of other choices—fortunately we have the Yorkshire Bank so we can shop around a little. So it must have had some effect, though it is difficult to quantify.

Q: So it is a question of competition really, rather than the size of the institution?

—*A:* Yes.

Q: You are interested in having a lot of people, never mind if their head offices are all in London and they are all enormous?

—*A:* There was a time when, at any rate in Yorkshire, it was reputed—and I have seen evidence of this myself—that the Yorkshire Bank was more liberal in policies about lending to small businesses, though it charged an extra ½ per cent or so for this liberality. Whether that is still true I am not sure but I have heard that they are coming more into line with all the other banks. Whether or not you can do anything about restoring or increasing competition in the high street banks I do not know—whether you could get the Trustee Savings Bank, for instance, to open up and start lending to small businesses.

Q: It is something to watch, surely, in legislation, that new legislation does not encourage this sort of process?

—*A:* Yes.

Mr Mills: It is a fact, is it not, that the Yorkshire Bank is owned by the clearers anyway?

—*A:* Yes.

Q: There is a strong prospect of the savings banks which are now in the personal lending sector going into corporate lending and, as you well know, in the north of England there is a very well established branch network. From your point of view would that as an alternative source of money be useful? Presumably you are saying it might well be useful, but it would be an alternative source with an established network of agencies that you could go to which is not part of the clearing bank established network.

—*A:* (*Mr Dauris*) We are always in favour of competition for supply to ourselves. I would like to come back to the first part of Dr Mitchell's question, the problem of setting up small companies, because certainly not enough have been set up to replace the ones that have died off for various reasons. The reason is that it is difficult for people to save up money by the middle of their working life when they have got fed up with the big firm they are working for to start up on their own, or perhaps to find a friend to join them for the same reason. Also because of the fiscal advantages of paying money into a pensions fund, as we said in our written evidence, one is dissuaded from the personal kind of saving which might have been made in the last century and the early part of this century which one could realise in order to buy a corner shop or something like that. If a man has his money locked up in a pension fund he cannot readily get at it even if he wants to. If there are small businesses about they tend to encourage other people to set up. Many people wanting to start up a business do so by seeking advice from a friend running a business. Also the more small businesses are likely to be set up the greater the proliferation of possible lending institutions might well become. So the one may well follow the other.

Dr Mitchell: Is there anything specific that you would like to see happen to encourage new businesses to start?

—*A:* (*Mr Wood*) Some things are already happening. I think there has been a change here. It is often small factors that have militated against this. For instance, one of the factors in my own field is the question of management education and training for small businesses. We spend in Britain at least £15 million a year on this education and the bulk of this subsidy goes to large businesses, because the courses tend to be constructed for the large business rather than the small one. In my institution and quite a number of others we have been trying to encourage the type of facility that suits the small businessman. One thing that we would like to do more of is running short courses on 'Starting running your own business'. The problem is that it is difficult under the rules of the Department of Education and Science and other educational organisations to run such courses on a normal educational fee basis. We have to do it on what is called a full cost basis. So if you want to start a business you pay the full cost of the course you come on, but if you are already in an established business you can be subsidised. What we have done recently, and I would like to see more of this, is to run some courses sponsored by the Training Services Agency to help people who are, as the euphemism goes, between jobs—redundant executives, in other words—to help them start businesses. The latest development, which is very encouraging, is that one large company, namely ICI, has taken an even more radical step: before they declare people redundant they are offering them the opportunity, whilst they are still in employment with ICI and have the security, to learn more about how to start and run their own business. I think if we could get more big businesses to do that kind of thing and help people to start their own business, what kind of approach to make to financial institutions, what kind of business to go into, we would see a big surge in the interest of older people starting new businesses.

Mr Graham: What is your view of the training as you see the results of it? What do you think of the training received by bank managers? Do they, for example, serve you well in terms of advice about many of the things that prove to be such a problem to you, much of the legislation that you receive? Could they act much more as a way in which these kinds of services could be concentrated, so that the man who runs a small business does not have to be the accountant, the lawyer, the salesman and the production manager, so that you could have some of these services concentrated in the bank? Would banks be a possible channel for this? And when you go to the banks to borrow money do they seem to be well appraised in order to assess technical projects?

—*A:* (*Mr Critchley*) I would have thought it was asking too much of a bank manager to expect him to perform this role. If you say who could perform the role, I think it is becoming so detailed and so abstruse that you have to have a specialist in each particular subject. For example, if you have a little shop and you have one man as head of one department and another man as head of another department, to move them around you might be breaking the law under the Employment Protection Act for all you know nowadays, so probably the only thing to do would be to go to a solicitor. By the time you had spent all this time going to a solicitor for that sort of thing, to an accountant for another sort of thing, to the bank manager for another sort of thing, and so on, you would spend most of your time out of the business and you would have run up bills all the way along. I am not being very constructive, but I do not think it could be done by the bank manager, it would really be asking too much of him.

Q: And on the separate question of whether the banks are able to assess projects, looking at the technical side of it, what is your opinion?

—*A:* (*Mr Dauris*) Do you mean financially?

Q: Assess them financially but also to understand what the technology is that is involved.

—*A:* (*Mr Critchley*) I would not have thought they were terribly good.

Mr Wood: I think it depends on what level. All the banks, to my knowledge, have people in their organisations who are experts in certain fields. There will be experts in the retail business or in the manufacturing business, not necessarily the manager of the high street bank. I think what we have to recognise is the change in the role of the high street bank manager, who used to be a sort of father figure but who because of banking technology is becoming not much more than an office manager. Therefore the banks are having to change the role of the local high street branch manager and are having to provide more specialised services. One of the banks—perhaps I had better not say which one—has set up a so-called business advisory service, which is staffed by ex-bank managers who have been trained specifically to help small businesses, not just with sources of finance but in terms of things like costing problems, helping to set up a budget, cash flow, and so on. That kind of thing is being done, but on a relatively small scale.

Mr Murray: Which bank is this?

—*A:* It is Barclays, although I think it is true to say that some of the other banks are doing similar things, but not perhaps quite to the same extent.

Sir John Prideaux: It would be quite wrong, Mr Chairman, to think that that was the property of one bank alone. As Mr Wood, who is a very good advocate, has said, it is quite well spread, and if one bank does one thing that the rest of the banks do not, if it is profitable they follow it quite soon.

—*A:* Actually it is not profitable on its own as a venture, but very long term.

Sir John Prideaux: No. Let us say useful, not profitable.

Chairman: There was a move some time ago to concentrate Stock Exchanges in London. Would that be detrimental to small companies?

—*A:* (*Mr Dauris*) It would have to be small quoted companies and we are not really dealing with companies quoted on any Stock Exchange, London or elsewhere.

Q: This morning there was some evidence of big companies occasionally when they need specialist work done, instead of setting up their own unit to do it and training people asking small businesses to take it on for them on a regular basis. Do you find that happens?

—*A:* I think it probably is done quite widely. Many small firms earn their living by supplying large ones, sometimes exclusively. This is very well known in the motoring industry. In my own industry, which is textiles, we certainly find among our customers nationalised industries and large companies, and we assume we are performing a service, sometimes warehousing their goods which we distribute for them because it is more economic for them to have us do it.

Q: What kind of textiles is it?

—*A:* Household textiles — bedding, towels, tablecloths.

Mr Wood: There is a change now, in that in Britain large companies have tended to do as many things as possible in-house themselves. If you take the chemical industry and contrast the chemical industry in Britain with the chemical industries in Germany, Japan and the United States, they tend there to hive off many of their activities, for instance maintenance, and put them out to a subcontractor, because they reckon that in that way they get better value for money then doing it for themselves and having all the trouble of managing it. I think there is a move in that direction in Britain.

Dr Mitchell: The Transport Act, did that, did it not, it hived off a lot of transport services?

—*A:* Yes.

Mr Brierley: I think it was said earlier that small companies did not want any discrimination in their favour. But is it not possible that, perhaps inadvertently, there is discrimination against them? What I am really thinking about, and much of the evidence has put this point, is the fact that thresholds, the level at which some forms of government aid are given, are frequently above the capacity of small firms to qualify for. Is that your experience?

—*A:* There is a point about thresholds, but I think there is an even more major one, which is that small firms, because the owner-manager is independent, are more reluctant to make use of that kind of facility. One of the things we do not know in this country is how much of the total amount of government aid that is made available for various firms goes to large companies and how much goes to small companies, because the figures are not kept in that way. I have asked questions about this. Under the Industry Act 1972 the figures are now kept and published on the basis of how much has gone to different regions, how much has gone to different sectors of the economy, types of business, how much in the form of supporting land and building as opposed to plant and equipment. But what we do not know is how much has gone to small firms and how much has gone to large firms, because the Industry Act did not ask for this information, and good civil servants do what they are told to do and not what they are not told to do and they have not kept this information. When Tony Benn was appointed Minister of Industry one of the things he asked for was this information. The information that is now being published gives a breakdown of the grants that are coming under the Industry Act by size of grant—not by size of company, but by size of grant. I have a long list. Unfortunately they established a cut-off point of £10,000; so we do not know the below figure. But one of these days we may be able to analyse the information and find out the facts. The facts are that undoubtedly in most cases large companies are getting a very much bigger share of almost any type of grant than smaller companies are.

Chairman: Thank you very much indeed, gentlemen.

(The witnesses withdrew)

Printed in England for Her Majesty's Stationery Office by Oyez Press Limited
Dd 586607 K14 11/77

UNIVERSITY OF YORK LIBRARY
Heslington, York.

Date of Return	Date of Return	Date of Return
CANCELLED 12 DEC 1978		
CANCELLED 12 DEC 1978		
26 MAR 1979 CANCELLED		
26 MAR 1979 CANCELLED		
17 DEC 1980		
25 MAR 1981		
-3 JUL 1996 CANCELLED		
CANCELLED 11 OCT 1996		